CALLOWAY CORNERS HISTORY

Empty for many years, the house became the birthplace of the fictitious Calloway sisters; Mariah, Jo, Tess and Eden of the four Harlequin Romance novels, each named for one of the sisters. The house was used on the cover art for each of the four novels. After meeting the author who originated the idea for the series, Penny Richards, the previous owners of the house decided to use the romance series' name for the Bed and Breakfast. Penny also wrote Eden as well as many other novels.

In 1993, Harlequin coordinated a release for the books with a contest for their readers, the winner to win a weekend for two at Calloway Corners along with a cash prize. While Harlequin was putting the finishing touches on the contest, the required administrative procedures were put into place to make Calloway Corners a "real" town. Fiction became fact on February 2, 1993 in Calloway Corners, Louisiana. The house is also pictured on the Northwest Louisiana page of the 1992 and 1993 Louisiana State Film Directory.

Calloway Corners is centrally located twenty-eight miles east of the river cities of Bossier City and Shreveport, where the excitement of riverboats on the Red River, thoroughbred horseracing at Harrah's Louisiana Downs, shopping at The Boardwalk on the river in Bossier City, the Louisiana State Fair and the annual end of year Independence Bowl awaits. The oldest town in Louisiana, historic Natchitoches, "City Of Lights", is only a short hour away. Less than half an hour away are antique shops, "Bonnie & Clyde Trade Days" in Arcadia, museums and many other local attractions.

Many claim that the house is haunted and, I must admit, there have been a few "unexplained" occurrences since we moved here in 2000 but none scary enough to make us leave!

INTRODUCTION

"EATING AND READING ARE TWO PLEASURES THAT COMBINE ADMIRABLY." C.S. LEWIS

This is not a "healthy eating" recipe book! It is intended to impart to the user a history and taste for a variety of foods; comfort, unique, gourmet, common and uncommon, that they would not otherwise have. The many deserts have a common theme; richness and goodness. The many other recipes also have a common theme; just dang good eating! So if you want to combine the tasty variety of recipes in this book with healthy eating; prepare them for special occasions which will give you the opportunity to impress friends, family, neighbors and "angels unaware". A meal to impress is about a sumptuous menu, enticing presentation, music appropriate for the occasion, refreshing drinks and the right ambiance. Like a precious gift, preparing a delicious meal is about making people feel extra special. With just the right combination of ambiance and culinary delights, you too can create a memorable, delicious, and sometimes romantic experience.

Romance is a powerful force that makes you feel connected to someone in a deeper way, and understanding your partner's "love language", is the key to lasting romance in a relationship. Physical Touch, as a gesture of love, is one of the more powerful "love languages". Men, generally, tend to respond to Physical Touch more, whereby a woman responds more to the Acts of Service "love language". Acts of Service, such as men being willing to sacrifice their time (i.e., help out around the house instead of playing golf) or Physical Touch, should always be freely given and received; never done on our own terms. The key is to love the other person in "their love language" and not our own. Love, after all, only displays its power as a verb; not as a noun. No one receives love by words, although words can be used to convey the feelings one has for another. It is only in the giving that love truly manifests itself.

INTRODUCTION (CONTINUED)

Some of the best stories, expressions of the heart and romances have been shared over a meal. From suppers around grandma's kitchen table to romantic, candle-light dinners, or the "last supper" Jesus had with his disciples, food has played, and continues to play, a central role in the most significant events in our lives. A shared table is a shared life. Many a meal has begun with a stranger and ended with a friend. And, sometimes.....to a romance!

This is my "food" love story. I had just began dating my future wife when my former wife sent me a pecan pie by way of my former step daughter. That same day, my bride to be brought me a pecan pie! I don't know if you are what you eat, but I do love a good pecan pie! In case you're wondering; the lovely lady I was dating (who's been my wife since 1992) had the winning pecan pie!

Love is in the giving. Learn how to make your partner feel seen, heard, understood and loved. Sharing a meal, created with love, can set the stage for all the above!

Some Food Quotes

Springtime a la Carte by O. Henry
"Sarah's fingers danced like midges above a summer stream. Down through the courses she worked, giving each item its position according to its length with an accurate eye. Just above the desserts came the list of vegetables. Carrots and peas, asparagus on toast, the perennial tomatoes and corn and succotash, lima beans, cabbage... and then..."

The Best Sauce by P.G. Wodehouse
"They are an acquired taste, I expect. Perhaps I am, too. Perhaps I am the human parsnip, and you will have to learn to love me."

A Word for Autumn by A.A. Milne
"Season of mists and mellow celery, then let it be. A pat of butter underneath the bough, a wedge of cheese, a loaf of bread and—Thou."

TABLE OF CONTENTS

Appetizers & Nibblers

SMOKED SALMON AND HERB CHEESE CROSTINI

Source: Author

Ingredients

1 white baguette, sliced into ½ inch thick slices

1 Armenian cucumber, thinly sliced   4 radishes, thinly sliced

Fresh dill weed   Freshly ground black pepper

1 avocado, thinly sliced   12 oz. smoked salmon, thinly sliced

Herb Cheese

Garlic & Fine Herbs Cheese

2 Tbsp. fresh dill weed, chopped

Freshly ground black pepper to taste

Sweet paprika

Preparation

Preheat the oven to 375°F.

Arrange the baguette slices on a large baking sheet. Bake until toasted, 10-12 minutes, flipping over halfway through baking. Remove and let cool completely.

Combine the cheese, dill weed and black pepper in a food processor. Process until smooth.

To assemble: spread the cheese mixture on the cooled baguette slices, top with several slices of radish, avocado, cucumber and a slice of smoked salmon. Garnish with dill sprigs and sweet paprika.

"First we eat. Then we do everything else." **M.F.K Fisher**

AHI TUNA CALLOWAY CORNERS STYLE

Trust me! This is delicious! If you were blindfolded, you would not even know you were eating seafood! My mouth is watering just thinking about it!

Source: Author

Ingredients

1 Tbsp ground black pepper

1 tsp Kosher salt

½ tsp garlic powder

½ tsp thyme

½ tsp oregano

½ tsp basil

1 tsp brown sugar

½ tsp soy lecithin

½ tsp coriander

Preparation

Mix together the above ingredients. Heat, over medium high heat, enough olive oil in a heavy skillet to coat the bottom of the skillet. Coat sides of yellow fin tuna with seasoning and sear on all sides for 30 seconds each. Let cool and slice in ¼ inch slices and serve with sauce.

Dipping Sauce:

Ingredients

¼ cup soy sauce   *   ¼ cup rice wine vinegar   *   ¼ cup water
2 tsp sugar   *   2 tsp fresh, grated ginger   *   ½ tsp sesame oil

Combine all ingredients and whisk until sugar is dissolved.

BRUSCHETTA AL POMODORO

Source: Olive Garden

Ingredients

4 Roma (plum) tomatoes, diced

2 garlic cloves, chopped

1 garlic clove, cut in half

Black pepper to taste

Salt to taste

10 medium fresh basil leaves, chopped

4 Tbsp extra virgin olive oil

8 slices crusty Italian bread

Extra virgin olive oil (to drizzle)

Preparation

Combine diced tomatoes and chopped garlic in a mixing bowl. Season with salt & pepper to taste. Add half of chopped basil and 4 Tbsp of extra virgin olive oil.

Drizzle both sides of bread slices with extra virgin olive oil. Grill bread lightly on both sides.

Rub grilled bread with cut half of garlic clove to infuse with flavor. Top each slice with tomato mixture.

Garnish with remaining chopped basil and serve immediately.

"If you really want to be a friend, invite people to your home and cook for them...the people who give others their food give them their heart." Author

CARPACCIO OF DIVER SCALLOP

A fresh and delicate appetizer: Scallop carpaccio recipe by chef Dwayne Cheer, from the world's top restaurant, Atmosphere, in the Burj Khalifa building in Dubai

Ingredients

For the carpaccio:

Scallop 5 pieces

Chive 1 tsp

Pomelo 1 tsp

Grapefruit ½ tsp

Olive oil 1 tsp

Lime juice 1 tsp

CARPACCIO OF DIVER SCALLOP

For the tempura rock shrimp:

Rock shrimp 3 pieces

Tempura batter 4 tsp

For the salad:

Shiso (a type of mint) ½ tsp

Basil ½ tsp

Olive oil 2 tsp

Lemon juice ½ tsp

1 Apple, Granny Smith variety

Coriander ½ tsp

Lemon cress ½ tsp

For the apple dressing:

Basil ½ tsp

Apple juice 4 tsp

Parsley ½ tsp

Olive oil 6 tsp

Green apple 1

Preparation

Over a flame, reduce the apple juice to 1/2 and cool it down, peel the apple and blend the whole apple and all the skin with basil and parsley.

Add the olive oil and strain the mixture.

Slice the fresh scallops in half or in thirds, depending on size, and marinate the scallops with Pomelo, lime, grapefruit, chives, salt and olive oil.

Arrange the marinated scallops nicely on the plate.

Mix all the cresses with finely sliced or chopped apple and place in center of the plate.

Place the fried rock shrimp on the scallops and dress the plate with apple dressing.

TOMATO BACON AND CHEESE BRUSCHETTA

Source: Author

Ingredients

French or Italian bread, cut in ½ inch slices

1 / 3 cup olive oil

6 Roma tomatoes, diced

1 ¼ cup feta cheese, diced

6 slices Wrights Smoked Bacon, fried crisp & crumbled

¼ tsp fresh ground pepper

2 Tbsp fresh basil, chopped

2 Tbsp fresh lemon balm, chopped

Preparation

Lightly brush one side of bread with olive oil. Place on ungreased baking sheet oil side up. Bake for 15 minutes or until lightly browned. Arrange toasts on serving tray.

In a bowl combine tomatoes, cheese, crumbled bacon, and pepper. Toss gently. Top toasts with tomato bacon mixture. Sprinkle basil and lemon balm on top and more black pepper if desired.

For added flavor spread pesto on bread before topping with bruschetta.

ESCARGOTS À LA BOURGUIGNONNE

Source: Dean & Deluca

Ingredients

1 garlic clove

3/8 tsp salt

1 stick butter, softened

1 ½ tsp shallot, finely minced

1 Tbsp fresh flat-leaf parsley, finely chopped

¼ tsp black pepper

1 Tbsp dry white wine

12 to 16 snails* (from a 7- to 8-oz can)

2 cups kosher salt (for stabilizing snail shells)

French bread

12 to 16 sterilized escargot shells*

Instructions

Place oven rack in middle position and preheat oven to 450°F.

Using a heavy knife, mince and mash garlic to a paste with 1/8 tsp salt.

In a small bowl with an electric mixer, beat together butter, shallot, garlic paste, parsley, remaining ¼ tsp salt, and pepper until combined well. Beat in wine until combined well.

Divide half of garlic butter among snail shells. Stuff 1 snail into each shell and top snails with remaining butter. Spread kosher salt in a shallow baking dish and nestle shells, butter sides up, in salt.

Bake snails until butter is melted and sizzling; 4 to 6 minutes. Serve immediately.

Snails in Wine & Garlic Butter

Source: Author

Ingredients

1 (7 ½ oz. can) snails

1 Tbsp dry white wine

Pinch of ground nutmeg

1 large shallot, finely chopped

¾ tsp dried chervil

1 stick butter, softened

½ tsp salt

2-3 garlic cloves, crushed

1 ½ Tbsp parsley, finely chopped

Preparation

Preheat oven to 450°F. Using an electric mixer on medium, beat butter in a medium bowl until smooth. Add wine, salt, pepper, nutmeg and chervil, then beat on medium until incorporated. Reduce speed to low and add garlic, shallot, and parsley; mix just until incorporated.

Spoon about 2 tsp. garlic-parsley butter in each cup, if using escargot dishes. Place snails in a single layer in a shallow baking dish or one in each cup of individual escargot dishes, then spoon in more garlic-parsley butter to mound over top. Set dishes in a shallow baking pan and bake until snails are sizzling, about 10 to 15 minutes.

Cheese Logs

Source: Carmella Brewster

Ingredients

1 (8 oz. pkg.) cream cheese, room temperature

2 cups cheddar cheese, shredded

½ tsp garlic powder

1 cup pecans, crushed

Chili powder

Directions

Mix cheeses well. Add garlic powder. Mix well.

Form into 4 logs, roll in chili powder then roll in crushed pecans.

Wrap in plastic wrap and chill until firm.

Serve with Ritz crackers.

GUACAMOLE

Source: Author

Ingredients

3 avocados - peeled, pitted and diced

¼ tsp salt

¼ tsp garlic powder

¼ tsp onion powder

½ tsp chili powder

1 tsp lemon juice

Preparation

In a small bowl, mix together the avocados, salt, pepper, garlic powder, onion powder, chili powder and lemon juice. Serve immediately or cover and chill in the refrigerator ½ hour before serving.

CORN DIP

Source: Ashleigh Watkins

Ingredients

1 bag (2 cups) shredded cheddar cheese

1 cup mayonnaise

8 oz. sour cream

1 (4 oz.) can chopped green chilies

2 cans Mexicorn (Fiesta), drained

4 oz. pepper Jack cheese, shredded

¼ cup green onions, chopped

Salt and pepper, to taste

Corn chips

Directions

In a large bowl, combine all ingredients except corn chips. Cover and refrigerate overnight. Serve with corn chips.

BEER RABBIT (WILLIAM RANDOLPH HEARST'S WELSH RAREBIT)

Source: Castle Fare; Hearst Castle, California

Ingredients

1 Tbsp butter

1 lb. cheddar cheese, grated

2/3 cup beer that has been open and warm

1 tsp dry mustard

1 tsp Worcestershire sauce

Dash cayenne pepper

¼ tsp paprika

1 egg, lightly beaten

Crisped crackers or toast

Directions

In a chafing dish or large double boiler placed over simmering water, melt the butter. Add the grated cheese and stir until it begins to melt then slowly add the beer, stirring. Add the seasonings. Add an egg and stir until it is combined with the mixture. Serve over the crackers or toast as soon as it is ready.

Pepper Jelly & Cream Cheese Spread

No recipe book from Louisiana would be complete without at least one recipe using Tabasco. The diet of the Reconstruction South was bland and monotonous, especially by Louisiana standards, so Edmund McIlhenny (or a New Orleans plantation owner named Maunsel White) decided to create a pepper sauce to give the food some flavor and excitement. Although White is believed to have originated the sauce 10 years earlier; McIlhenny sowed the seeds of Capsicum Frutescence Peppers on Avery Island, Louisiana and Tabasco sauce is now a brand of hot sauce made exclusively from tabasco peppers, vinegar, and salt. It is produced by McIlhenny Company of Avery Island, Louisiana.

Source: TABASCO®

Ingredients

1 (8 oz.) pkg. cream cheese

1 jar TABASCO® brand Original Spicy Pepper Jelly or Mild Jalapeño Pepper Jelly

Preparation

Place block of cream cheese on serving plate and pour TABASCO® Pepper Jelly over cream cheese. Serve as a spread for bagels or crackers. Get creative and shape the cream cheese using a mold.

CLAM BALLS

Source: Castle Fare; Hearst Castle, California

Ingredients

12 hardboiled eggs, chopped

1 Tbsp chives or green onions, minced

1 cup clams, drained and minced (or fresh clams, ground)

½ tsp salt

Black pepper, to taste

½ cup mayonnaise

2/3 cup cashews, finely chopped

Instructions

Combine all ingredients except nuts. Shape into small balls. Roll in nuts and refrigerate until served.

EMERALD DIP

Source: Author

Ingredients

1 slice bacon, cooked and crumbled

2 ripe avocados, peeled and mashed

1 jalapeno, seeded and finely minced

1 (8 oz.) pk. cream cheese

4 Tbsp mayonnaise

¼ tsp lemon juice

Salt and white pepper, to taste

Preparation

Mix all ingredients together and chill. Serve with chips or crackers.

BALONEY CAKE

After watching the movie, Sweet Home Alabama, I was curious as to what Baloney Cake was. I googled it and found this recipe which was passed on by Just A Pinch Recipes.

Source: Unknown

Ingredients

1 lb. sliced bologna

2 Tbsp onion, grated

1 (8oz.) pkg. cream cheese, softened

1 Tbsp Worcestershire sauce

1 pkg. Ritz crackers

Directions

Combine softened cream cheese, onion and Worcestershire sauce. Beat well. Place a slice of bologna on a plate and spread with cream cheese mix. Repeat process until all bologna is used. Ice like a cake with rest of cheese mixture. Garnish with Cheese Whiz. Cool in refrigerator.

Slice in thin slices and serve on crackers.

BACON WRAPPED MUSHROOMS & PINEAPPLE

Source: Author

Ingredients

Pineapple chunks

Fresh button mushrooms

½ pkg. good quality bacon

Preparation

Preheat the oven to 425°F. Spray a baking sheet with non-stick cooking spray.

Cut the bacon strips in half.

Remove stems from mushrooms. Place a pineapple chunk in each mushroom. Wrap enough bacon around each pineapple filled mushroom cap to overlap. Secure each appetizer with a toothpick and put on a baking sheet. Place the baking sheet in the preheated oven and bake for 20 minutes or until the bacon is browned.

Oyster Cocktail Sauce

Source: Author

Ingredients

1 cup ketchup

¼ cup Worcestershire sauce

1 cup lemon juice

½ tsp salt

¼ tsp white pepper

½ tsp Tabasco

1 tsp horseradish, adjust to taste

Instructions

Mix all ingredients together until well-combined.

Keep refrigerated.

"He was a bold man that first ate an oyster." Jonathan Swift

BRIE EN CROUTE

Source: Jash Bower

Ingredients

1 egg

1 Tbsp water

All-purpose flour

Puff pastry sheet, thawed

½ cup apricot preserves or other desired filling

½ cup nuts, chopped

1 (3 inch) wheel of Brie or Camembert cheese

Assorted appetizer crackers or baguettes

Instructions

Heat the oven to 400°F. Whisk together the egg and water in a small bowl.

Sprinkle the flour on the work surface. Unfold the pastry sheet on the work surface. Roll the pastry sheet into a 14-inch square. Spread the filling on the pastry to within 2 inches of the edge. Place the cheese in the center of the pastry. Sprinkle with chopped nuts. Fold the pastry up over the filling and cheese to cover. Trim the excess pastry and press to seal. Brush the seam with the egg mixture. Place seam-side down onto a baking sheet. Decorate with the pastry scraps, if desired. Brush with the egg mixture.

Bake for 20 minutes or until the pastry is golden brown. Let stand for 45 minutes. Serve with the crackers.

SWEET AND SAVORY HAM CHEESECAKE

Source: Author

Ingredients

Crust:

¼ cup sugar, granulated

¼ cup light brown sugar, packed

½ cup pecans, chopped

½ cup Ritz crackers, crushed

¼ cup butter, melted

Savory cheese filling:

1 (8 oz.) pkg. cream cheese

1 (8 oz.) pkg. smoked Gouda cheese, grated

¼ cup flour

3 large eggs

1 cup half and half

1 tsp salt

1 tsp white pepper

1 Tbsp sweet paprika

¼ tsp cayenne pepper

1 tsp fresh Italian oregano, minced

1 Tbsp garlic chives, minced

3 fresh sage leaves, minced

3 Tbsp fresh Italian parsley, minced

1 cup cooked ham, diced

Preparation

Preheat oven to 350°F.

For the crust: In a large bowl, mix together all ingredients until well combined. Spray a 9 inch springform pan with cooking spray. Press crust into the bottom of the springform pan. Set aside.

For the Savory cheese filling: Mix together cheeses and flour. Blend in remaining ingredients. Pour into the prepared springform pan. Bake at 350°F for 15 minutes. Reduce oven to 300°F and bake for 45 minutes or until a tester come out clean. Remove from the oven and allow to cool. Remove from springform pan and transfer to a serving dish. To serve, spread on appetizer crackers.

CRAWFISH PÂTÉ

Source: Author

Ingredients

1 lb. cooked crawfish tails

1 cup butter

¼ cup dry white wine

2 Tbsp lemon juice

2 Tbsp onion, grated

¼ tsp ground nutmeg

½ tsp dry mustard

¼ tsp cayenne pepper

Preparation

Put crawfish through finest blade of a food grinder or mince as fine as possible. Cream butter and blend in wine, lemon juice, onion nutmeg and cayenne. Add crawfish and beat until smooth. Serve with lightly toasted baguettes.

FOR RESERVATIONS CALL: 1-318-371-1331

NOTES

_____

_____

_____

_____

_____

_____

_____

_____

_____

_____

_____

_____

_____

_____

NOTES

_____

_____

_____

_____

_____

_____

_____

_____

_____

_____

_____

_____

_____

Breads

"Good bread is the most fundamentally satisfying of all foods; and good bread with fresh butter, the greatest of feasts."
James Beard

BARBARA'S BACK PORCH ROLLS

Ingredients

1 cup warm water

2 pkgs. yeast

1 cup shortening

1 cup sugar

1 tsp. salt

1 cup boiling water

2 eggs, beaten

6 cups flour

Directions

Dissolve yeast in warm water and set aside. In a large bowl, mix the shortening, sugar, salt and boiling water. Mix in the eggs. Add the yeast and the flour and mix well. Refrigerate overnight. Roll out and cut 2" rounds, placing each in a greased muffin pan. Let rise until doubled; about 3-4 hours. Bake at 425° for 7-8 minutes. Makes 4 dozen rolls.

CALLOWAY CORNERS SCONES

Source: Author

Ingredients

2 ½ cups flour

½ cup sugar

2 tsp. baking powder

½ tsp. salt

½ tsp. allspice

½ tsp. ground cardamom

½ tsp. ground coriander

2 Tbsp. orange zest (1 Tbsp. dried)

½ cup finely chopped walnuts

¼ cup butter

¼ cup dried cranberries

1 cup heavy cream (remove 2 Tbsp. & reserve)

Organic Sucanat (natural sugar cane sugar)

Preparation

In a large bowl combine the first 9 ingredients and mix well. Add butter and cut in with a pastry cutter until mixture is course and pebbly. Add the dried cranberries and heavy cream (less the reserved 2 Tbsp.), stirring until damp and crumbly.

Turn mixture onto a smooth surface (it will still be crumbly and dry in places) and kneed until it holds together well. Divide and shape into 2 six inch round disks approximately ½" to ¾" thick. Cut each into 12 pie shaped wedges and place on a lightly greased baking sheet (use cooking spray if desired).

Prick each wedge 4 times with a fork and brush with the reserved 2 Tbsp. of heavy cream. Sprinkle lightly with the Organic Sucanat, using approximately ¼ tsp. for every wedge.

Bake in a pre-heated oven at 425°F for 18 minutes. Place on wire racks to cool.

BRIOCHE

Source: Official Cookbook, 1984 Louisiana World Exposition

Ingredients

1 cup milk	1 stick butter
1 tsp salt	½ cup sugar
2 pkgs. Yeast	¼ cup warm water
4 eggs, beaten	1 tsp lemon peel, grated
5 to 6 cups flour	1 egg yolk
1 Tbsp milk	

Directions

Preheat oven to 425°F. Mix together egg yolk and 1 Tbsp milk.
Scald milk; stir in butter, salt and sugar. Cool to lukewarm.
Sprinkle yeast on warm water and stir to dissolve. Combine eggs,
lemon peel, yeast and milk mixture. Beat in flour a cup at a time.
The dough will be soft to handle and will not be kneaded. Grease
top of dough, cover and let rise in a warm place until doubled,
about 1 ½ to 2 hours.

Punch down and refrigerate 4 to 6 hours until dough can be
handled. Shape 2/3 of the dough into smooth balls about 1 ½ inches
in diameter. Shape remaining dough into ½ inch balls. Work
quickly as dough will soften. Place large balls in greased muffin tins.
Make a dent with finger in center of each large ball of dough and
place small ball in dent. Brush with the egg and milk mixture.
Cover and let rise until doubled, about 1 hour.

Bake at 425°F until brown, about 10 minutes. Remove from pans at
once and place on a wire rack. Serve warm.

Braided Walnut Anadama Bread

This bread is dangerously good!
Source: Author

Ingredients

1 pkg (¼ oz.) active dry yeast
1/3 cup dark molasses
¼ cup warm water (110° – 115°)
¼ cup butter, softened
1 tsp salt
1 cup warm milk (110° – 115°)
3 ½ - 4 cups flour
1 tsp. ground cardamom
1 cup walnuts, finely chopped
¼ cup and 1 Tbsp. Triple Sec
1 egg, beaten

Preparation

Dissolve yeast in warm water. Let set for 5 min. In large mixing bowl, combine butter, salt, milk, molasses and ¼ cup Triple Sec. Stir in yeast mixture, 2 cups flour, cardamom and walnuts. Beat until well mixed. Mix in enough remaining flour to form a soft dough. Turn dough out onto a floured surface and knead until smooth and elastic; about 6-8 minutes. Place dough in a greased bowl, turning once to grease all sides. Cover and let stand in a warm place until doubled in size; about two hours. Punch down and cut off 1/3rd of the dough. Set aside. Divide remaining dough into three equal parts, shaping each into a 14" rope. Pinch together all three at one end and braid. Pinch together the other end and place on a greased cookie sheet. Divide into three equal parts the remaining dough and braid. Place smaller braid on top of larger braid. Cover with a damp cloth and let rise until doubled in size; about one hour. Combine egg and 1 Tbsp. Triple Sec. Brush over entire loaf. Sprinkle with finely ground walnuts, if desired. Bake at 350°F for 30 minutes.

COLLARD GREENS CORNBREAD

Source: Author

Ingredients

4 cups frozen, chopped collard greens, thawed, drained

½ cup chopped green onions

3 eggs

½ cup milk

3 Tbsp all-purpose flour

1 tsp salt

½ tsp smoked paprika

¼ tsp onion powder

¼ tsp garlic powder

1 cup cheddar cheese   *Topping:*

1 pkg southern cornbread mix

½ cup sliced green onions

½ cup whole kernel corn, drained

1/3 cup milk

2 Tbsp butter, melted

Preparation

Heat oven to 350. Spray 11x7-inch baking dish with cooking spray. In large bowl, place collard greens and stir in green onions. In medium bowl, stir together eggs, milk, flour and seasonings. Stir in cheese and spread evenly in baking dish. Bake uncovered for 25 minutes or until lightly set. In large bowl, stir Topping ingredients until just moistened and spread evenly over mixture in baking dish. Bake 35 to 45 minutes longer or until a deep golden brown.

GRANDMA NEUSTROM'S SWEDISH RYE BREAD

(Recipe worked out by Uncle Howard Watkins, watching and learning)

Source: Carole Bumpus

Ingredients

Part 1:

2 cups rye flour

2 ½ cups hot water

½ Tbsp salt

1 Tbsp caraway seeds (optional, but why not use them)

½ cup dark molasses

Mix together these 5 ingredients and cool.

Part 2:

2 cups flour

1 ½ cups warm water (110° - 115°)

2 pkgs. yeast, dissolved in the warm water

Directions

Mix together these three ingredients and let rise until bubbly. Add to the above mixture and let rise until doubled. Add 5-5 ½ cups of white flour. Turn out onto a floured surface and knead until smooth and elastic. Place in a large greased bowl, cover and let rise in a warm place until doubled. Divide into four greased loaf pans and let rise again. Bake at 350° for 1 hour. Brush butter on tops and remove to wire racks to cool.

**Serve with butter dripping down the sides and a nice cup of coffee. Life can't get any sweeter than that. Wrap completely cooled loaves in plastic wrap and refrigerate. Can be frozen. (Carole Bumpus' note)

JALAPENO CORNBREAD

Source: Clara Wilson

Ingredients

1 cup yellow cornmeal

1 cup buttermilk

2 eggs, beaten

¾ tsp. salt

½ tsp soda

½ cup bacon drippings or cooking oil

1 can (17 oz.) cream style corn

1 lb. breakfast sausage

1 lb. cheddar cheese, shredded

1 onion, chopped

4-5 jalapeno peppers, chopped

Directions

In a mixing bowl, combine cornmeal, buttermilk, eggs, salt, soda, bacon drippings and corn. Mix well and set aside. Brown and crumble sausage, drain and set aside. Pour half of the cornmeal mixture into a greased 9x13x2 inch baking dish. Sprinkle with ½ of the cheese, spread the sausage over the mixture and add the rest of the cheese. Sprinkle the onion and jalapeno peppers over the cheese then add the remaining cornmeal mixture, spreading evenly. Bake at 350°F for 50 minutes.

BRAIDED ALMOND HERB BREAD

Source: Author

Ingredients

1 pkg (¼ oz.) active dry yeast	2 Tbsp. sugar
¼ cup warm water (110° – 115°)	¼ cup butter, softened
1 tsp salt	1 cup warm milk (110° – 115°)
3 ½ - 4 cups flour	½ tsp tarragon, crushed
½ tsp dill	½ tsp marjoram, crushed

½ tsp. ground cardamom

½ cup almonds, toasted & finely chopped

¼ cup and 1 Tbsp Amaretto liqueur   1 egg, beaten

Preparation

Dissolve yeast in warm water. Let set for 5 min. In large mixing bowl, combine butter, salt, milk and ¼ cup Amaretto liqueur. Stir in yeast mixture, 2 cups flour, herbs and almonds. Beat until well mixed. Mix in enough remaining flour to form a soft dough. Turn dough out onto a floured surface and knead until smooth and elastic; about 6-8 minutes. Place dough in a greased bowl, turning once to grease all sides. Cover and let stand in a warm place until doubled in size; about one hour. Punch down and cut off 1/3rd of the dough. Set aside. Divide remaining dough into three equal parts, shaping each into a 14" rope. Pinch together all three at one end and braid. Pinch together the other end and place on a greased cookie sheet. Divide into three equal parts the remaining dough and braid. Place smaller braid on top of larger braid. Cover with a damp cloth and let rise until doubled in size; about one hour. Combine egg and 1 Tbsp. Amaretto liqueur. Brush over entire loaf. Sprinkle with more finely ground almonds, if desired. Bake at 350° F for 30 minutes.

ALMOND FLOUR BREAD

A delicious low carb almond flour bread.

Source: Author

Ingredients

2 cups fine grained almond flour

4 Tbsp psyllium husk powder

1 tsp baking soda

1 tsp salt

4 large eggs

4 Tbsp olive oil

2 Tbsp Triple Sec

½ cup warm water

1 tsp fresh chopped herbs, optional

Preparation

Preheat the oven to 350°F. Line a bread pan with a parchment paper.

In a large bowl, stir together dry ingredients. Stir in the eggs, olive oil, Triple Sec, and herbs (if using). Add the warm water. Dough will look more "wet" than a traditional dough. Set the bread aside for 5 minutes to allow the psyllium husk powder to absorb the water.

Transfer the batter to prepared bread pan.

Bake for 45-55 minutes. The bread is done when a doneness tester inserted in the center comes out clean and the top is firm and crust-like. Allow the bread to cool before removing from the pan and slicing.

HOECAKES

Source: Author

Ingredients

1 cup all-purpose flour

1 cup cornmeal

2 tsp baking powder

½ tsp salt

¾ cup buttermilk

1/3 cup water

2 large eggs, beaten

¼ cup cooking oil or bacon drippings

1 Tbsp butter

Preparation

Line a baking sheet with paper towels and set aside. In a medium bowl, whisk together the flour, cornmeal, baking powder and salt. Add buttermilk, water and eggs; mix well. Heat oil and butter in a cast iron skillet over medium to medium high and drop batter by 1/8 cup measure into the hot skillet to form small patties.

Fry until brown and crisp, turn and brown the other side. Remove and let drain. Serve immediately with warm syrup or honey butter for breakfast or as a snack, or with a mess of greens.

HOT WATER CORNBREAD

Source: Author

Ingredients

2 cups cornmeal

1 Tbsp baking powder

½ tsp salt

1 ½ to 2 cups boiling water

Vegetable oil

Preparation

Pour about ½ inch of oil into a heavy-bottomed skillet. Heat the oil to about 350°F or until glistening but not smoking. In a large bowl combine the corn meal, baking powder and salt and mix with about 1 ½ cups of boiling water. Carefully stir to combine. The batter should be pourable. Add additional water until you reach the consistency of thick pancake batter. Different corn meals will require different amounts of water. Start with less and add more if you need it.

Once the oil is hot, pour about ¼ cup of the batter into the oil. Cook 3 to 5 minutes or until brown around the edges then carefully flip over and cook an additional 3 to 4 minutes. Work in batches, adding additional oil if necessary. Drain the cornbread on a plate lined with paper towels. Serve immediately with warm syrup or honey butter for breakfast or as a snack, or with a mess of greens.

CRACKLIN' BREAD

Source: Author

Ingredients

1 cup cracklins', crumbled

5 Tbsp bacon drippings, melted and divided

1 cup yellow cornmeal

1 cup all-purpose flour

2 tsp baking powder

1 tsp salt

¼ tsp baking soda

1 1/3 cups whole buttermilk

2 large eggs

Preparation

Preheat oven to 425°F.

In a food processor, pulse cracklins' until chopped.

In a 10-inch cast-iron skillet, heat 1 Tbsp bacon drippings over medium-high heat. Set aside.

In a medium bowl, combine cornmeal, flour, baking powder, salt, and baking soda. Add buttermilk, eggs, and 2 Tbsp bacon drippings. Stir in cracklins'.

Add remaining 2 Tbsp bacon drippings to pan. Place in oven until hot, about 4 minutes. Carefully pour batter into hot pan. Bake about 18 minutes or until firm and brown on top. Let cool 10 minutes before serving.

SOUTHERN CORNBREAD

Source: My Mother; Mary Wilson Herriage

Ingredients

¼ cup bacon drippings

1 cup all-purpose flour

1 cup cornmeal

1 Tbsp. baking powder

½ tsp salt

2 large eggs

1 cup buttermilk

Directions

Preheat oven to 425°F. Pour bacon drippings in a 10 inch cast iron skillet. Set in the oven to pre-heat skillet and drippings. While skillet is pre-heating, whisk flour, cornmeal, baking powder and salt in a large bowl. Add eggs, buttermilk, and bacon drippings from skillet and stir until combined. Pour batter into pre-heated skillet and spread evenly.

Bake cornbread for 25 minutes. Let cornbread cool slightly then remove to a serving platter.

"The North thinks it knows how to make corn bread, but this is a gross superstition. Perhaps no bread in the world is quite as good as Southern corn bread, and perhaps no bread in the world is quite as bad as the Northern imitation of it."
Mark Twain

"Any man that eats Chili and Cornbread can't be all bad."
Carroll Shelby

Southern Buttermilk Cornbread

Source: Author

This is a great cornbread to serve freshly baked with beans or greens or a big bowl of chili. It can be used to make a great stuffing, too! My mother ate it broken up in a glass of cold buttermilk!

This cornbread is the classic buttermilk cornbread you'll find throughout the South. There's generally no sugar added to Southern cornbread, but if you prefer a sweeter cornbread, add a tablespoon or two of sugar or honey.

Ingredients

¼ cup bacon drippings	2 cups white or yellow cornmeal
¼ cup all-purpose flour	2 ½ tsp baking powder
½ tsp baking soda	¾ tsp salt
1 ¼ cups buttermilk	2 large eggs

Preparation

Heat the oven to 425°F. Position the rack in the center of the oven. Pour bacon drippings in a 10 inch cast iron skillet and pre-heat in the oven.

In a large bowl, combine the cornmeal, flour, baking powder, soda, and salt. Whisk to blend thoroughly. Add the buttermilk, eggs, and bacon drippings from the pre-heated skillet. Add the buttermilk mixture to the dry mixture and stir just until blended. Carefully remove the hot cast iron pan from the oven and set it on a metal rack. Pour the batter into the hot skillet, spreading evenly. Return the skillet to the oven and bake for about 25 minutes, until golden brown.

Serve hot with soups, stew, chili, beans, greens or crumbled into a glass of cold buttermilk. A pan of cornbread, mixed with sautéed onions, celery, seasonings and chicken stock, also makes a great dressing to go with chicken, pork, or turkey.

KENTUCKY SPOONBREAD

Source: Taste of Home

Ingredients

4 cups milk

1 cup cornmeal

3 tsp sugar

1 tsp salt

½ tsp baking powder

2 Tbsp butter

3 eggs, separated

Directions

In a large saucepan, heat 3 cups milk over medium heat until bubbles form around sides of pan.

Meanwhile, in a small bowl, combine the cornmeal, sugar, salt and remaining milk until smooth. Slowly whisk cornmeal mixture into hot milk. Cook and stir until mixture comes to a boil. Reduce heat; simmer for 5 minutes, stirring constantly.

Remove from the heat. Sprinkle baking powder over the cornmeal mixture, then stir it in with the butter. In a small bowl, beat egg yolks; stir in a small amount of hot cornmeal mixture. Return all to the pan and mix well.

In a small bowl, beat egg whites until stiff peaks form. Fold a fourth of the egg whites into the cornmeal mixture. Fold in remaining egg whites until blended.

Transfer to a greased 2-1/2-qt. baking dish. Bake, uncovered, at 350F° for 40-45 minutes or until puffed and golden brown. Serve immediately.

PANETTONE ITALIAN SWEET BREAD

Author: Rosemary, An Italian in my Kitchen

Ingredients

Panettone:

3 ¼ cups all-purpose flour (sifted)

¼ cup + 2 Tbsp sugar

2/3 cup water (tepid)

½ cup butter, cut into small pieces

½ tsp salt

1 1/2 tsp dry active yeast

2 eggs

1 egg yolk

Zest of 1 orange and 1 lemon

1 tsp vanilla

1 cup chocolate chips, dried, chopped apricots or candied fruit or a mixture

Topping:

¼ cup + 1 Tbsp almond flour

1 Tbsp cornstarch

1/3 cup + 1 Tbsp sugar

1 egg white

Powdered sugar for dusting

¼ cup almonds, skinned (or more if desired)

Panettone Italian Sweet Bread

Instructions

In the bowl of the mixer with the paddle attached, add sifted flour, in the center add yeast, sugar, butter, eggs, yolk, zest, vanilla and half the water. Mix 20 seconds, then change to the dough hook and add the other half of the water and salt.

Mix for 15- 20 minutes, stopping after 10 minutes to scrape the hook and bowl.

After 20 minutes add either the chopped apricots, candied fruit or chocolate chips (or even a mixture if you wish) mix on low for a couple of minutes until combined.

Remove to a flat lightly floured board, lightly rub hand with butter and gather the dough into a ball. Place in a large oiled bowl, cover with plastic and a dish towel. Place in a draft free, warmish spot to rise. Let rise for 2-3 hours or until tripled in size.

Once risen, move back to a lightly floured flat surface, with hands lightly buttered and roll again into a ball, place in greased Panettone mold, cover with plastic and dish towel and let rise for an hour.

Topping:

In a small/medium bowl mix together almond flour, cornstarch, sugar and egg white. Set aside.

Pre-heat oven to 365°F.

Carefully brush risen Panettone with topping, top with almonds and sprinkle with powdered sugar. Bake for approximately 45-50 minutes using a toothpick for doneness. Let cool completely before cutting. Enjoy!

PANETTONE (ITALIAN CHRISTMAS BREAD)

Source: Cooking Light

This Italian bread is similar to a fruitcake and traditionally served during the holidays. The Christmas treat is typically baked into a tall, cylindrical shape (empty coffee cans work great as baking pans). While its origins are sketchy, one legend holds that in the late 1400s, a young Milanese nobleman fell in love with the daughter of a baker named Toni and created "Pan de Toni" to impress his love's father.

Ingredients

Marinated fruit:

1/3 cup golden raisins

1/3 cup dried apricots, chopped

1/3 cup dried tart cherries

¼ cup triple sec

Dough:

1 package dry yeast (about 2 ¼ tsp)

¼ tsp sugar

¼ cup warm water (100° to 110°)

3 ¾ cups all-purpose flour, divided

6 Tbsp butter, melted

¼ cup fat-free milk

¼ cup sugar

½ tsp salt

1 large egg

1 large egg yolk

2 Tbsp pine nuts

Cooking spray

1 tsp butter, melted

2 tsp turbinado sugar

Directions

To prepare marinated fruit, combine first 4 ingredients in a small bowl; let stand 1 hour. Drain fruit in a sieve over a bowl, reserving fruit and 2 teaspoons liqueur separately.

PANETTONE (ITALIAN CHRISTMAS BREAD)

To prepare dough, dissolve yeast and ¼ tsp sugar in warm water in a small bowl; let stand 5 minutes. Lightly spoon flour into dry measuring cups; level with a knife. Combine ½ cup flour and next 6 ingredients (½ cup flour through egg yolk) in a large bowl; beat at medium speed of a mixer 1 minute or until smooth. Add yeast mixture and ½ cup flour; beat 1 minute. Stir in marinated fruit, 2 ½ cups flour, and pine nuts. Turn dough out onto a lightly floured surface. Knead until smooth and elastic (about 8 minutes); add enough of remaining flour, 1 Tbsp at a time, to prevent dough from sticking to hands.

Place dough in a large bowl coated with cooking spray, turning to coat top. Cover and let rise in a warm place (85°F), free from drafts, about 1 ½ hours. Dough will not double in size. (Press two fingers into dough. If indentation remains, the dough has risen enough.)

Punch dough down; let rest 5 minutes. Divide in half, shaping each into a ball. Place balls into 2 (13-oz.) coffee cans coated with cooking spray. Cover and let rise 1 hour.

Preheat oven to 375F°.

Uncover dough. Place coffee cans on bottom rack in oven, and bake at 375F° for 30 minutes or until browned and loaf sounds hollow when tapped. Remove bread from cans, and cool on a wire rack. Combine reserved 2 tsp liqueur and 1 tsp butter; brush over loaves. Sprinkle evenly with turbinado sugar.

LIGHT BREAD HOT ROLLS

One of my fondest memories is of Sunday dinners with the smell of roast beef, gravy and black-eyed peas cooking and of these rolls baking. The only thing better was when it came time to eat!

Source: My Mother; Mary Wilson Herriage

Ingredients

2 cups warm water

1 pkg. yeast

¼ cup sugar

2 tsp salt

3 Tbsp shortening

6-8 cups all-purpose flour (enough for a stiff dough)

Directions

Preheat oven to 450°F.

Stir yeast into the warm water. Mix dry ingredients together. Cut in the shortening. Add yeast mixture and stir in until stiff enough to work with hands. Knead until dough springs back. Put into a greased bowl and let stand about one hour.

Lightly grease each of the cups in a muffin pan. Work dough down, pinch off into small balls and place 3 balls, seam side down, in each muffin cup. Cover the muffin pan with a light cloth, put it in a warm spot and let the rolls rise for another 60 minutes. Bake in 450°F oven until golden brown, about 15 to 20 minutes.

CLOVERLEAF DINNER ROLLS

Source: Author

Ingredients

3 cups all-purpose flour

1 cup milk, lukewarm

4 Tbsp butter, softened

2 Tbsp sugar

2 tsp yeast

1 tsp salt

2 Tbsp butter, melted

Preparation

Stir yeast into the warm milk until dissolved. In the bowl of a mixer, combine all of the dough ingredients and knead to make a smooth, slightly sticky dough that comes away from the sides of the bowl (about 6-7 minutes). Make a ball and place it in a lightly greased container. Cover and let rise until double in size, about 1 hour.

Brush a 12-cup muffin tin with 1 Tbsp melted butter and set aside.

When the dough has doubled, punch it down and divide it into 12 parts. Divide each part into three equal-sized pieces and roll each piece into small balls. Place 3 balls in each muffin cup. Cover the muffin tin with a light cloth, put it in a warm spot and let the rolls rise for another 60 minutes.

Preheat the oven to 350°F. Remove the cloth and bake the rolls until golden brown, about 20 to 25 minutes.

Remove the rolls from the oven, and brush with the remaining melted butter. Transfer them to a serving platter. Serve hot.

APRICOT ORANGE SCONES

Source: Unknown

Ingredients

1 ¾ cups all-purpose flour

¼ cup sugar

1 ½ tsp baking powder

¼ tsp salt

¼ cup sour cream

3 Tbsp orange juice

¾ cup dried apricots, finely chopped

1 Tbsp orange zest, freshly grated

½ tsp baking soda

½ stick cold butter

1 large egg, slightly beaten

1 tsp almond extract

Glaze:

1 cup powdered sugar

¼ tsp almond extract

1 Tbsp butter, softened

1 to 2 Tbsp milk

Directions

Preheat oven to 375°F.

Combine flour, apricots, sugar, orange zest, baking powder, baking soda and salt in bowl. Cut in ¼ cup cold butter with pastry blender or fork until mixture resembles coarse crumbs.

Combine sour cream, egg, orange juice and 1 teaspoon almond extract in another bowl. Stir into flour mixture 1 minute or just until moistened. Turn dough onto lightly floured surface; knead 5 to 8 times until smooth.

Pat dough to 7-inch circle on greased baking sheet. Score into 6 wedges; do not separate.

Bake 18-25 minutes or until lightly browned. Cool 10 minutes.

Combine powdered sugar, 1 teaspoon butter, 1/8 teaspoon almond flavoring and enough milk for desired glazing consistency in bowl. Drizzle over warm scones.

COCONUT BIMINI BREAD

Source: Just a Pinch

Ingredients

2 ¼ tsp instant dry yeast

4 ½ cups unbleached flour

1 tsp salt

¼ cup nonfat dry milk powder

1 / 3 cup sugar

1 cup coconut milk, warmed (100°F to 110°F)

3 Tbsp honey

3 Tbsp butter, softened

1 / 3 cup vegetable oil

3 eggs

Directions

Preheat oven to 350°F.

Mix yeast into the warm coconut milk. Mix all ingredients in a large bowl. Turn out onto a floured surface and knead together until a smooth dough forms. Add extra flour if necessary. Place dough into an oiled bowl, cover and let rise in a warm place for about 1 ½ hours.

When dough is approximately doubled in size, remove dough and place in oiled baking pans. Let dough rise in baking pans for 30 minutes. Slash the top with a sharp knife and then bake for 35 minutes or until browned on top and cooked through.

Note: Serve with conch stew, conch chowder or other soups and stews.

MONKEY BREAD

Claire Saffitz; Bon Appétit Test Kitchen

Ingredients

Dough:

2 sticks unsalted butter, chilled	⅓ cup whole milk
1 ¼-oz. active dry yeast, about 2¼ tsp	3 cups all-purpose flour
3 Tbsp sugar	1 tsp kosher salt
4 large eggs, room temperature	

Assembly:

¾ cup granulated sugar	1 Tbsp ground cinnamon
6 Tbsp unsalted butter, melted	Sanding or granulated sugar
Prepared caramel sauce (see page 345)	

Preparation

Dough:

Cut chilled butter into 1-inch pieces then beat in the bowl of a stand mixer fitted with the paddle attachment on medium-low speed until butter is smooth and pliable but still cold, about 1 minute. Scrape into a medium bowl; set aside. Save mixer bowl because you're going to use it again in a minute (no need to wash).

Gently heat milk in a small saucepan over low until warm to the touch but not steaming hot. It should be 110°F–115°F. Whisk milk and yeast in a small bowl to dissolve yeast, then let sit until foamy, about 5 minutes.

Meanwhile, whisk flour, sugar, and salt in reserved mixer bowl to combine. Add yeast mixture and eggs, fit bowl back onto mixer, and beat on low speed with dough hook, gradually increasing mixer speed to medium as dry ingredients are incorporated, until dough comes together around hook. Continue to mix on medium speed until dough is smooth, elastic, and no longer sticking to the sides of the bowl, about 5 minutes. Add more flour by the tablespoonful as needed if dough isn't pulling away from bowl cleanly. With motor running, gradually add reserved butter about a tablespoonful at a time, waiting until it is absorbed before adding

MONKEY BREAD

more. This process can take several minutes, so be patient. When you're done adding the butter, the dough will be extremely smooth, soft, and supple but not sticky. Place dough in a large buttered bowl and cover. Let sit in a warm, draft-free spot until nearly doubled in size, 55–65 minutes.

Uncover dough and punch down several times to deflate. Line a 13x9" baking dish with plastic wrap, leaving generous overhang on all sides. Place dough in pan and press into an even layer, working all the way to the sides of the pan. Fold plastic up and over dough, eliminating air pockets between dough and plastic. Chill dough in freezer until firm to the touch, 20–30 minutes, or 1 day ahead in the refrigerator.

Assembly: Mix granulated sugar and cinnamon in a medium bowl to combine. Lightly brush 10 inch tube pan with butter. Sprinkle with sanding sugar, tapping out excess; set aside. Remove dough from freezer and peel back plastic. Brush entire surface with melted butter and sprinkle generously with some cinnamon sugar. Shake excess sugar back into bowl, then invert baking pan and turn out dough onto work surface sugar side down. Remove plastic; discard. Brush other side of dough with butter and sprinkle with more cinnamon sugar. Use a pizza cutter or a chef's knife to cut dough into a 12x6 grid.

Working relatively quickly so dough doesn't become too soft, separate pieces and, working one at a time, roll lightly between your palms into balls, dusting with more cinnamon sugar as needed to prevent sticking. Place in prepared tube pan as you go. Cover pan with plastic wrap and let sit in a warm, draft-free spot until pieces have swelled to nearly double in size, 40–50 minutes. Preheat oven to 350° a little before monkey bread is ready to bake.

Remove plastic from pan and bake monkey bread until golden brown, 25–35 minutes. Let cool 10 minutes, then use a small offset spatula to loosen monkey bread from sides of pan. Pull bottom out from pan and use spatula to loosen bread from bottom. Slide bread back into pan; invert onto a plate and remove pan. Place a wire rack over bread and invert right side up onto rack. If using a Bundt pan, just invert directly onto wire rack. Let cool at least 15 minutes before serving.

Pour about ½ cup caramel sauce over monkey bread if desired.

OOEY GOOEY MONKEY BREAD

Source: Author

Ingredients

20 frozen yeast rolls thawed & quartered   1 cup granulated sugar

2 Tbsp ground cinnamon   1 cup light brown sugar, packed

1 ½ sticks butter   1/3 cup heavy cream

2 Tbsp brandy   1 tsp vanilla

1 cup pecan pieces

Preparation

Preheat Oven to 350°F.

Place the frozen yeast rolls in a single layer on a platter, and thaw on the counter for 30 minutes. Use a sharp knife and quarter each roll.

On the stove top, melt the brown sugar, butter and heavy cream together over medium-high heat. Bring to a boil, stirring constantly. Cook for 1 minute. Remove from the heat and stir in the brandy and vanilla.

Mix together 1 cup of granulated sugar and 2 Tbsp of ground cinnamon. Toss with the quartered rolls in a large plastic storage bag until evenly coated. Sprinkle 1/3 of the pecans on the bottom of the tube pan. Pour 1/3 of the caramel sauce over the pecans. Layer half of the quartered rolls on top of the pecans and sauce in the pan. Sprinkle the first layer of rolls with 1/3 of the remaining pecan pieces. Pour another 1/3 of the caramel sauce over this layer. Layer the remaining quartered rolls on top. Top with the last 1/3 cup of pecan pieces. Pour remaining caramel sauce over the top. Sprinkle any leftover cinnamon and sugar over all. Cover with a damp cloth and allow to rise for 45 minutes. Bake at 350°F for 35-40 minutes until golden brown. Cool for 5-10 minutes before carefully inverting onto a platter.

KEY LIME MUFFINS

Source: Café Nervosa; from the Sitcom, Frasier

Ingredients

2 cups all-purpose flour

1 Tbsp baking powder

½ tsp salt

1 cup sugar

1/3 cup milk

2 large eggs, lightly beaten

¼ cup vegetable oil

1 tsp grated lime rind

¼ cup key lime juice

Instructions

Combine first 4 ingredients in a large bowl; make a well in center of mixture. Combine milk and remaining ingredients; add to dry ingredients, stirring until moistened. Spoon into greased muffin pans, filling ¾ full. Bake at 400°F for 18 minutes or until browned. Remove from pans immediately.

CAPPUCCINO BISCOTTI WITH ORANGE ZEST

Source: Author

Ingredients

2 cups flour

½ tsp baking soda

1 cup sugar

2 tsp instant coffee granules

1 Tbsp dried orange zest

¼ cup cold butter, cut into ½ inch slices

2 Tbsp coffee liqueur

½ tsp baking powder

½ tsp salt

¼ cup cocoa powder

½ tsp ground cinnamon

½ cup chopped walnuts

3 eggs, lightly beaten

Preparation

Preheat oven to 350°F. Spray a large baking sheet with cooking spray.

In a large mixing bowl, combine flour, baking powder, baking soda, salt, sugar, cocoa powder, coffee granules, cinnamon and orange zest. Using a pastry cutter, cut in the butter until the mixture is crumbly.

Stir in walnuts, eggs and coffee liqueur until the dough is just moistened (add milk if more moisture is needed). Turn out onto a lightly floured surface, and knead lightly until the dough is soft and slightly sticky, about 8-10 times.

With floured hands shape dough into a 16 inch long roll. Place roll on a baking sheet coated with cooking spray, flatten roll to 1 inch thick.

Bake at 350°F for 30 minutes. Remove the roll to a wire rack and let cool for 10 minutes.

With a serrated knife, cut roll diagonally into ½ inch slices and place, cut sides down, on baking sheet. Return to the oven and bake at 350°F for 10 minutes. Turn slices over, and bake an additional 10 minutes (biscotti will be slightly soft in the center but will harden as they cool). Remove to a wire rack and let cool completely.

HAZELNUT TEA BREAD

Source: Author

Ingredients

½ cup chopped hazelnuts

1 ½ cups all-purpose flour

¾ cup sugar

1 tsp baking powder

1 tsp baking soda

½ tsp salt

½ tsp allspice

2 large eggs, lightly beaten

¼ cup milk

¼ cup butter, melted

½ tsp lemon zest

½ tsp vanilla

2 pears, peeled, seeded and diced

Preparation

Preheat oven to 350°F. Bake hazelnuts for 15 minutes, stirring once. Remove and set aside.

Combine flour, sugar, baking powder, baking soda, salt and allspice in a large bowl then add hazelnuts.

Combine eggs and milk in a small bowl and stir in butter, lemon zest and vanilla. Pour this mixture into the dry ingredients and stir just until blended. Fold in pears. Pour into a lightly greased loaf pan and bake for 1 hour or until a pick inserted in the center comes out clean. Remove from oven and let cool in the pan for 10 minutes. Remove from pan to a wire rack and let cool completely.

OLIVE GARDEN BREAD STICKS

Olive Garden doesn't give out their recipes, but this is so close, you won't know the difference.

Ingredients

1 cup + 2 Tbsp warm water	1 ¼ tsp active dry yeast
2 Tbsp granulated sugar, divided	3 - 3 ¼ cups all-purpose flour
1 ½ tsp salt	3 Tbsp oil

Garlic butter topping:

2 Tbsp butter	½ tsp salt
¼ tsp garlic powder	

Instructions

Add warm water, yeast and 1 tsp of the sugar to the bowl of a stand mixer and stir gently. Allow to rest for 10 minutes.

Add remaining sugar (1 Tbsp + 2 tsp sugar), 1 ½ cups flour, 1 ½ tsp salt and vegetable oil and mix on medium speed, to combine. Add another 1 ½ cups flour and knead mixture for 5-7 minutes, until the dough is smooth and elastic. The dough should pull away from the sides of the bowl but still be slightly sticky to the touch. Add remaining ¼ cup of flour, only if needed.

Transfer dough to a large, greased bowl and cover tightly with plastic wrap. Allow to rest in a warm place until double in size (about 1 to 1 ½ hours). Once risen, punch dough down and divide it into 12 equal parts. Roll each piece of dough into a 9 inch rope and transfer to a greased cookie sheet. Cover with plastic wrap and let rise again for 1 hour.

Bake breadsticks at 425°F for 10-12 minutes.

While the breadsticks bake, mix the garlic butter topping ingredients together. Brush butter mixture over the tops of the hot, cooked breadsticks.

RED LOBSTER CHEESE BISCUITS

Source: Allrecipes.com

Ingredients

2 cups all-purpose flour

1 cup cheddar cheese, shredded

1 Tbsp baking powder

1 tsp salt

½ tsp garlic powder

2/3 cup milk

1/3 cup butter

1 large egg

2 Tbsp butter, melted

Directions

Preheat oven to 400°F. Butter a baking sheet.

Combine flour, cheddar cheese, baking powder, salt, and garlic powder in a bowl.

Combine milk, 1/3 cup butter, and egg in a separate bowl. Mix into the flour mixture until chunky; be careful not to over-mix the batter.

Drop batter by Tbsp full onto the prepared baking sheet.

Bake in the preheated oven for 10 minutes. Brush melted butter on top and continue baking until golden brown, about 5 minutes more.

Cook's Note:

You can add about 1/2 tsp of garlic powder and/or 2 teaspoons dried parsley to the melted butter to brush on top of the biscuits.

NOTES

NOTES

_____

_____

_____

_____

_____

_____

_____

_____

_____

_____

_____

_____

_____

_____

_____

BREAKFAST

"If more of us valued food and cheer and song above hoarded gold, it would be a merrier world." **J.R.R. Tolkien**

BAKED CREPE OMELETS

Source: Author

Ingredients

8 large eggs   ¼ cup heavy cream

½ tsp Tarragon   ½ tsp salt

Pepper to taste

Filling:

1 cup thinly sliced and chopped ham   4 Tbsp butter

2 cups sliced baby portabella mushrooms   ½ tsp salt

1 small onion, finely chopped   ¼ cup white wine

1 cup Bellavitano Raspberry Sartori Cheese, grated   4 savory crepes

Preparation

Pre-heat oven to 350°F. Make Savory Crepes according to your favorite crepe recipe. Spray inside of 4 custard dishes with non-stick cooking spray. Carefully place one crepe inside of each dish, pressing into the sides and bottoms.

Mix together first 5 ingredients. Set aside. Grate cheese and set aside. In a medium skillet, melt the butter and sauté the onions over medium heat until tender. Add the mushrooms and continue cooking until tender; about 10 minutes. Add the wine and salt and continue cooking, stirring occasionally, until the liquid is gone; about 10 minutes. Remove from heat.

Pour half of the egg mixture into the four crepe shells in the custard dishes. Divide the mushroom mixture, the ham and the cheese evenly in the 4 crepe shells. Pour the rest of the egg mixture evenly into the 4 crepe shells. Bake for 25 minutes or until the eggs are set.

Remove from oven, turn crepe omelets out of the custard dishes onto individual plates (right side up), sprinkle lightly with paprika and serve.

HERB CRÊPES WITH DRIED FIGS & GOAT CHEESE

Source: Author

Ingredients

1 Tbsp. brandy

1 Tbsp raspberry vinaigrette

2 Tbsp. heavy cream

6 dried figs (diced)

1 cup baby spinach, stems removed

4 oz. goat cheese or feta cheese

Salt to taste

4 crêpes

Preparation

Make herb crêpes according to desired recipe. Heat brandy, vinaigrette and cream over medium heat. Stir in figs and spinach and cook for 5 minutes. Remove from heat. Remove spinach and let figs soak for 30 minutes. Chop spinach. Remove figs, reserving any left over liquid. Combine figs, spinach, cheese and seasoning and fill crêpes. Drizzle remaining liquid over crepes.

QUICHE LORRAINE

Source: Simpson's Restaurant, Carmel, CA

Ingredients

2 cups grated gruyere cheese (I have substituted asiago cheese and it's wonderful!)

1 Tbsp flour

6 slices bacon (I use Wrights thick sliced bacon)

½ cup onion, minced

3 eggs

2 cups heavy cream

¼ tsp salt

Pinch of cayenne pepper and nutmeg

Directions

Preheat oven to 400°F. Spray a 10 inch quiche dish with non-stick cooking spray. Place a pie shell in the dish and press to the bottom and sides. Prick bottom of pie shell with a fork and bake for 5 minutes. Remove from oven, prick bottom of pie shell again and bake for another 5 minutes. Remove from oven.

Dredge cheese with flour. Using a whisk, beat eggs, heavy cream, salt, cayenne pepper and nutmeg until well blended. Cut bacon into small pieces, brown in a small frying pan then remove to a small bowl, leaving the drippings in the pan. In the frying pan containing the drippings sauté the onions until tender. Spread onions evenly over the bottom of the pie crust. Sprinkle bacon evenly over the bottom of the pie crust. Spread cheese evenly in the pie crust. Pour egg mixture into the pie crust. Bake at 400°F for 15 minutes. Reduce to 325°F and bake for 30 minutes. Makes 6 generous servings. Sprinkle lightly with sweet paprika to serve.

BREAKFAST SOUFFLÉ FILLED MUSHROOMS

Source: Author

Ingredients

4 large portabella mushrooms

2 Tbsp butter

3 Tbsp flour

¾ cup cups hot milk

Salt to taste

White pepper to taste

Pinch of nutmeg

5 egg whites, stiffly beaten

1 egg yolk (reserve other four for sauce)

½ cup Parmesan cheese

½ lb. prosciutto or other ham

¼ cup white wine

Preparation

Preheat oven to 425°F. Cook butter and flour together for 2 minutes. Beat in the hot milk with a wire whisk; add ¼ cup white wine, a pinch of nutmeg, salt and pepper and bring to a boil stirring constantly for one minute. Remove pan from heat and beat in egg yolk. Stir in ¼ of the egg whites then fold in, very carefully, the rest of the egg whites and all but two Tbsp of the cheese.

Scoop out the mushrooms and place, hollow side up, in an oven proof dish which has been buttered. Place just enough soufflé mixture in each mushroom to barely fill. Place a layer of ham on each mushroom then heap remaining soufflé mixture equally on top of each mushroom.

BREAKFAST SOUFFLÉ FILLED MUSHROOMS

Sprinkle with the remaining cheese and bake at 425°F for 15 to 20 minutes until puffed and golden on top. Serve immediately with hollandaise sauce.

Hollandaise Sauce:

Ingredients

1 cup butter

4 egg yolks, lightly beaten

2 Tbsp lemon juice

1/8th tsp cayenne pepper

Preparation

Divide butter in half. Put half in a small saucepan with the egg yolks and lemon juice. Place pan over a low fire and stir constantly until the butter is melted. Add remaining butter and stir until thick. Remove from heat and add cayenne pepper. Serve at once over the soufflé filled mushrooms.

"Mushrooms are miniature pharmaceutical factories, and of the thousands of mushroom species in nature, our ancestors and modern scientists have identified several dozen that have a unique combination of talents that improve our health."
Paul Stamets

"Life is too short to stuff a mushroom."
Shirley Conran

"Marriage is like mushrooms: we notice too late if they are good or bad."
Woody Allen

BAKED FRENCH TOAST

Source: My friend, Rob Marrus, GBNF

Ingredients

2 Tbsp light corn syrup	½ stick butter
1 cup brown sugar, packed	Pinch of salt
12 slices cinnamon swirl bread, crusts removed	
6 eggs	1 ½ cups milk
1 tsp vanilla	

Directions

Combine corn syrup, butter and brown sugar in a small saucepan. Cook over low heat until syrupy. Pour into a 9 X 13 inch baking dish. Lay six slices of the bread on the syrup mixture.

Mix eggs, salt, milk and vanilla in a bowl. Pour ½ of this mixture evenly over the bread. Place remaining 6 slices of bread on top of the bread in the dish. Pour remaining egg mixture evenly over the bread slices. Cover and refrigerate overnight. Bake in preheated oven for 45 minutes at 350°F.

Strawberry Nut Sauce:

Ingredients

1 cup strawberry jam	¼ cup walnuts, chopped
2 tsp lemon juice	2 tsp corn starch
2/3 cup cold water	

Directions

Mix cornstarch and water and set aside. In a sauce pan, bring jam to a boil and add cornstarch mixture, stirring constantly. Bring back to a boil and simmer 3 minutes. Add lemon juice and chopped walnuts. Spoon approx. 1 Tbsp over each serving of French toast.

Irish Babies

Source: Author

Ingredients

¾ cup heavy cream

2 Tbsp flour

½ tsp salt

6 eggs

1 Tbsp Irish whiskey

¾ cup cooked ham, diced

4 Tbsp butter, divided

2 large apples, peeled, cored and sliced

2 Tbsp raspberry vinaigrette

1 Tbsp sugar

2 Tbsp Irish whiskey

¼ tsp cinnamon

Preparation

Preheat oven to 350°F. Place 4 individual casserole dishes in the oven for 5 minutes. Remove the dishes and place 1/2 Tbsp butter in each. Tip to coat sides (may substitute non-stick cooking spray). Divide ham evenly in the dishes. Pour batter evenly into the casserole dishes and bake for 15 minutes.

Meanwhile, heat 2 Tbsp butter in a medium frying pan. Add sliced apples and gently sauté. Add strawberry vinaigrette, sugar, Irish whiskey and cinnamon, stirring gently to incorporate. Spoon equal portions onto four plates. Carefully remove the Irish Babies from the casserole dishes and place one on top of the apples in each plate. Sprinkle with powdered sugar.

PAIN PERDU

Source: Author

Ingredients

3 eggs, beaten

¾ cup milk

¼ tsp salt

1 tsp sugar

1 tsp vanilla

½ tsp cinnamon

¼ tsp allspice

¼ tsp cardamom

12 thick slices French baguette (day old works best)

½ stick butter

Preparation

Mix together first 8 ingredients. Slice the French bread into slices that are at least 1-inch thick.

Soak each slice in the egg custard mixture. Turn the slices until all of the mixture has been absorbed into the bread. Depending on how stale the bread is, this may take from 5 to 10 minutes. Completely saturate the bread.

In a large skillet, melt the butter and fry bread slices over medium heat until golden brown and crusty

Traditionally, pain perdu is served with powdered sugar sprinkled over the top. If you want it to look like it would in the French Quarter, then dust away and enjoy. You can also top it with fresh fruit such as; sliced strawberries, blueberries, etc.

EGGS BENEDICT

Source: Author

Ingredients

3 English muffins

3 Tbsp butter, softened

1 tsp butter

6 thin slices Canadian-style bacon

6 eggs

4 tsp distilled white vinegar

Paprika

Chives, finely chopped

Preparation

Spread each muffin half with some of the 3 tablespoons butter; keep warm.

In 10-inch skillet, melt 1 teaspoon butter over medium heat. Cook bacon in butter until light brown on both sides; keep warm.

Wipe out skillet to clean; fill with 2 to 3 inches water. Add vinegar to water. Heat to boiling; reduce to simmering. Break cold eggs, one at a time, into custard cup or saucer. Holding dish close to water's surface, carefully slip eggs into water. Cook 3 to 5 minutes or until whites and yolks are firm, not runny (water should be gently simmering and not boiling). Remove with slotted spoon.

Place 1 slice bacon on each muffin half. Top with egg. Spoon your favorite Hollandaise Sauce over eggs (or see Hollandaise Sauce in Rubs & Seasonings). Sprinkle with paprika and chives.

STEAM FRIED EGGS

Source: Author

Ingredients

2 eggs

2 Tbsp butter

2 Tbsp water

Preparation

Over medium heat, melt butter in a cast iron (or non-stick) frying pan just large enough for the two eggs.

When pan is well heated, swirl it around to coat pan bottom and part way up the sides with butter. Carefully break eggs and place them in the in pan. Pour water around edges of the eggs and cover with a well-fitting lid, preferably a glass one you can see through.

When the whites look set and yellows begin to glaze over, lift lid and check for doneness of the whites. I like mine with the yellows runny and the whites set. Remove to a serving plate.

BASIC FRENCH OMELET

Source: Incredible Egg

Ingredients

2 eggs

2 Tbsp heavy cream

1/8 tsp salt

Dash pepper

1 tsp butter

1/3 cup filling, such as:

shredded cheese

finely chopped ham and spinach

Sweet paprika

Yields: 1 serving

Directions

Beat eggs, heavy cream, salt and pepper in small bowl until blended.

Heat butter in 6 to 8-inch nonstick omelet pan or skillet over medium-high heat until hot. Tilt pan to coat bottom. Pour in egg mixture. Mixture should set immediately at edges.

Gently push cooked portions from edges toward the center with inverted turner so that uncooked eggs can reach the hot pan surface. Continue cooking, tilting pan and gently moving cooked portions as needed.

When top surface of eggs is thickened and no visible liquid egg remains, place filling on one side of the omelet. FOLD omelet in half with turner. With a quick flip of the wrist, turn pan and invert or slide omelet onto plate. Dust with paprika. Serve immediately.

NOTES

NOTES

CAJUN & CREOLE

"I don't know why I order gumbo when I go to a Cajun restaurant. I already know that mine's the best." Author

HISTORY

No other state has a more varied or colorful past than Louisiana. The state has been governed under 10 different flags beginning in 1541 with Hernando de Soto's claim of the region for Spain. La Salle later claimed it for Bourbon France and over the years Louisiana was at one time or another subject to the Union Jack of Great Britain, the Tricolor of Napoleon, the Lone Star flag of the Republic of West Florida and the fifteen stars and stripes of the United States after Jefferson negotiated the purchase of Louisiana from France in 1803 as part of the Louisiana Purchase. With the acquisition of Louisiana, Jefferson nearly doubled the size of the fledgling U.S. and made it a world power. Later, 13 states or parts of states were carved out of the Louisiana Purchase territory. In 1812 Louisiana became the 18th state.

The city of New Orleans was founded in 1718, and just a few years later many African people were brought to the city as slaves. The mix of African, French, and Spanish influences gave Louisiana, and particularly the city of New Orleans, a unique culture. Today the Chitimacha, Coushatta, Jena Band of Choctaw Indians, Caddo and Tunica-Biloxi tribes still live in this state.

The French province of Acadia (today's Nova Scotia and surrounding regions) was settled in the 1600s by French colonists, but after becoming a British possession, the British authorities demanded that the Acadians renounce their Roman Catholic faith and swear allegiance to the Crown. The Acadians refused and during the mass exile that followed many ended up in Louisiana. Cajun is a corruption of the original French pronunciation of Acadian; A-ca-jan.

Cajun cooking may be a first cousin to the Creole cuisine of New Orleans, but there is none other quite like it in the world. Favorite Cajun dishes include jambalaya, gumbo, turtle sauce piquant, andouille sausage, boudin (a pork and rice sausage), Cochon du lait, soft-shell crab, stuffed crab, a hundred shrimp dishes, crawfish etoufee, crawfish bisque, crawfish pie, and dozens more.

JAMBALAYA

Source: Jerry Moncrief

Ingredients

1 lb. breakfast sausage

1 lb. smoked sausage, sliced

2-3 chicken breasts or one whole chicken

1 small box Uncle Ben's Long Grain & Wild Rice

2 bunches green onions, chopped, including tops

½ cup chopped celery

Water

1 cup white rice

½ tsp. salt

½ tsp. black pepper

½ tsp. garlic powder

¼ tsp. cayenne

Directions

Boil chicken, celery, salt and black pepper in enough water to cover until chicken is tender. Remove skin, de-bone and cut chicken into chunks. Set aside.

In a large skillet, brown and crumble breakfast sausage. Add onions and cook until just tender. Add chicken to sausage and onion mixture. Add enough water to remaining chicken broth to make 4 ½ cups and pour into skillet with chicken and sausage. Add seasoning from wild rice box, cayenne and garlic powder and bring to a boil.

Add wild rice, white rice and sliced smoked sausage. Cover and simmer for 20 minutes or until liquid is gone.

CRAWFISH & CORN MAQUE CHOUX

Maque choux is a traditional dish of South Louisiana. It is thought to be a combination of Creole and American Indian cultural influence, and the name is likely to have derived from the French interpretation of the Native American name.

Source: Author

Ingredients

½ lb. bacon, sliced in ½ inch pieces

1 large onion, diced

½ red bell pepper, diced

2 cloves garlic, minced

2 cups whole corn

1 cup heavy cream

1 tsp fresh thyme, chopped

2 Tbsp fresh Italian parsley, chopped   1 Tbsp fresh basil, chopped

1 lb. crawfish tails   1 green onion, finely chopped

Salt and freshly ground pepper   Cajun seasoning

Preparation

In a large enameled cast-iron skillet, cook the bacon over moderately low heat, stirring, until it's lightly crisp, about 5 minutes. Transfer the bacon to paper towels. Pour off all but 2 Tbsp of the bacon drippings.

Add onion and bell pepper. Sauté until tender, about 3 to 5 minutes. Add garlic and corn. Sauté 2 minutes. Add cream, thyme, parsley, basil and crawfish tails. Simmer until sauce thickens, about 5 minutes. Mix in green onion and season to taste with salt, pepper and Cajun seasoning, if desired.

LAGNIAPPE QUICHE

Source: Author

Ingredients

5 eggs	1 tsp. Tony Chachere's
1 cup cooked rice	½ tsp. dried tarragon
1 ¼ cup half and half	½ tsp. dried basil
½ cup ham, diced	2 Tbsp. honey mustard
½ pkg. frozen crawfish tails (thawed)	2 cups cheese, shredded
1 small onion, finely chopped	1 pre-formed pie crust

Preparation

Place pie crust in a 10" quiche dish and prick across the bottom with a fork. Preheat oven to 450°F and bake for 5 minutes. Remove from oven; carefully prick pie crust again with a fork and bake for another 5 minutes. Reduce oven to 350°F.

In a large sauce pan over medium heat, sauté onions in one Tbsp. butter until tender. Add rice, ham, crawfish tails, Tony Chachere's, tarragon and basil. Mix together and cook 5 minutes or until heated through. In a medium size bowl beat eggs then add the half and half and honey mustard. Mix together until blended. Spread 1 cup of the shredded cheese on the pie crust then add the rice mixture and spread evenly. Pour the egg mixture over the rice and gently mix together taking care not to disturb the cheese. Bake in the pre-heated 350°F oven for 25 to 30 minutes or until the quiche mixture doesn't jiggle in the middle. Spread the remaining 1 cup of shredded cheese over the top and bake for an additional 5 minutes. Slice as you would a pie and serve hot.

Rabbit and Andouille Sausage Jambalaya

Source: Author

Ingredients

1 lb. breakfast sausage   1 lb. andouille sausage, sliced

2 rabbits

1 small box Uncle Ben's Long Grain & Wild Rice

2 bunches green onions, chopped, including tops

½ cup chopped celery

Chicken broth

1 cup white rice

½ tsp. salt

½ tsp. black pepper

½ tsp. garlic powder

¼ tsp. cayenne

Preparation

Boil rabbit, celery, salt and black pepper in enough water to cover until rabbit is tender. De-bone and cut rabbit into chunks. Set aside.

In large skillet, over medium heat, brown and crumble breakfast sausage. Add onions and cook until just tender. Add rabbit to sausage and onion mixture. Add enough chicken broth to remaining rabbit broth to make 4 ½ cups and pour into skillet with rabbit and sausage. Add seasoning from wild rice box, cayenne and garlic powder and bring to a boil.

Add wild rice, white rice and sliced andouille sausage. Cover and simmer for 20 minutes or until liquid is gone.

CRAWFISH CHEESECAKE WITH PECAN CRUST

Source: Author

Ingredients

Pecan Crust:

¾ cup pecans   1 cup all-purpose flour

½ tsp salt   5 Tbsp unsalted butter, cold

3 Tbsp ice water

Preparation

Finely chop pecans and mix with flour and salt. Add butter and cut
into flour mixture until you have crumbs about the size of a pea.
Add ice water and work with your fingers until incorporated evenly. Dough will still be fairly crumbly. Press into sides and bottom of
a 9" spring form pan. Bake in a 350°F oven for about 20 minutes.
Allow crust to cool.

Filling:

½ small onion, finely chopped   ½ pound crawfish tails, chopped

8 oz. cream cheese, room temp.   3 oz. Creole cream cheese

2 eggs   Salt and white pepper to taste

Favorite hot sauce to taste

Sauté onion in a small amount of butter until translucent. Add
crawfish and cook until just heated through. Remove from heat and
set aside.

In mixer, blend cream cheese until smooth. Add Creole cream
cheese and then eggs one at a time. Fold in crawfish mixture.

CRAWFISH CHEESECAKE WITH PECAN CRUST

Season to taste with salt, white pepper and hot sauce. Pour into prepared, cooled crust and bake at 300°F for about 30 minutes or until set and firm to touch.

Sauce:

2 Tbsp chopped shallots

4 oz. mixed wild mushrooms (or whatever you can find)

1 Tbsp lemon juice

3 oz. Worcestershire sauce

1 oz. hot sauce

3 oz. heavy cream

3 Tsp butter, softened

Salt & pepper to taste

Sauté shallots until translucent. Add the mushrooms and cook until just cooked through. Add lemon juice, Worcestershire sauce and hot sauce, and reduce by ¾. Add heavy cream and reduce by half. Wisk in the butter. Serve on the side to be added as desired.

NEW ORLEANS STYLE BARBEQUE SHRIMP

Source: Author

Ingredients

1 pound (21-25 count) shrimp, heads remove, peeled, tails on

Bbq sauce:

2 cloves garlic, minced

1 medium onion, finely chopped

4 Tbsp olive oil	2 Tbsp lemon juice
1 cup white wine	1 cup water
2 Tbsp Worcestershire Sauce	1 tsp. Bitters
1 Tbsp mustard	2 Tbsp ketchup
¼ cup Organic Sucanat	½ tsp. cayenne pepper
2 Tbsp CC Spice (recipe in Rubs & Seasonings)	1 bay leaf
2 tsp. salt	½ tsp. black pepper
1 stick butter	French bread for serving

Preparation

Peel the shrimp, leaving tails attached. Coat the shrimp with CC Spice and refrigerate while making the sauce. Heat 2 Tbsp. olive oil over high heat in a large pot. Add onions and garlic and sauté until tender.

Add the lemon juice, wine, water, Worcestershire Sauce, Bitters, ketchup, mustard, Organic Sucanat, cayenne pepper, 2 Tbsp. CC Spice, the bay leaf, salt and black pepper. Stir well and bring to a boil. Reduce heat and simmer for 30 minutes. Remove bay leaf. Add butter and cook an additional 2 minutes until butter is thoroughly melted and blended in.

Heat the remaining 2 Tbsp. of oil in a large skillet over high heat. Add the seasoned shrimp and sauté them for 2 minutes, turning once, shaking the skillet occasionally. Be careful not to overcook shrimp or they will become tough. Add the barbeque sauce. Stir and simmer for 3 minutes. Remove the shrimp to a warm platter with tongs and serve in a plate over grits with barbeque sauce spooned over the top. Serve with French bread.

CRAWFISH BREAD

Source: New Orleans JAZZ FEST

Ingredients

1 pound crawfish tails, coarsely chopped

1 loaf French bread

½ stick butter

½ cup onions, chopped

½ cup celery, chopped

2 cloves garlic, minced

¼ cup yellow bell pepper, chopped

½ tsp dry mustard

½ cup BLUE PLATE mayonnaise

1/3 cup Monterey jack cheese, grated (pepper jack for bigger kick)

1/3 cup Cheddar cheese, grated

Directions

Slice French bread lengthwise down one side and scoop out inside of loaf. In large skillet, melt butter over medium high heat and sauté onions, celery, bell pepper and garlic until tender. Add crawfish and cook until heated through. Blend in dry mustard and mayonnaise. Add cheeses and blend until melted. Spread crawfish mixture inside the bread and close halves back together. Butter top of loaf, wrap in foil and bake on BBQ pit or in a 350°F oven for 20-3- minutes. Cut into slices and serve hot.

CRAWFISH ETOUFEE

Source: Author

Ingredients

1 stick butter	¼ cup flour
1 medium green bell pepper, diced	2 medium onions, diced
2 stalks celery, chopped	3 cloves garlic, minced
1 can tomato sauce	2 tsp Worcestershire sauce
1 tsp. Kitchen Bouquet	½ tsp. thyme
1 tsp. basil	1 tsp. parsley

1 bay leaf

1 cup Crawfish or chicken stock; adjust to desired consistency

1 cup white wine	1 pound crawfish tails
2 green onions, chopped	½ tsp black pepper
¼ tsp cayenne pepper	Salt to taste

Preparation

In a large Dutch oven or heavy bottomed saucepan combine melted butter and flour until smooth. Cook on medium heat, stirring continuously, for about 10-12 minutes, until you have achieved desired color. Add the onion, garlic, green pepper and celery and cook for 8-10 minutes, stirring frequently. Add tomato sauce, Worcestershire sauce, thyme, basil, parsley, bay leaf and let simmer for 30 minutes. Gradually pour in the stock and wine, bring to a boil and let it simmer for 5 minutes. Add the crawfish and Kitchen Bouquet and simmer for 3-4 more minutes. Don't overcook crawfish. Stir in, green onions.

Serve over hot cooked rice.

"What did you said? Cook without wine? C'mon now, how you gonna did that, huh?" Justin Wilson

CRAWFISH BISQUE

Source: Author

Ingredients

½ stick butter

¼ cup olive oil

½ cup flower

2 large onions, chopped

1 bell pepper, seeded & chopped

2 celery ribs, minced

4 cloves garlic, minced

1 lb. crawfish tails

3 cups shellfish stock (preferred) or other stock

1 ½ tsp salt or to taste

½ tsp black pepper or to taste

2 Tbsp smoked paprika

½ tsp. cayenne

1 tsp. thyme

¼ cup fresh parsley

2 bay leaves

½ cup heavy cream

1 tsp. Tabasco

½ cup white wine

1 Tbsp lemon juice

¼ cup chives

Preparation

Melt butter in a saucepan over medium. Whisk in flour until combined. Cook, stirring constantly, until roux is pale brown, about 10 minutes. Add onion, bell pepper, celery, garlic, salt, black pepper, paprika and cayenne pepper, and cook, stirring occasionally, 5 minutes. Increase heat to medium-high. Stir in stock, parsley, thyme, bay leaves, and ¼ cup white wine, and cook 10 minutes. Add half of crawfish, and cook 2 minutes.

Remove from heat and remove bay leaves. Using a submersible emulsifier puree until smooth, about 30 seconds. Return heat to medium-low. Stir in cream, lemon juice, Tabasco, and remaining crawfish and the remaining white wine. Bring to a low simmer, and cook until heated, about 5 minutes.

If you want to take the time to make a traditional crawfish bisque with stuffed crawfish heads, look up a recipe and add the stuffed heads according to the recipe.

FRIED EGGPLANT WITH CRAWFISH ETOUFEE

This dish is a rich and elegant appetizer, but would make a filling entrée by serving two fried eggplant rounds with the same amount of crawfish etoufee.

Source: George Graham - AcadianaTable.com

Ingredients

Etoufee:

1 stick unsalted butter	1 cup diced yellow onion
½ cup diced green bell pepper	½ cup diced celery
½ Tbsp minced garlic	1 lb. Louisiana crawfish tail meat
1 Tbsp all-purpose flour	½ cup seafood stock
½ tsp. cayenne pepper	Kosher salt and freshly ground black pepper

Dash of hot sauce

Eggplant:

1 large eggplant	Kosher salt
Peanut oil	1 cup all-purpose flour
1 Tbsp Acadiana Table Cajun Seasoning Blend	1 large egg, beaten
½ cup whole milk	1 tsp hot sauce
1 cup unseasoned bread crumbs	½ cup green onion tops, diced

Instructions

Etoufee:

In a large cast-iron skillet over medium-high heat, melt the butter. Add the onion, bell pepper, and celery, and sauté until the onions turn translucent, about 5 minutes. Add the garlic, lower the heat to simmer, and stir to combine. Add the crawfish tail meat and stir to combine. Sprinkle the flour over the mixture, stir to incorporate, and add the stock. Stir until the stock thickens into a tight sauce-like

FRIED EGGPLANT WITH CRAWFISH ETOUFEE

consistency, about 5 minutes. Let simmer for 5 minutes longer and then turn off the heat. Keep warm until ready to serve.

Eggplant:

Slice the eggplant into 4 rounds of uniform 1-inch thickness. Place on a plate lined with paper towels. Sprinkle both sides with salt and place in the refrigerator for at least 1 hour or overnight.

In a large pot with at least 3 inches of oil over medium-high heat, bring the temperature of the oil to 350°F.

Remove the eggplant from the refrigerator and using paper towels remove any excess moisture or surface salt.

In a shallow bowl, add the flour and seasoning. Stir to combine.

In a shallow bowl, add the egg, milk, and hot sauce; whisk to combine.

In a shallow bowl, add the bread crumbs.

Dip each eggplant round into the flour; add to the egg mixture; and coat with the bread crumbs.

Add the coated eggplant to the hot grease and fry until golden brown on both sides, 5 to 8 minutes. Remove and drain on paper towels. Lightly sprinkle with salt.

For serving, place 2 eggplant rounds on each plate and spoon a generous portion of etoufee over each. Sprinkle with green onion tops and serve with rice.

"When you cut that eggplant up and you roast it in the oven and you make the tomato sauce and you put it on top, your soul is in that food, and there's something about that that can never be made by a company that has three million employees."
Mario Batali
Ingredients for: Acadiana Table Cajun Seasoning Blend in Rubs & Seasonings.

TEXAS GUMBO

I'm a native West Texan so I use a few additional ingredients, like Jimmy Dean sausage, which creates a richer flavored gumbo.

Source: Author

Ingredients

1 large chicken, boned and skin removed	1 cup butter
1 cup flour	2 lb. smoked sausage

1 pkg. Jimmy Dean breakfast sausage (what makes it Texas gumbo)

2 large onions, chopped	4 cloves garlic, minced
4 ribs celery, chopped	1 bell pepper, chopped
4 cups okra, cut up	2 bay leaves
½ tsp. thyme	½ tsp. oregano
½ tsp. marjoram	½ tsp. basil
2 Tbsp. parsley	1 cup dry white wine
Salt, cayenne & black pepper to taste	2 Tbsp. olive oil

6 cups chicken broth (add water if additional liquid is needed)

Preparation

Prepare all of the vegetables and set aside to be added later. Keep the okra separate from the other vegetables. Slice the smoked sausage into ¼ inch slices and set aside to be added later. In a large pot melt the butter then stir in the flour to make a roux. Cook over medium heat, stirring frequently, until the roux is the color of medium to dark chocolate. While the roux is cooking, pour the olive oil in a large skillet and brown the chicken. When the chicken is brown, remove it from the skillet and cut it into bite sized pieces and set aside. In the same skillet, cook the Jimmy Dean sausage, mashing and cutting it until it is in pieces the size if chili meat.

TEXAS GUMBO

Cook until it starts to brown, then remove the sausage from the skillet (leaving the grease) and set it aside. Add the okra to the skillet and cook until it starts to brown and is no longer slimy. Remove the okra from the skillet and set it aside. When the roux looks brown enough, add all of the vegetables, except the okra, stirring them into the roux and cook until tender. Add the chicken broth slowly, stirring to mix together well. Add water at this time if more liquid is needed. You can now add all of the other ingredients. Bring to a boil then reduce the heat and simmer for 30 minutes, adjusting the salt and pepper to taste. Let set for at least an hour, then skim off all of the fat that has risen to the top and discard. Serve with cooked rice, crackers and filet' powder. Enjoy!

Note: With this recipe, my wife and I won the Taste of Louisiana Cook-off at Scott's Cycles in Bossier City, Louisiana in 2016. This is the trophy we won. It's made from 1948 Harley Pan Head parts except for the WW II gas grenade used for the gas tank.

CRAWFISH BISQUE

Perhaps the grandest dish in all of Cajun and Creole cuisine. This spicy, hearty bisque is sometimes served as thin as a soup, sometimes even thicker than an etoufee -- adjust the consistency to suit your taste. What makes it unique among all bisques in the culinary world is the addition of the stuffed crawfish heads (shells, actually) with crawfish dressing ... heavenly.

Source: Chuck Taggart; gumbopages.com

For the bisque:

20 pounds live crawfish	3 lemons, quartered
4 packets Zatarain's Crab, Shrimp and Crawfish Boil seasoning	
6 Tbsp butter	½ cup peanut oil
1 cup flour	2 large onions, finely minced
1 large bell pepper, finely minced	3 ribs celery, finely minced
4 cloves garlic, finely minced	5 cups shellfish stock or water
1 Tbsp salt, or to taste	Freshly ground black pepper, to taste
1 Tbsp Creole seasoning	2 Tbsp cayenne pepper
2 tsp thyme	½ cup chopped green onion tops
½ cup chopped parsley	5 dozen stuffed crawfish heads (see below)

About 7 ½ cups cooked Louisiana long-grain white rice

Prepare a large crawfish-boiling pot with enough water for boiling the crawfish; add Zatarain's and lemons and bring to a boil. Drop the crawfish in live, and boil for 10 minutes. Ice down the boil and let the crawfish soak in the cold spiced water; the longer you let them soak, the more seasoning will be absorbed.

Break off the tails. Peel the tails, removing the vein but reserving the little flap of crawfish meat that's over the vein. Remove the crawfish fat from the heads (the little yellow glob that's worth its

CRAWFISH BISQUE

weight in gold) and reserve in a separate container.

Clean 5 dozen crawfish heads for stuffing. The so-called "head" is actually the large red thorax shell. Remove all inside parts, including the eyes and antennae. What should remain is a little tube with two open ends and one open side. Be careful; the shell must be scraped clean on the inside and it can be a bit rough on the fingers. (I'm told that a beer can opener makes this job easier.) Divide the crawfish fat and tails evenly, reserving half for the bisque and half for the stuffing.

Prepare the stuffed crawfish heads according to the recipe below. This is very labor-intensive, and takes a long time; most folks I know take two days to make crawfish bisque, cooking the crawfish, cleaning the heads and stuffing them the day before, and cooking the bisque on the second day. Recruit some help if you can. Place the stuffed heads in a pan and refrigerate.

To prepare the bisque, make a roux with the butter, oil and flour. Cook over low-medium heat, being careful not to scorch the butter, until the roux turns light brown. Stir CONSTANTLY. This means constantly, without stopping for anything. Add the onions, bell pepper, celery and garlic, and continue to cook, stirring constantly, until the vegetables are soft and the roux is peanut butter-colored. Remove from heat and cool, continuing to stir.

Gradually and carefully add the stock or water (stock preferably) and combine thoroughly, making a nice gravy. Add half of the crawfish tails and crawfish fat, Creole seasoning, salt and peppers, and cook over low heat for 15 minutes. If you've got a little leftover crawfish stuffing, add it to the pot as well, as it adds more body and flavor.

Add the baked or sautéed crawfish heads, and cook over low heat for 30 minutes. Add the onion tops and parsley just before serving.

(Continued on next page)

CRAWFISH BISQUE

To serve, mound about ¾ cup rice in large bowl, and divide the bisque evenly between them. Serve 6 stuffed crawfish heads with each serving. Don't worry about table manners; you almost have to use your fingers to get the stuffing out of the heads, and I've seen some folks (like me) inserting tongue into crawfish head to lick all the stuffing out. If you want to be more dainty, the tail end of your fork or spoon, or the end of a butter knife, helps get the stuffing out more easily. Make sure everyone gets the same number of heads, or fights will break out; they're that good. I'm told that tradition requires the empty heads to be placed around the rim of the bowl, so that some don't get more than others. It's easier to count them quickly that way.

For the stuffed crawfish heads:

¼ cup oil	½ cup flour
2 medium onions, finely minced	1 large bell pepper, finely minced
¾ cup stock or water	2 tsp salt
Freshly ground black pepper	1 ½ tsp cayenne pepper
2 large eggs, well beaten	2 cups plain French bread crumbs
¼ cup chopped parsley	¼ cup minced green onions with tops
4 Tbsp butter, melted	5 dozen cleaned crawfish heads
Flour for dusting	

Make a roux with the oil and flour. Add onions and bell peppers and cook until tender, stirring constantly. Mince or grind the remaining half of the crawfish tails and add to the roux-onion mixture. Add the remaining crawfish fat and simmer for 15 minutes.

Add stock, salt, peppers, breadcrumbs, eggs, parsley, green onions and butter. Combine thoroughly, adjusting the consistency with more stock or more bread crumbs as needed.

CRAWFISH CAROLYN

This dish comes from the menu of Christian's Restaurant, although it's been quite a few years and I'm not sure if they still serve it. It's still mighty good, though, and quite rich. You can vary the amount of cayenne pepper to suit your own palate; be careful not to overdo it, but the cream will help take the bite off it somewhat.

For the cream sauce:

3 cups heavy whipping cream   2 cups shellfish stock or water

¼ cup brandy   1 ½ cups blonde roux (¾ cup oil, ¾ cup flour)

1 cup grated Parmigiana Reggiano cheese (or domestic Parmesan, but for God's sakes don't use that crap from the green can)

For the crawfish:

2 Tbsp unsalted butter   ½ small onion, finely chopped

¼ green bell pepper, finely chopped ½ stalk celery, finely chopped

3 cloves garlic, minced   ¼ cup flat-leaf parsley, finely chopped

¼ cup green onion, thinly sliced   2 tsp fresh thyme (1 tsp dried)

½ to 1 ½ tsp cayenne pepper, to taste   Salt and pepper, to taste

1 pound crawfish tails

Heat the cream with the stock or water, then add the cheese and brandy and bring to a boil. Stir in the roux and simmer for 15 minutes; keep warm.

Heat the butter in a skillet, then add the finely chopped onions, garlic, bell pepper and celery. Sauté for about 5 minutes until soft, translucent and fragrant. Add the crawfish, salt, thyme, red and black peppers. Cook uncovered for about 5 minutes, then mix in the cream sauce.

Divide the crawfish mixture into four small gratin dishes, then top with more grated Parmesan cheese. Place under the broiler for a minute or so until the top gets slightly browned and bubbly, and serve immediately.

MR. B'S RISOTTO

By Judy Walker

NOLA.com; The Times-Picayune

Mr. B's Risotto was demonstrated by executive chef Michelle McRaney and her executive sous chef, Vincent Sciarrotta, on the second Friday at the Food Heritage stage in 2013. The restaurant makes several versions: Garlic, crawfish with sautéed, diced onion, red and green diced bell peppers, jumbo lump crabmeat and asparagus, wild mushrooms with vegetable stock, corn and oven-dried tomatoes and lobster. McRaney and Sciarrotta made the crawfish version, with sautéed diced onion, red and green diced bell peppers, and crawfish. You can add ½ to 1 pound extra ingredients, at the end of the cooking process. If you wish to duplicate their crawfish version, be sure the cooked mixture is drained well before serving.

Mr. B's Bistro; New Orleans

Ingredients

7 cups chicken stock	1 stick plus 2 Tbsp unsalted butter
2 Tbsp olive oil	2 medium onions, diced
1 lb. Arborio rice	¼ cup white wine
¼ cup freshly grated Parmesan cheese	

Instructions

In a large saucepan, heat stock, covered, until hot. Reduce heat to low and keep at a simmer, covered.

In a large heavy-bottomed pan, melt 2 tablespoons butter over medium heat. Add oil and heat until hot but not smoking. Add onion and cook, stirring, until translucent, about 5 minutes. Add rice and cook, stirring with a wooden spoon, 1 to 2 minutes, or until rice is coated in oil.

COCHON DE LAIT (CAJUN ROAST PIG)

Outdoor Cooking Louisiana-Style

Cochon de lait is one of Acadiana's most famous and most delectable dishes -- marinated, pit-roasted young suckling pig, sliced thin and served with gravy, on a plate or on a po-boy. The mere aroma of this dish is enough to make your knees buckle, not to mention the taste. (See how to do it next two pages)

COCHON DE LAIT (CAJUN ROAST PIG)

The Cochon de lait is a Louisiana tradition and one of the main social events of the Cajun and Creoles. Remember that each pig is
different and will require varying seasoning amounts and cooking
times. Any measurements given here are approximate and will
work best on a 50-pound pig.

Source: Gary; modified from recipes by John Folse and Chuck Taggart

Ingredients

1 50-pound pig	5 Tbsp salt
1 Tbsp black pepper	1 Tbsp garlic
1 Tbsp paprika	1 Tbsp chili powder
4 cups melted butter	2 bottles beer
Hot sauce	¼ cup garlic

Preparation

Traditional Cochon de Lait starts with selecting the ideal, fresh
suckling pig. A 25-75 pound pig (dressed out) is preferred. Make
sure your butcher properly prepares the carcass for open-pit roasting. Season the pig well inside and out with salt, pepper, garlic,
paprika and chili powder. Reserve half of the seasonings for use later in the cooking.

Combine butter, beer, hot sauce and ¼ cup granulated garlic. Use
more or less of each ingredient depending on the size of pig. Inject
front and rear hams and tenderloin with this infused liquid. This
seasoning process helps bring out the full flavor of the pig and en-
hances the natural juices, resulting in a full-flavored, tender and
delicious pig. For best results, season the pig the day before roasting.

Using a meat saw, cut through backbone at neck and tail. Lay pig
open flat. Stretch the pig between to pieces of heavy wire mesh (the

COCHON DE LAIT (CAJUN ROAST PIG)

mesh type used in concrete construction). Secure the sides and corners with bailing wire. Next, wire a 1 inch pipe on each long side to support pig over the fire over a hardwood fire made preferably with oak or pecan wood. Dig a 10 to 12 inch deep pit about 3 feet by 4 feet to serve as a fire pit. Build a low wall encircling the pit with concrete blocks or bricks. Lay sheet metal or tin against this wall and down the sides of the fire pit.

Start your fire and allow to burn down to a good bed of hot coals. Place the pig over the pit, with the ends of the pipe resting on the concrete blocks. Pig should be 15 to 20 inches above the coals. Turn the roasting rack about every half hour. Total cooking time with vary according to weight of the pig, but you should allow 6 - 7 hours for a 25 - 50 pound pig, and 8 - 9 hours for a 50 - 75 pound one.

Many Cajuns consider the Cracklin' skin the best part of the Cochon De Lait. To get the skin croquant (crispy) build a very intense fire, and bring up a strong flame, just before the pig is going to come off the fire. When you hear the last of the grease popping, bubbles will rise on the skin, and it's time to turn over the pig over.

Take the rack away from the fire and lay it on a clean flat surface for a few minutes to prepare for serving.

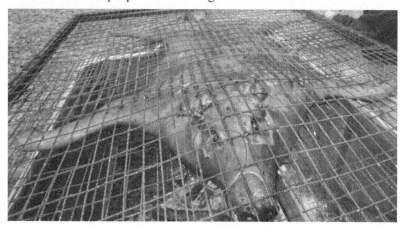

CAJUN SHEPHERD'S PIE

Source: Author

Ingredients

1 lb. pork, ground

1 lb. alligator, chopped

¼ cup bacon drippings

1 medium onion, diced

1 stalk celery, finely chopped

2 cloves garlic, minced

½ cup green bell pepper, finely chopped

1 cup carrots, diced

2 Tbsp all-purpose flour

2 mirlitons, cooked and chopped

2 Tbsp tomato paste

1 Tbsp Worcestershire sauce

½ tsp Tabasco sauce

1 tsp salt

1 tsp dried basil

½ tsp dried oregano

1 Tbsp dried parsley

½ tsp dried thyme

¼ tsp white pepper

½ tsp onion powder

¼ tsp garlic powder

Cajun Seasoning, to taste

10 oz. frozen green peas

10 oz. frozen corn

1 lb. pkg. crawfish tails

½ cup chicken broth

3 cups sweet potatoes, cooked, mashed

Paprika

Preparation

Marinate alligator in buttermilk, to cover, for ½ hour; drain and rinse.

Cook whole mirlitons in boiling water while alligator is marinating, about 25 minutes. Remove from water, cool enough to handle and chop.

Preheat oven to 400°F.

CAJUN SHEPHERD'S PIE

Heat bacon drippings in a large skillet over medium heat. Sauté onion, celery, bell pepper, carrots and garlic until tender. Remove from skillet, leaving remaining drippings in skillet, and set aside.

Add alligator and cook until just done. Add pork, breaking apart, until meat is crumbled and starts to brown. Sprinkle meat with the flour and toss to coat, continuing to cook for another minute. Return vegetables to skillet with the meat and add chopped mirlitons.

Add the tomato paste, Worcestershire, Tabasco, salt, basil, oregano, parsley, thyme, pepper, onion powder, garlic powder and Cajun Seasoning and stir to combine. Bring to a boil, reduce the heat to low, cover and simmer slowly 10 to 12 minutes or until the sauce is thickened slightly. Stir the corn, peas and crawfish into the meat mixture and spread evenly into a 2 quart casserole dish.

Combine the chicken broth with the mashed sweet potatoes and spread on top, starting around the edges to create a seal to prevent the mixture from bubbling up and smooth with a rubber spatula. Place on a half sheet pan on the middle rack of the oven and bake for 25 minutes or just until the potatoes begin to brown. Remove to a cooling rack for at least 15 minutes before serving.

DAUBE GLACE

Daube was introduced to New Orleans by the French Creoles who brought the preparation from their native France, where there are many regional versions of the dish. The Creoles went a step further and created Daube Glace which is a jellied dish served cold for breakfast or brunch.

What makes this dish unique from an ordinary Pot Roast is the larding of the roast with seasoned salt pork which flavors the meat from the inside while it cooks. Be sure and do this the night before cooking!

Source: Mary Moore Bremer

Ingredients

4 lbs. rump	¼ lb. Salt bacon, cut into thin strips (½" X 3")
¼ tsp cayenne	1 tsp salt
½ tsp black pepper	3 fresh bay leaves, finely chopped
1 Tbsp Fresh Thyme, finely chopped	4 Garlic Cloves
1/8 tsp ground cloves	¼ tsp allspice
2 large onions	

Directions

Take four pounds of rump, lard it with one quarter pound of salt bacon which has been cut into strips three inches long, and one half inch thick, and has been rolled in the flavoring mixture. Make incisions in the meat about 1½ inches apart and three inches long, and insert these flavored strips of fat. It is best if this can be put in a porcelain vessel and kept for twenty-four hours. If not convenient to do this, cook at once. Take two large onions, slice, and put in saucepan with one tablespoon of lard. When slightly brown, lay the larded rump of beef on top of this, cover closely and let simmer slowly till well brown. Then add the remainder of the mixture of flavorings in which you have rolled your larding strips. Add five

DAUBE GLACE

carrots, diced, two turnips cut the same way and two large chopped onions. Let the whole brown, keeping well covered, and cook slowly over low flame. Always cover tightly. After ten minutes, turn daube and let simmer ten minutes more. Then add sufficient hot water to cover. Season high; cover pot tight, turn flame low and cook slowly till tender. This takes about four hours. Serve cold.

Glace for cold daube:

This is made by boiling pig's feet and a small piece of veal, seasoned highly with herbs and sufficient water, until it forms a jelly. This, poured over the hot daube before it is put in ice box, and served very cold, makes a wonderful dish.

Garnish with curly parsley and slices of lemon.

CRAWFISH ETOUFEE

Source: Onnie Walker

Ingredients

6 Tbsp butter

4 Tbsp all-purpose flour

1 cup onion, chopped

6 green onions with tops, chopped

½ cup bell pepper, chopped

½ cup celery, chopped

2 cups chicken broth

2 to 3 lbs. crawfish tail meat

¼ cup fresh parsley, chopped

Salt and pepper, to taste

1 bay leaf

Tabasco, to taste

Directions

In a large heavy skillet, melt butter; stir in flour. Cook and stir over low heat for about 20 minutes until a rich brown. Add vegetables and cook until tender. Stir in chicken broth and seasonings. Simmer about 10 minutes, add crawfish tails and simmer about 10 minutes more. Adjust seasonings, to taste. Add some Tony Chachere's and a little fresh squeezed lemon juice, if desired.

Discard bay leaf and serve over hot rice.

"I live in Connecticut, but eventually I'd like to move back to New Orleans. I grew up there; the pace is a bit slower. Plus, I love crawfish and po'boys."

Harry Connick, Jr.

RED BEANS, SAUSAGE AND RICE

Although born and partly raised in West Texas, I still grew up eating red beans, but we ate ours with cornbread and fried potatoes. The sausage and rice didn't get added until we moved to Louisiana in 1961. That's the way I've eaten them since except for the years I lived in California when I reverted back to eating them with cornbread and fried potatoes. My kids loved them and always wanted me to cook "beans and spuds" for them. This, however, is the way I've cooked them since moving back to Louisiana in 1991.

Source: Author

Ingredients

2 cups dried pinto beans	1 large onion, chopped
2 cloves garlic, minced	1 ham hock
½ bell pepper, chopped	1 bay leaf
½ tsp marjoram	½ tsp dried basil
½ tsp dried oregano	1 Tbsp dried parsley
Salt and black pepper, to taste	Cayenne pepper, to taste
1 lb. smoked sausage, sliced ¼ inch thick	1 Tbsp Kitchen Bouquet

Preparation

Pick through beans, removing any foreign matter and bad beans. In a large pot, rinse beans 3 times, draining after each rinse. **_"Do not soak beans overnight and drain them"_**! Doing that removes much of the flavor.

In a large, heavy pot, brown sausage in 1 tablespoon of oil until slightly crisp. Add 3 to 4 quarts of water and all of the above ingredients except the smoked sausage and Kitchen Bouquet. Cook beans until tender, about 3 to 4 hours.

Add smoked sausage and Kitchen Bouquet, adjust seasoning and cook 15 minutes more. Serve over cooked rice.

MIRLITON CASSEROLE

"Mirliton is better known as chayote, and records show it was grown in New Orleans from as early as 1867. According to mirliton enthusiast Lance Hill, its early popularity was likely related to the close connection the city had with the Caribbean, which began the long history of backyard mirliton vines in New Orleans that continues to this day. In 2005, Hurricane Katrina wiped out many of these backyard vines, but community groups are working to bring back the traditional Louisiana mirliton, which is included in Slow Food USA's Ark of Taste."

Source: Author

Ingredients

5 medium mirlitons	1 Tbsp crab boil (liquid)
1 stick butter	2 medium onions, diced
¼ cup celery, diced	2 cloves garlic, minced
1 cup green onions, sliced	¼ cup parsley, chopped
Salt and black pepper to taste	1 cup cheddar cheese, shredded
¼ tsp cayenne pepper	½ cup bread crumbs

Preparation

Preheat oven to 350°F. Place mirlitons in a large pot and cover with salted water and crab boil. Bring to a boil and cook approximately 25 minutes or until tender. Drain mirlitons and discard water. Halve, discard the seeds, cube then set aside. In a large skillet, melt butter over medium heat. Add onions, celery, minced garlic and green onions. Sauté 3 to 5 minutes or until tender. Add cubed mirlitons, cheese and parsley then season to taste with salt, black pepper and cayenne pepper, mixing well. Pour into a greased 9 x 13 inch casserole dish and sprinkle with bread crumbs. Bake for 20 to 25 minutes or until lightly browned.

STUFFED MIRLITONS

Source: Rouses Markets

Ingredients

6 fresh mirlitons	1 Tbsp Extra Virgin olive oil
1 medium onion, chopped	1 rib celery, chopped
1 bay leaf	½ tsp dried thyme
Salt and black pepper, to taste	Cajun seasonings, to taste

¾ lb. medium-sized wild-caught Gulf shrimp, peeled and deveined

¾ lb. Louisiana crawfish tails   ¾ lb. lump Gulf crabmeat

Directions

Preheat oven to 350°F.

In a heavy pot, bring about 2 inches of salted water to a boil. Drop whole mirlitons in water, cover, and reduce heat. Simmer until mirlitons are tender, about 45 minutes. Remove from pot and set aside to cool.

Cut mirlitons in half, lengthwise, and remove the seeds. Scoop out the flesh, keeping the shell intact. Rough chop the flesh and set aside.

In a large skillet over medium heat, warm one tablespoon of olive oil. Add onions, mirliton flesh, bay leaf, and thyme and cook until soft, about 5 minutes. Add shrimp, and cook until the shrimp are just pink. Remove from heat, and fold in crabmeat and crawfish tails. Remove bay leaf and season with salt, pepper and Cajun seasonings.

Preheat oven to 350°F. Place mirliton shells in a roasting pan, flesh side up. Spoon seafood mixture into the shells, and top with a light coating of breadcrumbs. Bake until the breadcrumbs are lightly browned, about 30 minutes.

NEW ORLEANS STYLE SHRIMP AND GRITS

Source: Author

Ingredients

Grits:

1 cup stone-ground grits	2 cups water
2 cups whole milk	½ tsp salt

Sauce:

1 ½ oz. breakfast sausage, uncooked	1 stick butter
1 Tbsp all-purpose flour	1 clove garlic, minced
1 tsp Worcestershire sauce	½ tsp fish sauce
½ cup dry white wine	½ cup water
½ tsp Kitchen Bouquet	1 tsp brown sugar, packed
2 oz. Tasso ham, minced	½ tsp salt

2 tsp Cajun Seasoning (recipe in Rubs & Seasonings)

2 lbs. large shrimp, peeled and deveined

5 Tbsp butter for finishing dish

Instructions

Add 1 cup of grits to 2 cups of water, 2 cups of milk and ½ tsp salt. Bring to a boil. Reduce heat to low and simmer for 30 minutes, stirring occasionally to prevent sticking.

Cook the sausage over medium heat, mashing it to separate into as small pieces as possible. When just starting to brown, remove from heat and set aside.

In a large skillet, over medium heat, melt the 1 stick of butter. Stir in the 1 Tbsp flour and cook for 3 to 5 minutes, stirring frequently. Add the garlic and sauté until the garlic becomes fragrant. Whisk in the wine and water, stirring to blend well. Add Worcestershire

NEW ORLEANS STYLE SHRIMP AND GRITS

Sauce, fish sauce, sugar, Kitchen Bouquet, ham, sausage, salt and Cajun seasoning. When the sauce begins to bubble, add the shrimp. Flip the shrimp when it begins to turn pink and curl. Cook for one minute more and remove shrimp.

Continue to cook the sauce for 5 more minutes, then remove from the stove. Add the 5 Tbsp butter and stir until the butter melts into the sauce. The sauce should be slightly thick.

"They tried opening a Red Lobster in Lafayette — man, that place closed in less than a year. Cajuns won't eat no frozen shrimp." Local Resident

"A Cajun will share a recipe with you, but they'll always leave out one ingredient." Tourist couple from Baton Rouge

"The first person to eat an oyster was either really brave or else really hungry" Oysterman; Houma, Louisiana

"It's very hard having a restaurant down here. Cooking for people who know how to cook is hard." Restaurant Cook, Vermillion Parish

NOTES

NOTES

_____

_____

_____

_____

_____

_____

_____

_____

_____

_____

_____

_____

_____

_____

CANDIES

"All you need is love. But a little chocolate now and then doesn't hurt." Charles M. Schulz

CHEWY PECAN PRALINES

A rich, creamy, praline filled with pecans.

Source: Author

Ingredients

1 cups granulated sugar

1 cup brown sugar

2 cups light corn syrup

1 pound butter

2 cups heavy cream

2 Tbsp. buttermilk

2 teaspoons vanilla extract

½ tsp cinnamon

8 cups pecans coarsely chopped

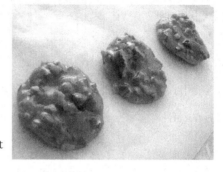

Preparation

Line cookie sheets with foil (preferably non-stick foil) and spray with cooking spray. Combine sugars and corn syrup. Cook sugar/corn syrup mixture over medium low heat until the candy thermometer registers 250°F. Stir often. Remove sugar/corn syrup mixture from burner.

Add butter. Stir until butter is melted. Slowly stir in heavy cream and 2 Tbsp buttermilk. Return mixture to the burner and cook stirring constantly until the candy thermometer reads 242°F. Remove mixture from heat.

Stir in vanilla extract and cinnamon. Stir in chopped pecans Drop onto prepared cookie sheets and let cool completely. Wrap pralines in plastic wrap or wax paper.

YIELD: 5 dozen

TEXAS CHEWY PRALINES

Source: Lammes

Ingredients

1 cup white sugar

1 cup brown sugar

2 cups light corn syrup

1 lb. butter

2 cups heavy cream

2 tsp vanilla extract

8 cups pecans

Directions

Line 2 baking sheets with aluminum foil.

Coat with nonstick cooking spray or use release aluminum foil.

In a large saucepan over medium heat, combine sugars and corn syrup.

Heat to 250 degrees F (120 degrees C).

Remove from heat, and stir in butter until melted.

Gradually stir in cream.

Return to heat.

Cook, stirring constantly, until temperature reaches 242 degrees F (116 degrees C)

Remove from heat, and stir in vanilla and pecans.

Drop by spoonful onto prepared pans.

Cool completely, then wrap each piece individually with plastic.

DIVINITY

Source: My Mother; Mary Wilson Herriage

Ingredients

2 ½ cups granulated sugar

½ cup cold water

½ cup light corn syrup

2 egg whites, room temperature

1 cup pecans, chopped

1 tsp vanilla

Instructions

In a heavy saucepan over medium heat, stir together the sugar, corn syrup, and water. Stir only until sugar has dissolved. Do not stir after this point. Cook syrup mixture until it reaches 250°F on a candy thermometer, bringing it to a hard ball stage.

While the syrup is cooking, beat the egg whites until stiff peaks form. Once the sugar mixture reaches 250°F, carefully pour a slow steady stream of syrup into the stiffly beaten egg whites, beating constantly at high speed. Add the vanilla and continue to beat until mixture holds its shape, approximately 5 minutes. Stir in pecans.

Using 2 spoons, drop the divinity onto waxed paper, using 1 spoon to push the candy off the other. This may take a little practice because the technique is to twirl the pushing spoon, making the candy look like the top of a soft serve ice cream. If the candy becomes too stiff, add a few drops of hot water. You will need to work fast when making this type of candy.

Divinity can be finicky about setting up on humid days so you might not want to try this recipe for the first time on a rainy day.

DATE NUT LOAF

This stuff is wonderful, and I'm not a big fan of dates! Date Nut Roll Candy is a traditional, Southern candy served during the holidays.

Source: My Mother's Sister; Aunt Grace

Ingredients

2 cups granulated sugar

¾ cup Carnation Evaporated milk

¼ cup water

1 pkg. dried dates, chopped

1 Tbsp butter

1 tsp vanilla

1 cup pecans, chopped

Instructions

Stir milk, sugar and butter together in a heavy saucepan over medium high heat. Cook until a soft ball forms when dropped in cold water. Add dates and cook for 10 minutes or until the temperature reaches 235°F on a candy thermometer or when drops of the mixture into a bowl of cold water forms a soft ball.

Remove from heat and add butter, vanilla and pecans. Beat until creamy.

Carefully spread across a wet cloth and roll up smoothly, about 2 inches round. Store in the refrigerator (rolled in the wet cloth), and it will keep for weeks. Otherwise, it becomes hard and sugary." Take out and slice off a piece (or pieces), as desired, to eat.

MAMA'S FAVORITE PECAN BRITTLE

Source: My Mother; Mary Wilson Herriage

Ingredients

½ cup "red" (dark) Karo Syrup

1 ½ cups sugar

2/3 cup water

1 ½ cups peanuts

2 tsp. soda, "scant"

Directions

Cook all together until peanuts pop, stirring continuously. Continuing to stir, add 2 "scant" tsp soda. Pour into a buttered dish, spreading evenly. When nearly cool, turn the brittle over to finish cooling.

Break into pieces and eat.

PEANUT BRITTLE

Source: Aunt Bernice; Colorado City, Texas

Ingredients

2 cups sugar

1 cup corn syrup

½ cup water

1 tsp vanilla

1 tsp soda

Directions

Cook sugar, syrup and water until it "spins a thread". Add peanuts and cook until they pop open and mixture turns a light golden brown. Remove from the fire and stir in vanilla and soda. Pour into a large buttered dish to cool.

Break candy into pieces to eat.

CHOCOLATE COVERED MARZIPAN SQUARES

Source: Author

Ingredients

2 lbs. Marzipan, homemade or store-bought

9 oz. Dark chocolate

2 Tbsp butter

½ cup heavy cream

½ tsp orange extract

2 tsp Vanilla

Preparation

Knead the marzipan lightly until pliable. Evenly press the marzipan into a parchment lined 8 x 8 square pan. Press with the back of a spoon to make an even base. Place in the fridge for 10 minutes.

Chocolate topping:

Add the chocolate, butter and cream into a double boiler or microwave safe bowl. Melt until completely dissolved. Add orange extract and vanilla and stir until smooth. Pour over the Marzipan base. Spread evenly all over the marzipan. Cover with plastic again and let set in the fridge for at least 4 to 5 hours or overnight.

When completely set lift the parchment paper and take the whole block out of the pan. Divide the block into half, then fourths, then each of those into squares to get even pieces.

NOTES

NOTES

CASSEROLES

Green Bean Casserole

"Admit it. You love that green bean casserole!

You know the one I'm talking about. The green beans, Campbell's mushroom soup and French's Fried Onion Rings that graces so many Thanksgiving tables. One national survey reports that half the families in America have eaten this oddly likable casserole that has become a holiday staple.

Dorcas Reilly, who invented one of 20th-century America's classic dishes with her green-bean casserole, passed away on October 15, 2018 at the age of 92. The dish (originally known as the green-bean bake) was created in 1955, and like a lot of classics from that era, it was the product of a corporate test kitchen."

Ingredients

1 (10 ¾ oz.) can Campbell's condensed cream of mushroom soup

¾ cup milk

1/8 tsp. pepper

2 (14.5 oz.) cans Del Monte cut green beans, drained

1 1/3 cups French's fried onions

Directions

Preheat oven to 350°F. In a 1 ½ quart casserole, combine soup, milk and pepper until well blended. Stir in beans and 2/3 cup fried onions.

Bake, uncovered, for 30 minutes or until hot and bubbly. Stir. Sprinkle with remaining 2/3 cup fried onions. Bake 5 minutes or until onions are golden.

"My most memorable meal is every Thanksgiving. I love the food: The turkey and stuffing, the sweet potatoes, the mashed potatoes, the Campbell's green bean casserole; and of course, the pumpkin pie." Douglas Conant

HEARTY BAKED MACARONI AND CHEESE

Source: Author

Ingredients

16 oz. elbow macaroni, cooked

1 tsp olive oil

6 Tbsp butter

1/3 cup all-purpose flour

3 cups whole milk

1 cup heavy whipping cream

4 cups cheddar cheese, shredded

2 cups Asiago cheese, shredded

Salt and pepper to taste

½ tsp smoked paprika

1 ½ cups panko crumbs

4 Tbsp butter, melted

½ cup Parmesan cheese, shredded

¼ tsp smoked paprika

Instructions

Preheat oven to 350°F. Lightly grease a large 3 qts or 4 qts baking dish and set aside. Combine shredded cheeses in a large bowl and set aside.

Cook pasta according to the package instructions. Remove from heat, drain, and place in a large bowl. Drizzle pasta with olive oil and stir to coat pasta. Set aside.

Melt butter in a deep saucepan, Dutch oven, or stock pot. Whisk in flour over medium heat and continue whisking for about 1 minute until bubbly and golden. Gradually whisk in the milk and heavy cream until nice and smooth. Continue whisking until you see bubbles on the surface and then continue cooking and whisking for another 2 minutes. Whisk in salt and pepper.

Add half of the shredded cheese and whisk until smooth. Add the other half of the shredded cheese and continue whisking until creamy and smooth. Sauce should be nice and thick. Stir in the cooled pasta until combined and pasta is fully coated with the cheese sauce. Pour into the prepared baking dish.

In a small bowl, combine panko crumbs, Parmesan cheese, melted butter and paprika. Sprinkle over the top and bake until bubbly and golden brown, about 30 minutes. Serve immediately.

SAUSAGE CASSEROLE

Source: Terri Ainsworth, courtesy of Robin Nation

Ingredients

1 lb. hot pork sausage

1 lb. mild pork sausage

6 oz. roll garlic cheese, grated

2 cups grits, cooked

1 ¾ cups milk

1 stick butter, melted

1 (8 oz.) pkg. cornbread mix

6 eggs, lightly beaten

¼ tsp Worcestershire

¼ tsp Tabasco

8 oz. cheddar cheese, grated

Directions

Brown sausage in a large skillet, stirring until it crumbles. Spread evenly in a greased 9 X 13 baking dish. Sprinkle garlic cheese over sausage.

Combine remaining ingredients and pour over sausage. Cover and chill 8 to 10 hours. Set out at room temperature for 30 minutes. Bake at 350°F for 45 minutes. Sprinkle cheddar cheese over top the last 5 minutes of baking.

"I wonder if there is a person on Earth who is consoled by a casserole."

Katja Millay, The Sea of Tranquility

GOULASH

Goulash is a great comfort food. It is warm, delicious, filling, hearty, easy to prepare and is the perfect family meal after a busy day!

Source: Gary

Ingredients

2 pounds ground beef

1 onion, chopped

1 (14.5 oz. can) whole corn, undrained

1 (14.5 oz. can) diced tomatoes, undrained

3 cups water

2 tsp salt

1 (16 oz. box) elbow macaroni

Preparation

In a Dutch oven or large saucepan, cook ground beef over medium heat until starting to brown. Drain grease. Add onion and cook for 3 minutes, or until soft tender.

Add diced tomatoes, corn, water, salt and elbow macaroni to the pan. Mix well and bring to a boil. Reduce to medium-low heat, cover pan and simmer for 25-30 minutes or until macaroni is cooked.

CURRIED FRUIT BAKE

Source: Coy Gorman

Ingredients

1 large can peach slices

1 large can pear halves

1 large can apricot halves

1 large can pineapple chunks

½ cup maraschino cherries

2 bananas

½ cup brown sugar, packed

2 Tbsp corn starch

1 Tbsp curry powder

1 stick butter, melted

Directions

Preheat oven to 400°F.

Drain juice from all canned fruit and save. Arrange canned fruit in a large baking dish. Slice bananas on top of the fruit in the dish. In a small saucepan, combine the drained juices, brown sugar, corn-starch, curry powder and butter. Bring to a boil and pour on top of fruit. Add the cherries and bake for 40 minutes at 350°F.

Serves 8 to 10

"The secret of happiness is variety, but the secret of variety, like the secret of all spices, is knowing when to use it."

Daniel Gilbert

HOT CORN CASSEROLE

Source: Carla

Ingredients

1 stick butter

1 Tbsp sugar

1 (8 oz.) pkg. cream cheese

1 can Mexican corn

1 can white corn

1 pablano pepper, seeded and minced

½ tsp salt

½ tsp black pepper

1 tsp cayenne pepper

Tony Chachere's

Flour

Directions

Combine butter, cream cheese and sugar. Add remaining ingredients and mix well. Pour into a casserole dish and sprinkle Tony Chachere's on top. Bake in a 425°F oven for 30 minutes or until bubbly in center.

BUTTERNUT SQUASH CASSEROLE

Source: Parents Magazine

Ingredients

½ (2 cups) butternut squash, peeled and cut into ½ inch cubes

2 tsp olive oil

¼ tsp salt

½ lb. whole-wheat elbows

2 Tbsp butter

2 Tbsp flour

1 ½ cups reduced-fat milk

1 ¾ cups low-fat white cheddar cheese, shredded and divided

Directions

Preheat oven to 375 degrees F. Toss squash with oil and salt on a foil-lined tray. Bake for 20 minutes or until tender, set aside.

Cook pasta for 2 minutes less than package directions call for; drain and place in a bowl with squash. Meanwhile, melt butter over low heat. Whisk in flour; cook for 2 minutes.

Slowly whisk in milk. Bring mixture to a boil, then simmer. Cook 3 minutes, stirring occasionally. Add 1 ½ cups cheese; stir until melted. Stir cheese sauce in pasta and squash.

Spoon into 6 greased, individual ramekins. Sprinkle on remaining cheese. Bake 10 minutes.

NOTES

_____

_____

_____

_____

_____

_____

_____

_____

_____

_____

_____

_____

_____

_____

_____

NOTES

COOKIES

"A gourmet who thinks of calories is like a tart who looks at her watch." James Beard

SNICKERDOODLES

Source: Clara Wilson

Ingredients

½ cup butter

½ cup shortening

1 ½ cup sugar

2 eggs

2 ¾ cups flour

2 tsp cream of tartar

1 tsp soda

¼ tsp salt

2 tsp vanilla

Cinnamon Sugar Coating:

2 Tbsp sugar

2 tsp cinnamon

Directions

Cream shortening, butter and sugar. Add eggs and vanilla, mixing well. Mix together flour, cream of tartar, soda and salt and blend with the creamed mixture. Chill dough, form into 1 inch balls, roll in sugar & cinnamon mixture and bake on cookie sheets at 325°F for 10-12 minutes. Remove immediately.

ORANGE BALLS

Source: Author

Ingredients

1 (12 oz. box) vanilla wafers

1 ½ cup pecans, toasted & finely chopped

1 cup sugar

2 Tbsp Grand Marnier

¼ cup orange juice concentrate

1 stick butter, melted

Shredded coconut

Preparation

Combine first 6 ingredients, roll into 1 inch balls, roll in shredded coconut and place on a cookie sheet. After set, transfer to a storage container.

WALNUT OATMEAL RAISIN COOKIES

Source: Author

Ingredients

1 cup all-purpose flour	½ tsp ground cinnamon
½ tsp baking soda	¼ tsp salt
1 stick butter, softened	½ cup brown sugar
¼ cup sugar	1 large egg
1 tsp vanilla	1 ½ cups old-fashioned rolled oats
½ cup raisins	½ cup walnuts, chopped

Preparation

In a large bowl, whisk together the flour, cinnamon, baking soda, and salt. Set aside.

In a large mixing bowl using an electric mixer, cream together the butter, brown sugar, and granulated sugar for 1 to 2 minutes until well combined. Add the egg and vanilla extract and mix until fully combined. Slowly mix in the flour mixture and continue mixing until just combined, then mix in the oats, raisins and walnuts until fully combined, making sure to scrape down the sides of the bowl as needed.

Preheat oven to 350°F.

Using a cookie scoop, drop the dough onto prepared baking sheets. Roll the cookie dough into balls and very gently press down with your hand to flatten each ball of cookie dough slightly. Make sure to leave a little room between each ball of cookie dough as they will spread a little while they bake.

Bake in separate batches at 350°F for 10-12 minutes or until the edges of the cookies are lightly golden brown and the top is set. Remove from the oven and cool on the baking sheet for 5 minutes, then transfer the cookies to a wire rack to finish cooling.

CHEWY ALMOND MARZIPAN BARS

Ingredients

2/3 cup sugar

½ cup butter, room temperature

½ tsp almond extract

½ cup almond flour

¼ tsp sea salt

½ cup slivered almonds, toasted

1/3 cup marzipan

1 large egg

1 ¼ cups all-purpose flour

2 tsp baking powder

1 Tbsp cream

Instructions

Place a rack in the center of your oven and preheat oven to 325°F. Line a 9×13 baking pan with parchment paper, leaving an overhang on two opposite sides.

In a medium bowl, combine the flour, almond flour, baking powder and salt, stir and set aside. In the bowl of your mixer, beat on medium speed the butter and the sugar, until the mixture is creamy. Add the marzipan and beat until the marzipan has been incorporated into the butter and sugar mixture and no lumps remain. Add the egg and the almond extract and then beat until the batter is light and fluffy. Beating on low speed, add the flour mixture and beat until incorporated to the batter.

Evenly press the dough into the bottom of the lined pan. Using a pastry brush, brush the cream on top of the dough. Sprinkle the dough with the toasted slivered almonds and lightly press them into the top. Bake for 18 min, or until just barely beginning to color around the edges. The top should be dry to the touch. Over-baking these will yield crunchy cookies.

Let them cool in the pan for 5 minutes and then using the overhang of the parchment paper, lift them out of the pan and put them on a wire rack to cool. Once cool, cut with a sharp knife into 18 pieces or more.

CRISPY TEA CAKES

Source: Valeria (Val) Corley

Ingredients

1 cup granulated sugar

1 cup powdered sugar

2 sticks butter, softened

1 cup vegetable oil

2 eggs

1 tsp vanilla

4 cups all-purpose flour

1 tsp cream of tarter

1 tsp baking soda

½ tsp salt

1 tsp lemon zest (optional)

Instructions

Preheat oven to 350°F. In large mixing bowl, cream together both sugars and the butter. Add oil, eggs and vanilla and beat again. Combine dry ingredients and add to the sugar mixture, beating until fully incorporated, scraping down sides as needed. Drop dough by Tbsp size balls onto greased cookie sheet. Dip the bottom of a glass in sugar and press down lightly on each dough ball to flatten, dipping in sugar after each one.

Bake at 350°F for 12 to 15 minutes, or until lightly browned on the edges. Cool completely and then store in an airtight container until they disappear.

If you want them to be crispy, be sure and bake them until there is a light browning around the edges.

KAHLUA BROWNIES

In the early '80s, we made our first trip across the border. Everyone had told us to bring back Mexican vanilla and Kahlua. So we did. This recipe, which might have come from a press release years ago, was the result of that first trek. These are adult brownies, made only for special occasions. The secret is baking them until just done, so they are moist and slightly chewy.

Kitty Crider; Austin American Statesman

Ingredients

1 ½ cups all-purpose flour

½ tsp salt

3 oz. unsweetened baking chocolate

2 cups sugar

¾ cup walnuts, chopped

Heat oven to 350°F.

½ tsp baking powder

½ cup butter

3 large eggs

¼ cup Kahlua

1 Tbsp. Kahlua for tops of bars

Directions

Line a 9-inch-square cake pan with greased parchment or foil. Resift flour with baking powder and salt. Set aside.

In a saucepan over low heat, melt the butter and chocolate, stirring frequently until smooth. Remove the saucepan from heat, and let cool.

Beat eggs and sugar until light. Mix in cooled chocolate mixture and ¼ cup Kahlua. Add flour mixture and mix well. Stir in walnuts. Turn into a greased cake pan. Bake in center of oven for 30 minutes or until top springs back when touched lightly in center and edges begin to pull away from pan. Be careful not to overbake.

Remove from oven and cool in pan. When cold, brush top with the remaining 1 Tbsp. of Kahlua. Let stand until cold before cutting into squares.

TEXAS GOVERNOR'S MANSION COWBOY COOKIES

Cowboy cookies tend to be hearty, with oatmeal, nuts, coconut, chips and more. This version, from the Texas Governor's Mansion, is no exception. The dense dough is so filled with goodies it barely holds together. But that's why they taste good. This cowboy cookie recipe makes a lot, so unless you are feeding a busload of Texas guests, you might want to cut the recipe in half. (It is sometimes known as Laura Bush's Cowboy Cookies because it was featured in Family Circle magazine.)

Kitty Crider; Austin American Statesman

Ingredients

3 cups all-purpose flour   1 Tbsp. baking powder

1 Tbsp. baking soda   1 Tbsp. ground cinnamon

1 tsp. salt   1 ½ cups (3 sticks) butter, at room temperature

1 ½ cups granulated sugar   1 ½ cups light-brown sugar, packed

3 eggs   1 Tbsp. vanilla

3 cups semisweet chocolate chips   3 cups old-fashioned rolled oats

2 cups sweetened flake coconut   2 cups (8 oz.) pecans, chopped

Directions

Heat oven to 350°F. Mix flour, baking powder, baking soda, cinnamon and salt in bowl. In 8-quart bowl, beat butter on medium speed until smooth and creamy, 1 minute. Gradually beat in sugars: beat to combine, 2 minutes. Add eggs, one at a time, beating after each. Beat in vanilla. Stir in flour mixture until just combined. Add chocolate chips, oats, coconut and pecans. For each cookie, drop ¼ cup dough onto ungreased baking sheets, spacing 3 inches apart. Bake until edges are lightly browned; rotate sheets halfway through. Time will vary depending on size. Very large cookies will take 17 to 20 minutes; smaller ones 12 to 16.

BANANA NUT BREAD BROWNIES

Source: Clara Wilson

Ingredients

2 sticks butter, softened

1 ½ cups sugar

2 eggs

1 cup yogurt or sour cream

3 bananas, mashed

2 cups all-purpose flour

¾ tsp salt

1 tsp baking soda

2 tsp vanilla

½ cup walnuts, chopped

Frosting:

1 stick butter

3 cups powdered sugar

3 Tbsp milk

1 ½ tsp vanilla

Instructions

Preheat oven to 375°F. Grease a 9 X 13 inch pan.

In a large bowl, beat together sugar, sour cream, butter, and eggs until creamy. Add bananas, flour, baking soda, salt, and vanilla and blend until well mixed, about 1 minute. Stir in walnuts.

Spread batter evenly into pan. Bake 25 minutes or until golden brown. Cool until just warm and frost with frosting.

PECAN TARTS

Source: Pat Brandon

Ingredients

3 oz. cream cheese, softened

½ cup butter, softened

1 cup all-purpose flour

¼ tsp salt

Filling:

1 large egg

¾ cup packed dark brown sugar

1 Tbsp butter, softened

1 tsp vanilla extract

2/3 cup pecans, chopped

Directions

In a small bowl, beat cream cheese and butter until fluffy; blend in flour and salt. Refrigerate for 1 hour. Shape into 1-in. balls; press onto the bottom and up the sides of greased mini-muffin cups.

For filling, in a small bowl, beat the egg. Add brown sugar, butter and vanilla; mix well. Stir in pecans. Spoon into tart shells.

Bake at 325°F for 25-30 minutes. Cool for 15 minutes before carefully removing from pans. Garnish with maraschino cherries if desired.

"Pecans are not cheap, my hons. In fact, in the South, the street value of shelled pecans just before holiday baking season is roughly that of crack cocaine. Do not confuse the two. It is almost impossible to make a decent crack cocaine tassie, I am told." Celia Rivenbark

OATMEAL COOKIES

Source: Valeria (Val) Corley

Ingredients

3 sticks butter

2 cups light brown sugar, firmly packed

2 eggs

2 tsp vanilla

1 ½ cups all-purpose flour

¼ tsp nutmeg

1 tsp cinnamon, heaping

1 tsp salt

1 tsp baking soda

1 cup raisins

1 cup pecans chopped

7 cups Quaker old-fashioned oats

(amount may vary)

Instructions

Melt butter in microwave. Mixing by hand, add brown sugar, eggs, vanilla, flour, nutmeg, cinnamon, salt and soda. Add in pecans and raisins. Stir in oatmeal until batter is stiff. Wet hands before forming cookies. Drop onto cookie sheets that have been sprayed with Baker's Joy. Bake at 325°F for 25 minutes.

Yield 18 large cookies.

THE NEIMAN MARCUS CHOCOLATE CHIP COOKIE

You may know the urban myth about our signature cookie. We're providing the recipe in part to refute that myth. Print it for yourself or pass it along to friends and family — it's absolutely free, and absolutely delicious.

Source: Neiman Marcus Café; Dallas, Texas

Ingredients

½ cup (1 stick) butter, softened   1 cup light brown sugar

3 Tbsp granulated sugar   1 large egg

2 tsp vanilla extract   1 ¾ cups all-purpose flour

½ tsp baking powder   ½ tsp baking soda

½ tsp salt   1 ½ tsp instant espresso coffee powder

1 ½ cups semi-sweet chocolate chips

Directions

Preheat oven to 300°F. Cream the butter with the sugars using an electric mixer on medium speed until fluffy (approximately 30 seconds). Beat in the egg and the vanilla extract for another 30 seconds.

In a medium bowl, sift together the dry ingredients and beat into the butter mixture at low speed for about 15 seconds. Stir in the espresso coffee powder and chocolate chips.

Using a 1 oz. scoop or a 2 Tbsp measure, drop cookie dough onto a greased cookie sheet about 3 inches apart. Gently press down on the dough with the back of a spoon to spread out into a 2 inch circle. Bake for about 20 minutes or until nicely browned around the edges. Bake a little longer for a crispier cookie.

Yield: 2 dozen cookies

THE $250 COOKIE

Almost everybody has heard the one about the woman lunching at the Neiman Marcus Cafe in Dallas, who enjoyed the chocolate chip cookies so much that she asked for the recipe. For "only two-fifty," the waitress said, it was hers. But when the credit card bill arrived, the woman found the total near $300. Turns out the recipe cost $250, the story goes. In 1997, after years of enduring the myth, Neiman Marcus came up with a recipe – and gave it out for free. It's a delicious variation on chocolate chip cookies, using ground oatmeal, nuts and adding extra chocolate with a grated Hershey bar.

Ingredients

1 cup butter	1 cup dark brown sugar, packed
1 cup granulated sugar	2 eggs
1 tsp vanilla	2 ½ cups oatmeal
2 cups flour	½ tsp salt
1 tsp baking soda	1 tsp baking powder
1 ½ tsp instant espresso coffee powder	12 oz. chocolate chips
1 (4 oz.) milk chocolate bar	1 ½ cups chopped nuts

Preparation

Heat oven to 375 degrees.

Cream together butter and both sugars. Stir in eggs and vanilla.

Finely grind oatmeal in a blender or food processor. Combine the oatmeal, flour, salt, baking powder, soda and coffee granules in a medium bowl, and slowly add it to the wet ingredients. Beat just until combined. Grate chocolate bar using a micro plane grater and add it, along with chocolate chips and nuts to the batter. Mix just to combine.

Drop by heaping Tbsp, 2 inches apart, on a greased cookie sheet. Bake for 10 minutes.

CHOCOLATE CHIP COOKIES

Source: My friend; Rob Marrus, GBNF

Ingredients

2 cups butter

1 cup white sugar

1 cup brown sugar, packed

2 eggs

2 tsp vanilla

2 ½ cups flour

2 ½ cups oatmeal

3 cups all-purpose flour

½ tsp salt

1 tsp baking soda

12 oz. chocolate chips

1 (12 oz.) semi-sweet chocolate chips

2 cups pecans coarsely chopped

Preparation

Heat oven to 325°F.

Cream together butter and both sugars. Beat in eggs and vanilla.

In another bowl, combine the flour, baking soda and salt. Gradually add flour mixture into the batter. Mix in the chocolate chips and pecans. Mix just to combine.

Drop by ¼ cup or ice cream scoop, 2 inches apart, on a greased cookie sheet. Bake for 10 minutes or until golden brown. Makes about 24.

NOTES

NOTES

_____

_____

_____

_____

_____

_____

_____

_____

_____

_____

_____

_____

_____

_____

DESSERTS

BONBON CAKE

Source: Author

The cake pictured on the Dessert Index page is one that I modified from a recipe of my Grandma Moon's which she gave me around 1995. Her cake would have been flat with a 4 inch round raised section in the center (making it look like a flat topped hat) and did not include the two chocolate layers. Also, she used a different filling between the layers. Even though it did not have the shape of a bonbon candy, she did call hers a bonbon cake. I make it about once every 2 to 3 years for Christmas.

Don't bother turning the pages looking for the recipe as it is not included. There are a couple of reasons that I did not include the recipe. 1 - It is very time prohibitive to make this cake, requiring 4 to 5 hours preparation and baking plus an overnight stay in the refrigerator, which is why I make it only once every 2 to 3 years. Oh, the cake is worth the effort if you want to give something which is unique and almost divine! Yes, I said divine and not that other "d" word that is being used and misused adnauseam. This cake is fantastically delicious! 2 - I have shared the recipe with a few other people over the years and no one has attempted to make it. So, I have decided that it is my "legacy" recipe. It will be passed down from generation to generation as it was passed on to me; or not.

So, there's the picture of my Bonbon Cake. It is the gift of an enigma (try saying that fast) which I bestow upon you. Perhaps someone out there will solve it or create one of their own.

"The only time to eat diet food is while you're waiting for the steak to cook." Julia Child

"Seize the moment. Remember all those women on the 'Titanic' who waved off the dessert cart!" Erma Bombeck

CARAMEL FLAN (CRÈME CARAMEL)

Source: Unknown

Ingredients

¾ cup sugar

4 eggs

1 (14 oz.) can condensed milk

1 (12 oz.) can evaporated milk

1 Tbsp vanilla extract

Boiling water, for baking in larger pan

Directions

Preheat oven to 325°F.

Brown sugar in a saucepan till a medium dark golden brown, but not burnt and then quickly transfer to the bottom of a 10 inch baking dish (you may add a few tablespoons of water to help it melt).

In a large bowl beat the eggs and then add the 2 cans of milk and vanilla extract, mixing well.

Pour mixture into baking dish and place dish in a larger pan.

Add the boiling water until half way up the sides of the baking dish.

Place in the oven and bake for approximately 45 - 55 minutes. The center should be soft and firm but not liquidly. Let cool before serving.

Baked Custard with Caramel Sauce (Leche Asada)

Ingredients

3 orange slices, cut 1/4-inch-thick

1 1/2 cups plus 2 tbsp. sugar

1 tsp. vanilla extract

4 large eggs

2 cups whole milk

1 cup fresh orange juice

1/2 tsp. kosher salt

Instructions

Heat the oven to 325°. In an 8-inch square baking dish, sprinkle the orange slices with 2 tablespoons sugar. Drizzle with the orange juice and cover with foil. Bake until very soft, about 40 minutes. Transfer to a rack and let cool. Refrigerate the orange slices in the dish and keep the oven at 325°.

In a medium saucepan, heat 1 cup sugar over medium-high and cook, stirring with a heatproof spatula, until the sugar turns dark amber. Remove from the heat and quickly pour the caramel evenly over the bottom of a deep 8-inch pie dish. Let stand for 10 minutes until the caramel hardens.

In a small saucepan, combine the milk with the vanilla and salt and then heat over medium. Cook, stirring, until the salt dissolves and the milk just begins to simmer. Remove from the heat and let cool. In a large bowl, whisk the remaining 1/2 cup sugar with the eggs until just combined. While whisking, slowly pour the warm milk into the eggs and stir until the sugar dissolves. Pour the custard over the caramel and then place the dish inside a large roasting pan.

Transfer the roasting pan to the oven rack and then pour enough boiling water to come halfway up the side of the pie dish. Bake until the custard is set on the edges but still slightly loose in the center, about 1 hour. Transfer the roasting pan to a rack and then lift the pie dish from the water bath and set it on a rack to cool completely. Refrigerate the custard at least 4 hours or overnight.

To serve, invert a serving plate on top of the pie dish, and then flip the two together and allow the custard and its caramel sauce to fall onto the plate. Lift the orange slices from their syrup and cut each into 6 wedges. Cut the custard into wedges and then garnish each with some of the orange wedges. This classic custard is ubiquitous in Chile.

CHEF JOHN'S CRÈME CARAMEL

Source: Chef John

"Crème caramel belongs on the short list for 'World's Greatest Dessert.' The way the almost-burnt caramel layer gets fused on, and becomes one with, the creamy custard is nothing short of magic."

Ingredients

Cooking spray

½ cup sugar

1 large egg

3 large egg yolks

¼ tsp salt

¼ cup sugar

½ cup crème fraiche

½ cup whole milk

1 tsp vanilla extract

½ tsp Grand Marnier

Directions

Preheat oven to 325°F. Lightly spray 4 heatproof 6.5-oz. ramekins with vegetable spray. Place ramekins in a casserole dish.

Place ½ cup sugar in a small, heavy, dry skillet over medium heat. When sugar begins to melt around the edges, gently shake the pan continually, swirling sugar around, until all the sugar melts; don't use utensils to stir. When sugar is completely melted and dark brown, remove the pan from heat.

Quickly pour equal amounts of caramel syrup into the 4 prepared ramekins.

CHEF JOHN'S CRÈME CARAMEL

Place 1 egg and 3 egg yolks in a bowl with a pinch of salt and ¼ cup sugar. Whisk until sugar is dissolved and mixture becomes frothy, about 1 minute.

Spoon the crème fraiche into the egg mixture; add the milk, vanilla, and Grand Marnier. Whisk together until ingredients are completely mixed.

Ladle mixture into the prepared ramekins, filling them about 2/3 to ¾ full.

Fill casserole with hot tap water to reach halfway up the sides of the ramekins. Place casserole on middle rack of preheated oven.

Bake until just barely set, 45 to 50 minutes. You can start checking for doneness at about 40 minutes.

Using tongs, remove the ramekins from the casserole to a cooling rack. When just slightly warm, run a sharp paring knife around the edge of each custard.

To unmold, cover ramekin with a small plate, then invert. Chill before serving.

Chef John's Crème Fraiche

Ingredients

2 cups heavy cream

3 Tbsp cultured buttermilk

Directions

Combine cream and buttermilk in a glass jar. Cover tightly with cheesecloth (or any breathable material) and let sit at room temperature (70 to 75°F (21 to 24°C)) for 24 hours. Stir, screw on lid, and refrigerate for 24 hours before using.

LATIN FLAN

Source: Jennifer Segal

Ingredients

2/3 cup sugar

2 large eggs plus 5 yolks

1 (14 oz.) can sweetened condensed milk

1 (12 oz.) can evaporated milk   ½ cup whole milk

2 tsp vanilla extract   ½ tsp salt

1 Tbsp Bourbon (see note)

Instructions

(This recipe should be made at least one day before serving.) Adjust a rack to the middle position and preheat the oven to 300°F.

Stir together the sugar and ¼ cup water in a medium heavy saucepan until the sugar is completely moistened. Bring to boil over medium-high heat and cook, without stirring, until the mixture begins to turn golden. Gently swirling the pan, continue to cook until sugar is a honey color. Remove from the heat and swirl the pan until the sugar is reddish-amber and fragrant, 15 to 20 seconds. Carefully swirl in 2 tablespoons of warm tap water until incorporated – be careful as the mixture will bubble and steam. This whole process should take less than 10 minutes.

Pour the caramel into an 8½ x 4½-inch loaf pan; do not scrape out the saucepan. Set the loaf pan aside.

Whisk the eggs and yolks in large bowl until combined. Add the sweetened condensed milk, evaporated milk, whole milk, vanilla, Bourbon, and salt and whisk until incorporated. Strain the mixture through a fine-mesh strainer into a large bowl to remove any bits of egg; then pour the strained custard into the loaf pan over the caramel.

LATIN FLAN

Place the loaf pan in the center of a 9x13-inch baking or roasting pan (preferably with high sides) to make a water bath. Place the nested pans in the oven; then, using a tea kettle or pitcher, pour hot water around the loaf pan until it reaches about halfway up the sides of the loaf pan. Bake for 75 - 90 minutes, until the custard is set around the edges but still a bit jiggly in the center. (Don't worry that it seems undercooked. The custard will continue to cook as it cools, and the center will set completely -- I promise!) Carefully remove the pans from the oven and leave the flan in the water bath for 1 hour to cool.

Remove the loaf pan from the water bath and wipe the pan dry. Cover tightly with plastic wrap and chill in the fridge overnight or up to 4 days.

To unmold the flan, carefully slide a sharp knife around the edges of the pan. Invert a platter with a raised rim (to contain the liquid caramel) on top of the flan and turn the pan and platter over. If the flan doesn't release immediately, let it sit inverted for a minute and it should slide out. When the flan is released, remove the loaf pan. Using rubber spatula, scrape the residual caramel onto the platter. You won't be able to release all of the caramel – that's okay. Slice the flan and spoon the sauce over individual portions. (Leftover flan may be covered loosely with plastic wrap and refrigerated.)

Note: If you would like to omit the Bourbon, replace with an additional 2 teaspoons of vanilla extract.

FRENCH CAFE AU LAIT CRÈME BRULEE

Source: The Spruce Eats

A soft, silky crème cooked to just past setting point and topped with a crunchy, glass like topping is what makes a classic Crème Brulee one the most loved of all French desserts. The Crème can be found in most European countries, and other continents, which is no surprise, it is one of the best.

Coffee and its culinary partner, cream, meld together smoothly in this cafe au lait crème brulee recipe. This crème is not overly sweet and is the classic after-dinner flavor pairing.

A classic French brulee is made in a shallow dish, but over time the method of making in a ramekin had grown in popularity. If you do make this in a shallow dish, reduce the cooking time by at least 15 minutes.

What You'll Need

10 egg yolks

½ cup plus ¼ cup granulated sugar, divided

2 cups heavy cream

½ cup strongly-brewed espresso, cooled to room temperature

How to Make It

Preheat the oven to 300°F.

Arrange 6 custard cups in a large pan with sides at least 1 ½ inches deep (see note above about shallow or deep cooking).

Whisk the egg yolks in a large bowl until they turn frothy and bright yellow. Slowly whisk ½ cup sugar, the cream, and espresso into the beaten eggs. Beat the mixture for 90 seconds at least.

Pour the eggs and cream through a medium-mesh sieve into a large (4 cup) liquid measuring cup.

Divide the mixture between the 6 custard cups. Fill the large pan holding your cups with boiling water half-way up the sides of the ramekins to create a Bain-Marie or water bath for the cooking. Creating this bath around the crèmes stops them from curdling during cooking.

French Cafe au Lait Crème Brulee

If you are lucky enough to have a steam oven, use that instead.

Bake the custard in the hot-water bath for 55 minutes to 1 hour, until the custard is set but still moves a bit in the center when jiggled. Cool the custard in the water bath for 20 minutes, and then refrigerate them until they are chilled.

Sprinkle the remaining 1/4 cup granulated sugar over tops of the custards and caramelize the sugar with a small, handheld kitchen torch. Serve immediately.

This coffee crème Brulee recipe makes 6 servings.

Alternative Flavorings for Cafe Crème Brulee

Ring the changes by switching the added flavors of your crème.

Alternatively you can use a splash of Grand Marnier or other liqueurs in the classic crème brulee (not for children, though). Rather than using lemon or orange try the flavored drinks to create the changes.

Again, perhaps not one for children but as great as the dessert is choosing a splash of Lavender or adding extra vanilla.

SAUTERNES CUSTARD WITH ARMAGNAC-SOAKED PRUNES

Source: At Lunch with the Ghosts of Bloomsbury

In lieu of vanilla sugar, you can substitute ¾ cup sugar and 1 tsp. vanilla extract.

Featured in: At Lunch with the Ghosts of Bloomsbury

Ingredients

2 bags English breakfast tea

1 lemon

1 cup (7 ½ oz.) Agen prunes

2/3 cup Armagnac

9 large egg yolks

1 2/3 cups sauternes

1 orange

1 cup (8 oz.) granulated sugar

1 stick cinnamon

¾ cup vanilla sugar

3 whole large eggs

1 2/3 cups heavy cream

Instructions

In a small saucepan, bring 2 ½ cups water to a boil. Remove from the heat and add the tea bags. Let the tea steep for 2 minutes, and then remove the bags and discard. Using a vegetable peeler, peel 3 strips of zest from the orange and 2 strips from the lemon; reserve the fruit for another use.

Stir the citrus strips into the tea along with ½ cup granulated sugar, the prunes, and the cinnamon and bring to a boil. Reduce the heat to maintain a gentle simmer and cook the prunes until slightly softened, about 5 minutes. Remove the pan from the heat and let the prunes cool in their liquid. Stir in the Armagnac and pour the prunes and liquid in a glass jar or plastic container. Seal the container and refrigerate the prunes at least 24 hours, or preferably up to 5 days, before using.

Heat the oven to 300°F and arrange six 8-oz. ramekins in a 9-by-13-inch baking dish. In a small skillet, stir the remaining ½ cup granulated sugar with 5 tablespoons water and bring to a boil. Cook, without stirring, until the sugar turns dark amber, about 7 minutes, and then remove the skillet from the heat. Quickly pour the caramel evenly into the ramekins and let cool.

SAUTERNES CUSTARD WITH ARMAGNAC-SOAKED PRUNES

In a large bowl, whisk the vanilla sugar with the egg yolks and whole eggs until smooth. In a small saucepan, heat the sauternes until warm and pour into the eggs, whisking steadily. Heat the cream in the same manner and pour into the custard and stir until the sugar dissolves. Pour the custard evenly into the ramekins and place the baking dish in the oven. Pour enough boiling water into the baking dish to come halfway up the sides of the ramekins and bake until the custards are set but jiggle slightly in the center, about 30 minutes.

Transfer the baking dish to a rack and carefully remove the ramekins from the water bath. Let the custards cool to room temperature and then refrigerate for at least 8 hours or overnight. To serve, run a paring knife around the edge of each ramekin, invert the custard onto a dessert plate, and spoon 3 to 5 prunes and their liquid alongside the custard.

GJETOST CRÈME BRULEE

Source: Amy Thielen

Gjetost is a traditional Norwegian cheese with a fudgy texture and cara-melized flavor.

Ingredients

2 Tbsp red currant compote	1 cup milk
1 ½ Tbsp cornstarch	2 Tbsp unsalted butter
1 cup heavy cream	1/3 cup light brown sugar, plus 1 Tbsp
2 ½ cups shredded gjetost (about 8.8 oz.)	1 tsp vanilla extract
¼ tsp. kosher salt	2 Tbsp granulated sugar

Instructions

Divide compote between 6 (6-oz.) ramekins.

In a small bowl, mix ¼ cup milk with the cornstarch and set aside.

Melt butter in a small skillet over medium-high. Continue cooking until browned and nutty, about 6 minutes, and set aside.

In a 4-qt. saucepan, combine the remaining ¾ cup milk with the cream and 1/3 cup brown sugar over medium-high. Bring to a simmer, then add the gjetost. Whisk until melted, about 3 minutes. Add in the milk and cornstarch mixture and continue whisking until thick, about 3 minutes. Remove from heat and stir in the brown butter, vanilla, and salt.

Divide the pudding mixture between ramekins and smooth the tops. Re-frigerate until cool, about 1 hour.

To serve, mix remaining 1 Tbsp brown sugar and the granulated sugar together. Divide the sugar mixture between each pudding evenly and bru-lee.

Caramel Apple Cobbler

Source: Author

Ingredients

1 cup sugar for caramel

1 cup sugar for Crust

½ cup (1 stick) butter, softened

2 cups flour

2 tsp baking powder

½ tsp salt

1 cup milk

1 cup apples, sliced (or other fruit compatible with caramel)

¼ cup water

Preparation

Spread 1 cup sugar evenly in a 9 by 13 baking dish and place in the preheated oven until melted and golden, about 15 minutes. Remove from oven. Let cool. Spread sliced apples evenly over the caramel and add the ¼ cup water to help dissolve the caramel as it bakes.

Cream remaining cup of sugar and butter. Mix dry ingredients and add alternately with milk. Spoon crust mixture evenly over the cooled caramelized sugar and apples.

Topping:

½ cup sugar

1 Tbsp corn starch

1 cup boiling water

Mix dry ingredients and sprinkle over batter. Drizzle boiling water over all. Bake at 350°F for 1 hour or until golden brown.

BANANAS FOSTER BREAD PUDDING
WITH BANANA-RUM CUSTARD SAUCE

Source: Author

Bread Pudding:

Ingredients

1 loaf French bread	1 quart half and half
5 eggs, separated	2 egg whites (reserve yolks for sauce)
1 ½ cups sugar	2 Tbsp dark brown sugar
¼ cup butter, melted	1 Tbsp vanilla
1 tsp. almond extract	2 tsp. cinnamon
¼ cup dark rum	¼ cup crème de banana liqueur
3 bananas, mashed	3 bananas, sliced diagonally

1 cup dried cranberries, soaked in rum for at least 1 hour

3 Tbsp melted butter

Preparation

Preheat oven to 350 F. Mix sugars and ¼ cup melted butter and beat until light. Mix in egg yolks. Add milk, liqueurs, extracts, cinnamon and the mashed bananas, mixing well.

Tear or cut French bread into chunks and place into a large bowl. Pour the egg mixture over the bread and mix well. Crush with hands to make sure milk has soaked through. Add the cranberries and sliced bananas. With a mixer, beat the seven egg whites until stiff peaks form, then fold into the bread pudding mixture. Pour 3 Tbsp melted butter into a heavy 9 x 14 baking dish and coat bottom and sides. Pour the bread pudding mixture into the dish, then cover with foil and place into a Bain-Marie (or put the dish into a larger pan and pour hot water into the pan about ¾ way up the side of the baking dish). Bake at 350 F for one hour. Remove foil and finish baking until center is set, about 15 minutes (longer if necessary).

BANANAS FOSTER BREAD PUDDING
WITH BANANA-RUM CUSTARD SAUCE

Banana-Rum Custard Sauce:

Ingredients

1 cup evaporated milk	1 cup whole milk
2 egg yolks	¾ cups sugar
3 Tbsp corn starch	½ tsp. vanilla
¼ tsp. almond extract	¼ cup dark rum
¼ cup crème de banana liqueur	4 Tbsp butter
1 cup dark brown sugar, packed	1 Tbsp dark rum
1 Tbsp crème de banana liqueur	Custard Sauce
1 cup chopped pecans	

Preparation

First 9 ingredients – Custard Sauce: Beat the egg yolks and sugar together until light yellow, then add milk and mix well. Mix corn starch in 3 Tbsp cold water, mixing until dissolved, then add to egg mixture along with extracts and liqueurs. Bring water to boil and cook in a double boiler over med/high heat until thickened and sauce coats a spoon.

Remaining ingredients – Bananas Foster Sauce: Melt butter, add the brown sugar and cook over medium heat until sugar has dissolved and melted. Add the liqueurs mixing well. Stirring constantly, add the custard sauce and the pecans. Cook for one minute.

Slice the pudding into individual servings. Place a pool of the sauce into a dessert bowl then a slice of bread pudding. Drizzle more sauce over the top. Enjoy

TUJAGUE'S PECAN PIE

"When the French settled in New Orleans they discovered the pecan. And they promptly made good use of it by creating pecan brittle, pecan pralines, pecan sauce and of course pecan pie. The first pecans I ever ate came from my Grandmother's pecan tree in her backyard. Every Christmas she would send a 50 pound gunny sack of pecans to my mother." Malcolm Hébert

"This recipe for pecan pie is from my mother's uncle whose family owned Tujague's restaurant in New Orleans for more than 70 years."

Source: Christopher Hébert

Ingredients

1 (9-inch) pie shell, unbaked

3 eggs

1 cup sugar

2/3 cup dark corn syrup

2 Tbsp butter, melted

1 tsp vanilla extract

1/8 tsp salt

3 Tbsp Armagnac or other brandy

1 ½ cups pecan halves

Instructions

Preheat the oven to 400°F. In a glass mixing bowl beat the eggs, blending in the sugar, syrup, butter, vanilla, salt, Armagnac and pecans. Pour the mixture into the pie shell and bake 10 minutes. Lower the oven to 350°F and bake 30 minutes or until a wooden skewer or knife inserted into the pie comes out clean. Cool on a wire rack. Serves 6-8.

THE CAMELLIA GRILL'S PECAN PIE

The Camellia Grill's pecan pie is justifiably famous; oodles of 'em are eaten in-house at this beloved and venerable Uptown New Orleans eatery, and they say they ship pies all over the country. They used to hand out a little card with the recipe, but they don't anymore. Here's what was on the card!

Source: Chuck Taggart; gumbopages.com

Ingredients

4 eggs

¼ tsp salt

¼ cup butter, melted

1 ¼ cups light corn syrup

1 ¼ cups brown sugar, firmly packed

1 tsp vanilla extract

1 unbaked 9-inch pie shell

1 cup pecans, chopped

Directions

Beat eggs with a wire whisk or fork. Add salt, butter, syrup, sugar and vanilla; mix well. Pour into pastry shell; sprinkle with pecans. Bake at 350°F for 45-50 minutes.

BAPTIST CAFÉ MOCHA PECAN PIE

Source: Unknown

Ingredients

1 9-inch unbaked pie shell

1 ¼-cup sugar

¼ cup melted butter

4 eggs, beaten

1 cup light corn syrup

1 tsp. vanilla

3 Tbsp coffee syrup or strong coffee (Kahlua if you aren't Baptist)

3 Tbsp chocolate syrup

At least 1 cup of pecan halves

Directions

Beat eggs with a wire whisk or fork. Add remaining ingredients and mix well. Pour into pastry shell and bake in a pre-heated oven at 350 degrees for 45 to 50 minutes or until filling no longer jiggles in the middle.

PECAN PIE

Source: Clara Wilson

Ingredients

1 cup sugar

½ stick melted butter

3 eggs, beaten

½ cup light corn syrup

At least 1 cup pecans, chopped

Directions

Mix together all ingredients and pour into a deep pie crust. Bake in a preheated oven at 350°F for 30 to 45 minutes or until set.

Jeff Tweedy, "Pecan Pie"

As I walk along and stumble,
Trains rumble in my head.
As I breathe along and grumble,
I think about you instead.
And a piece of pecan pie
And you, that's all I want.
Just a piece of pecan pie.
And all I want is you.

Sometimes I get so hungry
I think about pie all day.
Just a little whipped cream
And honey, I'm on my way
And a piece of pecan pie
And you, that's all I want.
Just a piece of pecan pie.
And all I want is you.

PECAN, COGNAC, BUTTERSCOTCH BREAD PUDDING

Source: Bon Appetite

Ingredients

Butterscotch Sauce:

1 cup light brown sugar, packed	½ cup light corn syrup
3 Tbsp unsalted butter	1 ½ tsp kosher salt
½ cup heavy cream	1 Tbsp cognac

Pudding:

12 cups day-old white bread, crusts removed, cut into ½ inch cubes

½ cup unsalted butter, melted	2 Tbsp plus 1 ½ cups sugar
5 large eggs	4 cups heavy cream
1 ½ Tbsp poppy seeds	Pinch of kosher salt
3 Tbsp cognac	½ vanilla bean, split lengthwise
2 cups pecan pieces	

Preparation

Butterscotch Sauce:

Bring brown sugar, corn syrup, butter, and salt to a boil in a medium saucepan over medium-high heat, whisking to dissolve sugar. Boil until mixture is syrupy and measures 1 ½ cups, about 3 minutes. Remove from heat; add cream and cognac and stir until smooth. Let cool.

Pudding:

Toss bread, melted butter, and 2 Tbsp sugar in a large bowl and set aside. Using an electric mixer, beat eggs and remaining 1 ½ cups sugar in another large bowl until pale yellow and fluffy, about 3 minutes. Add cream, poppy seeds, and salt; beat to blend. Place

PECAN, COGNAC, BUTTERSCOTCH, BREAD PUDDING

cognac in a small bowl; scrape in seeds from ½ vanilla bean. Whisk to distribute seeds, then add to egg mixture, whisking to blend well. Pour egg mixture over bread mixture in bowl. Add pecans and toss to coat well. Transfer mixture to a 13x9x2 inch glass or ceramic baking dish, spreading out in an even layer. Cover with plastic wrap and chill overnight.

Preheat oven to 325°F. Remove plastic wrap and bake until top is browned in spots and a tester inserted into center comes out clean, 1 ¼ to 1 ½ hours. Serve bread pudding with butterscotch sauce.

"Family is like a pecan pie. Something sweet holding all the nuts together." Unknown

"I just clipped 2 articles from a current magazine. One is a diet guaranteed to drop 5 pounds off my body in a weekend. The other is a recipe for a 6 minute pecan pie." Erma Bombeck

CHOCOLATE BOURBON PECAN PIE

Source: Author

Ingredients

1 refrigerated piecrust, uncooked

1 ½ cups pecans, chopped

1 cup semisweet chocolate morsels

1 cup dark corn syrup

½ cup granulated sugar

½ cup brown sugar, firmly packed

¼ cup bourbon

4 large eggs

¼ cup butter, melted

2 tsp dried orange zest

2 tsp vanilla

½ tsp salt

Preparation

Preheat oven to 325°F. Carefully press piecrust into a 9-inch pie plate. Shape edges to pie plate and crimp. Sprinkle pecans and chocolate evenly onto bottom of piecrust.

Stir together corn syrup and next 3 ingredients in a large saucepan, and bring to a boil over medium heat. Cook, stirring constantly, 3 minutes. Remove from heat.

Whisk together eggs and next 4 ingredients. Gradually whisk one-fourth of hot corn syrup mixture into egg mixture and add to remaining hot corn syrup mixture, whisking constantly. Pour filling into prepared piecrust.

Bake at 325°F for 55 minutes or until set. Cool pie on a wire rack.

Black Russian Cake

Source: Author

Ingredients

1 small box instant chocolate fudge pudding

2 cups milk

1 box dark chocolate cake mix

2 eggs

½ cup vegetable oil

¼ cup Kahlua

¼ cup vodka

¾ cup water

1 tsp vanilla

2 Tbsp orange zest

1½ cups chocolate chips

For the glaze:

1 can dark chocolate frosting

2 Tbsp. Kahlua

½ tsp vanilla

Preparation

Preheat oven to 350°F. Grease and flour a Bundt pan.

In a large mixing bowl, beat pudding mix and milk with whisk for 2 minutes. Add dry cake mix, eggs, oil, Kahlua, vodka, water, vanilla and orange zest to pudding and mix until well blended. Add chocolate chips and stir with a spoon. Pour batter into greased and floured Bundt pan and bake at 350°F for 50 to 60 minutes or until a toothpick comes out clean. Cool in Bundt pan for half an hour and turn onto wire rack. Continue to cool on wire rack for another hour. In the meantime, make the glaze.

In a microwave-safe bowl, heat the frosting for 30 seconds then stir. Heat for an additional 30 seconds and stir until frosting is smooth. Add Kahlua and vanilla to the melted frosting and beat with a whisk until well blended. Set aside glaze until cake is cooled.

When cake is completely cool, put on a serving platter and top with glaze. Use any remaining glaze as topping when serving cake.

THE RICH HISTORY OF A FAVORITE DESSERT

Cheesecake is a beloved dessert around the world. While many assume that it has its origins in New York, it actually dates back much further. Let's go back over 4,000 years to ancient Greece! Sit back, grab a creamy slice of cheesecake and learn all about this dessert's rich history.

Cheesecake Travels the Globe

The first "cheese cake" may have been created on the Greek island of Samos. Physical anthropologists excavated cheese molds there which were dated circa 2,000 B.C. Cheese and cheese products had most likely been around for thousands of years before this, but earlier than this goes into prehistory (that period in human history before the invention of writing) so we will never really know. In Greece, cheesecake was considered to be a good source of energy, and there is evidence that it was served to athletes during the first Olympic Games in 776 B.C. Greek brides and grooms were also known to use cheesecake as a wedding cake. The simple ingredients of flour, wheat, honey and cheese were formed into a cake and baked – a far cry from the more complicated recipes available today!

The writer Athenaeus is credited for writing the first Greek cheesecake recipe in 230 A.D. (By this time, the Greeks had been serving cheesecake for over 2,000 years but this is the oldest known surviving Greek recipe!) It was also pretty basic - pound the cheese until it is smooth and pasty - mix the pounded cheese in a brass pan with honey and spring wheat flour - heat the cheese cake "in one mass" - allow to cool then serve.

When the Romans conquered Greece, the cheesecake recipe was just one spoil of war. They modified it including crushed cheese and eggs. These ingredients were baked under a hot brick and it was served warm. Occasionally, the Romans would put the cheese filling in a pastry. The Romans called their cheese cake "libuma" and they served it on special occasions. Marcus Cato, a Roman politician in the first century B.C., is credited as recording the oldest known Roman cheesecake recipe.

As the Romans expanded their empire, they brought cheesecake recipes to the Europeans. Great Britain and Eastern Europe began experimenting with ways to put their own unique spin on cheesecake. In each country of Europe, the recipes started taking on different cultural shapes, using ingredients native to each region. In 1545, the first cookbook was printed.

The Rich History of a Favorite Dessert

It described the cheesecake as a flour-based sweet food. Even Henry VIII's chef did his part to shape the cheesecake recipe. Apparently, his chef cut up cheese into very small pieces and soaked those pieces in milk for three hours. Then, he strained the mixture and added eggs, butter and sugar.

It was not until the 18th century, however, that cheesecake would start to look like something we recognize in the United States today. Around this time, Europeans began to use beaten eggs instead of yeast to make their breads and cakes rise. Removing the overpowering yeast flavor made cheesecake taste more like a dessert treat. When Europeans immigrated to America, some brought their cheesecake recipes along.

Cream cheese was an American addition to the cake, and it has since become a staple ingredient in the United States. In 1872, a New York dairy farmer was attempting to replicate the French cheese Neufchatel. Instead, he accidentally discovered a process which resulted in the creation of cream cheese. Three years later, cream cheese was packaged in foil and distributed to local stores under the Philadelphia Cream Cheese brand. The Philadelphia Cream Cheese brand was purchased in 1903 by the Phoenix Cheese Company, and then it was purchased in 1928 by the Kraft Cheese Company. Kraft continues to make this very same delicious Philadelphia Cream Cheese that we are all familiar with today.

Of course, no story of cheesecake is complete without delving into the origins of the New York style cheesecake. The Classic New York style cheesecake is served with just the cake – no fruit, chocolate or caramel is served on the top or on the side. This famously smooth-tasting cake gets its signature flavor from extra egg yolks in the cream cheese cake mix.

By the 1900s, New Yorkers were in love with this dessert. Virtually every restaurant had its own version of cheesecake on their menu. New Yorkers have vied for bragging rights for having the original recipe ever since. Even though he is best known for his signature sandwiches, Arnold Reuben (1883-1970) is generally credited for creating the New York Style cheesecake. Reuben was born in Germany and he came to America when he was young. The story goes that Reuben was invited to a dinner party where the hostess served a cheese pie. Allegedly, he was so intrigued by this dish that he experimented with the recipe until he came up with the beloved NY Style cheesecake.

LINDY'S CHEESECAKE

Ingredients

2 ½ pounds or 5 (8-ounce) blocks cream cheese

1 ¾ cups sugar   3 tablespoons flour

1½ tsp orange rind, grated   1½ tsp lemon rind, grated

¼ teaspoon vanilla extract   5 eggs

2 egg yolks   ¼ cup heavy cream

Cookie dough crust:

1 cup sifted all-purpose flour   ¼ cup sugar

1 tsp lemon rind, grated   Pinch vanilla bean (inside pulp)

1 egg yolk   ¼ cup butter

Directions

For the filling, combine cheese, sugar, flour, grated orange and lemon rind and vanilla.

Add eggs and egg yolks, one at a time, stirring lightly after each addition. Stir in cream.

To make the crust, combine flour, sugar, lemon rind and vanilla, make a well in center and add egg yolk and butter. Work together quickly with hands until well blended.

Wrap in waxed paper and chill thoroughly in refrigerator for about 1 hour.

Roll out 1/8-inch thick and place over oiled bottom of a 9-inch spring form cake pan. Trim off the dough by running a rolling pin over sharp edge.

Bake at 400 degrees for 20 minutes or until light gold. Cool. Butter sides of cake form and place over base. Roll remaining dough 1/8-inch thick and cut to fit the sides of the oiled band. Fill form with cheese mixture.

LINDY'S CHEESECAKE

Bake at 550°F degrees for 12 to 15 minutes. Reduce temperature to low (200°F) and continue baking 1 hour. Cool before cutting.

Author Dan Freedman's note: I tried this myself. Main takeaway: You really do have to pay attention to details. When recipe says "sifted flour," it means "sifted flour." And when it says bake bottom crust 20 minutes or until light gold, that means check it every 5 minutes or so.

Also, the cookie dough recipe doesn't appear to yield enough for much side crust, so I doubled it. Richard Cohen said he just pressed the dough extra thin against the bottom and sides of the pan and there was enough.

In addition to following the directions exactly, Richard (Cohen) suggests stirring the batter very slowly to avoid bubble formation, and paying special attention to directions about timing and oven temperature.

Back in the day, Lindy's truly was the toast of Broadway, the place to see and be seen for stars, celebs, cops, crooks and, well, Runyonesque characters of every shape and size.

Author Damon Runyon was a regular, basing his cast of thousands — Milk Ear Willy and Harry the Horse among them — on actual Lindy's personages.

"Guys and Dolls," the 1950s-vintage Broadway musical hit based on Runyon's writings, featured Nathan Detroit (nom de guerre for prohibition-era gangster Arnold Rothstein) extolling the culinary excellence of the cheesecake at "Mindy's."

From opening day in 1921 to its ultimate demise in 1969, Lindy's featured the pantheon of great Jewish delicacies — corned beef, pickled herring, sturgeon and gefilte fish. But it was the cheesecake that kept the likes of Milton Berle, Ed Sullivan, Phil Silvers, Walter Winchell and Al Jolson coming back for more.

CHOCOLATE RASPBERRY CHEESECAKE

Source: Author

Ingredients

1 ½ cups chocolate cookies, crushed   ½ cup chopped walnuts

½ stick butter, melted   1 ¼ cups sugar

4 (8 oz. pkg.) cream cheese, softened   1 cup crème fraiche

1 teaspoon vanilla extract   3 large eggs, lightly beaten

½ cup semisweet chocolate chips ½ cup seedless raspberry preserves

Topping:

½ cup semisweet chocolate chips   1 / 3rd cup heavy cream

Fresh raspberries and whipped cream, optional

Preparation

Preheat oven to 325°F. Place a greased, 10 inch, springform pan on a double thickness of heavy-duty foil (about 18 in. square). Securely wrap foil around pan. Combine cookie crumbs, chopped walnuts and melted butter. Press onto the bottom and ¼ way up the sides of the pan.

In a large bowl, beat cream cheese and sugar until smooth. Beat in sour cream and vanilla. Add eggs; beat on low speed until just combined. Set aside 1 ½ cups; pour remaining batter into pan.

Melt chocolate and stir in preserves until blended. Stir in reserved batter until just blended. Drop by tablespoonful over the plain batter. Swirl gently. Place springform pan in a larger pan and add 1 inch of hot water.

Bake at 325°F for 65-75 minutes or until center is just set and top appears dull. Remove springform pan from water bath and remove foil. Cool cheesecake on a wire rack for 10 minutes. Carefully run a knife around edge of pan to loosen. Cool 1 hour longer.

Almond-Amaretto Cheesecake

Source: Bacardi Rum Bottle

Ingredients

40 NILLA Wafers, finely crushed

¾ cup toasted almonds, finely chopped   1/3 cup sugar

¼ cup plus 2 Tbsp butter, melted   No-Stick cooking spray

3 (8-ounce) packages cream cheese, room temperature

1 cup sugar   4 eggs, room temperature

1/3 cup whipping cream, room temperature

¼ cup amaretto almond-flavored liqueur   1 tsp vanilla

2 cups sour cream   1 Tbsp amaretto almond-flavored liqueur

¼ cup sugar   1 tsp vanilla extract

Sliced or slivered toasted almonds (garnish)

Directions

Combine first 4 ingredients. Press into bottom and 1 ¾ inches up side of a 9-inch springform pan which has been coated well with cooking spray. In a large mixing bowl, beat together cream cheese and 1 cup sugar until light and fluffy. Add eggs, one at a time, beating well after each addition. Lower speed to medium; add whipping cream, ¼ cup amaretto, and 1 tsp vanilla, mixing well. Pour into prepared crust and bake at 350°F for 15 minutes. Reduce oven to 225°F; bake for 1 hour and 20 minutes or until set. Cool on a rack for 5 minutes. Combine next 4 ingredients. Spread evenly on cake; cook 5 additional minutes. Cool; cover lightly and chill over-night. To serve, remove from pan onto a serving dish. Garnish with almonds. Yield: 16 to 18 servings.

GRAND MARNIER STRAWBERRY CHEESECAKE

I subscribed to Bon Appétit Magazine for many years while I was honing my culinary skills. It was my favorite "food" magazine. I was just discovering cheesecake (the first I ever ate was at a food bar in L.A. International Airport in the late 60s while waiting for a flight) and this was one of my favorite cheesecake recipes back in the day.

GRAND MARNIER STRAWBERRY CHEESECAKE

Source: Bon Apetite Magazine

Ingredients

2 cups graham cracker crumbs	¾ cup finely chopped pecans
2 tablespoons grated orange rind	¼ cup brown sugar, packed
1 teaspoon cinnamon	½ cup butter, melted
No-Stick cooking spray	1 cup brown sugar, packed

3 (8-ounce) packages cream cheese, room temperature

4 eggs, room temperature   1/3 cup whipping cream, room temperature

¼ cup Grand Marnier or other orange-flavored liqueur

1 teaspoon vanilla extract	2 cups sour cream
1 tablespoon Grand Marnier	¼ cup brown sugar, packed
1 teaspoon vanilla extract	Fresh strawberries

Strawberry glaze

Directions

Combine first 6 ingredients. Press into bottom and 1 ¾ inches up side of a 9-inch springform pan which has been coated well with cooking spray.

In a large mixing bowl, beat together cream cheese and 1 cup sugar until light and fluffy. Add eggs, one at a time, beating well after each addition. Lower speed to medium; add whipping cream, ¼ cup Grand Marnier, and 1 teaspoon vanilla, mixing well. Pour into prepared crust and bake at 350°F for 15 minutes. Reduce oven to 225°F; bake for 1 hour and 20 minutes or until set. Cool on a rack for 5 minutes.

Combine next 4 ingredients. Spread evenly on cake; cook 5 additional minutes. Cool; cover lightly and chill over-night. To serve, remove from pan onto a serving dish. Garnish with the strawberries and strawberry glaze. Yield: 16 to 18 servings.

LIMONCELLO BLUEBERRY CHEESECAKE

Source: Author

Ingredients

Crust:

2 cups graham cracker crumbs	½ cup chopped walnuts
6 Tbsp butter, melted	¼ cup brown sugar, packed

Filling:

4 (8 oz. pkg.) cream cheese, softened	1 cup sugar
½ cup heavy whipping cream	5 eggs, lightly beaten
¼ cup lemon juice	2 Tbsp all-purpose flour
1 Tbsp lemon peel, grated	2 ½ tsp vanilla extract
¼ cup Limoncello	1 cup blueberries

Preparation

Preheat oven to 325°F. Grease the bottom and sides of a 10-inch springform pan. In a small bowl, combine graham cracker crumbs, chopped walnuts, butter and sugar. Press onto bottom and 2 in. up sides of the springform pan. Bake 10 minutes. Cool on a wire rack. Tightly seal outside of springform pan with a slow cooker liner then aluminum foil and set in a larger pan. Fill larger pan 2/3rds up the side of the springform pan with warm water.

In a large bowl, beat cream cheese and sugar until smooth. Add eggs; beat on low speed just until combined. Beat in cream, lemon juice, flour, lemon peel, vanilla and Limoncello. Pour into crust. Evenly spread blueberries over top of filling (they will settle into the cheesecake).

Bake 55-65 minutes or until center is set. Remove cake from oven. Gently spread sour cream over top of cake. Return to oven and bake about 12 minutes. Cool on a wire rack 30 minutes. Carefully

LIMONCELLO BLUEBERRY CHEESECAKE

run a knife around edge of pan to loosen; cool 1 hour.

Sour Cream Topping:

1 pint sour cream

3 Tbsp sugar

1 tsp vanilla extract

Strawberry Glaze:

½ cup strawberry glaze

1 Tbsp Limoncello

1 tsp corn starch

Make glaze by blending in Limoncello and corn starch until smooth. Bring to a boil, stirring constantly, until thickened. Cook 3 minutes. Chill until cool but not set. Spread top of cheesecake with strawberry glaze.

Fruit Topping:

Fresh blueberries

Fresh strawberries, sliced

Arrange fruit evenly on top of cheesecake. Chill several hours or over-night.

"Because you don't live near a bakery doesn't mean you have to go without cheesecake." **Hedy Lamarr**

"Who knows how to make love stay? Tell love you are going to the Junior's Deli on Flatbush Avenue in Brooklyn to pick up a cheesecake, and if love stays, it can have half." **Tom Robbins**

CARAMEL MACCHIATO CHEESECAKE

Source: Author

Ingredients

Crust:

½ cup butter, melted   2 Tbsp sugar

½ cup walnuts, finely chopped   2 Tbsp fresh orange zest

Filling:

3 (8 oz.) pkg. cream cheese, softened   1 cup sugar

3 eggs   1 (8 oz.) container sour cream

¼ cup espresso, brewed   2 tsp vanilla extract

2 Tbsp Kahlua   Pressurized whipped cream

Caramel ice cream topping

Preparation

Preheat oven to 350°F. Lightly coat a 9-inch springform pan with nonstick cooking spray.

Mix together the graham cracker crumbs, melted butter, 2 Tbsp sugar, ground walnuts and orange zest until well combined. Press into the bottom of the springform pan, and 1 inch up the sides. Bake for 8 minutes, then remove to cool on a wire rack. Reduce oven temperature to 325°F.

Beat the softened cream cheese in a large mixing bowl until smooth. Gradually add 1 cup of sugar, beating until combined. Add eggs one at a time, beating well after each addition. Stir in sour cream, espresso, vanilla and Kahlua. Pour batter into cooled crust.

Bake for 1 hour and 5 minutes, turn oven off and allow to rest for 15 minutes. Remove from the oven and run a knife around the edge. Cool cheesecake on a wire rack to room temperature, then cover with plastic wrap, and chill in the refrigerator for 8 hours.

THE CHEESECAKE FACTORY BANANA CREAM CHEESECAKE

Ingredients

20 vanilla sandwich cookies

3 pkg. cream cheese, softened

2 Tbsp cornstarch

2 bananas, mashed

2 tsp vanilla

¼ cup butter, melted

2/3 cup sugar

3 eggs

½ cup whipping cream

Preparation

Preheat oven to 350°F.

Place cookies in a blender; process with on/off pulse until finely crushed. Add margarine; process with pulses until blended. Press crumb mixture onto bottom of 10" springform pan; refrigerate.

Beat cream cheese in large bowl with electric mixer at medium speed until creamy. Add sugar and cornstarch; beat until blended. Add eggs, one at a time, beating well after each addition. Beat in bananas, whipping cream, and vanilla. Pour cream cheese mixture into prepared crust.

Place pan on cookie sheet and bake 15 minutes. Reduce oven temperature to 200°F (DO NOT forget to reduce temperature - very important) and continue baking 75 minutes or until center is almost set.

Loosen edge of cheesecake; cool completely on wire rack before removing rim of pan. Refrigerate cheesecake, uncovered, 6 hours or overnight. Top with a layer of Bavarian cream. Allow cheesecake to stand at room temperature 15 minutes before serving.

PRALINE CHEESECAKE KING CAKE

Source: Author

Ingredients

Cookie dough crust:

1 1/3 cup flour	1 tsp cream of tartar
1 tsp dried lemon zest	½ tsp soda
¼ tsp salt	¼ cup butter
¼ cup shortening	¾ cup sugar
1 egg	1 tsp vanilla

Praline Filling:

½ cup sugar, granulated	½ cup light brown sugar, packed
1 cup pecans, chopped	½ cup all-purpose flour
½ cup butter, melted	½ tsp vanilla

Cream cheese filling:

3 (8-ounce pkg.) cream cheese	¾ cups sugar
2 Tbsp flour	1 Tbsp orange rind, grated
1 Tbsp lemon rind, grated	3 eggs
1 egg yolk	¼ cup heavy cream
1 tsp vanilla	

Creamy glaze:

1 ½ cups powdered sugar	3 Tbsp butter, melted
1 Tbsp fresh lemon juice	½ tsp vanilla
1 to 2 Tbsp milk	

Purple, green, and gold tinted sparkling sugar sprinkles

PRALINE CHEESECAKE KING CAKE

Preparation

To make the crust: Mix together flour, cream of tartar, dried lemon zest, soda and salt. Set aside. Cream shortening, butter and sugar. Add eggs and vanilla, mixing well. Blend dry ingredients with the creamed mixture.

For Praline filling: Combine the sugar, brown sugar, chopped pecans and ½ cup flour. Pour ½ cup melted butter over the praline mixture, add vanilla and mix until crumbly.

For cream cheese filling: Combine cream cheese, sugar, flour, grated orange and lemon rind. Add eggs and egg yolks, one at a time, stirring lightly after each addition. Stir in cream and vanilla.

For creamy glaze: Whisk together all ingredients except milk. Add milk, a little at a time, until of a thick and creamy consistency.

Spray a 10 inch springform pan with nonstick cooking spray. Spread dough over bottom of the pan, pressing it out smoothly (dough will rise to about a ½ to ¾ inch thickness while baking). Bake crust at 350°F for 30 minutes or until beginning to brown around the edges and becoming light gold on top. Check frequently so you don't overcook. Cool.

Sprinkle praline filling evenly over the cooled cookie dough layer. Pour cream cheese filling over the praline filling and baked cookie dough. Stick a plastic baby in there if you want.

Bake at 350°F for 15 minutes. Reduce temperature to 300°F and continue baking for 1 hour. Cool. Remove from spring form pan and transfer to a serving plate. Let cool completely. Drizzle creamy glaze evenly over cooled cheesecake. Sprinkle with green, purple and gold colored sugars, alternating colors and forming bands. Chill in refrigerator overnight before serving.

SECRET GARDEN PIE

Source: Author

Ingredients

1 envelope unflavored gelatin	¼ cup sugar
1 ½ cups milk	3 egg yolks, lightly beaten
¼ tsp salt	2 Tbsp Grand Marnier
1 tsp vanilla	1 (8 oz.) pkg. cream cheese, softened
½ cup sugar	1 cup macaroons, crumbled
½ cup pecans, finely chopped	¼ cup dried cranberries, chopped
2 Tbsp Amaretto Liqueur	3 egg whites
¼ cup sugar	1 cup fresh strawberries, sliced
1 cup whipping cream	2 Tbsp fresh orange zest

Preparation

In a saucepan, combine gelatin and ¼ cup sugar. Add milk, egg yolks and salt. Cook, stirring, until mixture is slightly thickened and gelatin is dissolved. Stir in Grand Marnier and vanilla. Chill until partially set.

While gelatin mixture is chilling, cream together cream cheese and ½ cup sugar. Blend in macaroon crumbs, ½ cup pecans, cranberries and Amaretto Liqueur.

In a mixing bowl, beat egg whites to soft peaks. Gradually add ¼ cup sugar, beating to form stiff peaks. Fold into gelatin/cream cheese mixture. Turn mixture into a baked 9 inch pastry shell, spreading smoothly. Arrange sliced strawberries on top. Whip the cream to soft peaks and spoon on top. Garnish with orange zest.

TARTE AU LA BOUILLIE

After pressing out the dough for her Tarte au la Bouillie (a traditional Cajun custard pie), Alzina Toups saves the scraps and makes them into cookies. "Old timers called them Pillowcase Cookies," she says. "When the oystermen went out, they'd nail a sack of them to the back of the boat. When they wanted a cookie, there they were."

Source: Alzina Toups; Cajun's Joy Cookin' 'n Eatin'

Ingredients

½ cup sugar

5 Tbsp cornstarch

3 cups cold half-and-half

1 tsp vanilla

Instructions

Preheat oven to 350°F.

In a small bowl, combine sugar and cornstarch. In another small bowl, add half-and-half. Stir cornstarch mixture into the half-and-half.

In a medium saucepan, cook half-and-half mixture over medium heat, stirring constantly, until thickened. Stir in vanilla. Remove from heat. Once slightly cooled, place plastic wrap over surface to prevent skin from forming.

Sweet Dough:

On a well-floured surface, roll Sweet Dough into a 13-inch circle; transfer to a 10-inch deep-dish pie plate. Add half-and-half mixture, and fold remaining dough over onto the half-and-half mixture.

Bake until crust is golden brown, about 25 to 30 minutes. Let pie cool to room temperature, then refrigerate 4 hours before slicing.

NANAIMO BARS

Nanaimo Bars are one of Canada's favorite confections. The beautiful City of Nanaimo, British Columbia has claimed them as their own. The story goes that a Nanaimo housewife entered a recipe for a chocolate square in a magazine contest. She called her recipe 'Nanaimo Bars'. She won the contest, and her "Nanaimo Bars" eventually became popular throughout Canada, as did the town they were named after. These no-bake, three layered bars are famous for a reason, they are delicious. They start with a Graham Cracker Crumb base, followed by a layer of custard buttercream, and the crowning glory is a smooth and glossy layer of dark chocolate.

Bottom Layer:

½ cup butter   ¼ cup sugar

1/3 cup unsweetened cocoa powder (regular or Dutch-processed)

1 large egg, lightly beaten   1 tsp pure vanilla extract

2 cups Graham Cracker Crumbs

1 cup dried coconut (shredded or flaked)

½ cup walnuts, coarsely chopped

Middle Layer:

¼ cup butter, room temperature   2 to 3 Tbsp cream

2 Tbsp vanilla custard powder or vanilla pudding powder

½ tsp pure vanilla extract   2 cups powdered sugar

Top Layer:

4 oz. semisweet chocolate   1 Tbsp butter

Line the bottom and sides of a 9 inch square pan with foil.

Bottom Layer: In a saucepan over medium low heat, melt the butter. Remove from heat and whisk, or stir, in the sugar and cocoa

NANAIMO BARS

powder and then gradually whisk in the beaten egg. Return the saucepan to low heat and cook, stirring constantly, until the mixture thickens (1 - 2 minutes). Remove from heat and stir in the vanilla extract, graham cracker crumbs, coconut, and chopped nuts. Press the mixture evenly onto the bottom of the prepared pan. Cover with plastic wrap and refrigerate until firm (about one hour).

Middle Layer: In your electric stand mixer, fitted with the paddle attachment (or with a hand mixer), beat the butter until smooth and creamy. Add the remaining ingredients and beat until the mixture is smooth. If the mixture is too thick to spread, add a little more milk. Spread the filling evenly over the bottom layer, cover, and refrigerate until firm (about 30 minutes).

Top Layer: Chop the chocolate into small pieces. Then, in a heat-proof bowl, over a saucepan of simmering water, melt the chocolate and butter. Spread the melted chocolate evenly over the filling and refrigerate for about 10 minutes or just until the chocolate has set. Using a sharp knife, cut into squares.

BANANA PUDDING

Source: Clara Wilson

There are as many ways to make banana pudding as there cooks. This is the banana pudding my wife and I grew up with....just plain ole' banana pudding.

Ingredients

½ cup sugar

1/3 cup all-purpose flour

Dash of salt

3 eggs, beaten

½ tsp vanilla

Vanilla wafers

2 cups milk

Medium ripe bananas

Directions

Combine sugar, flour and salt in the top of a double boiler. Stir in beaten eggs and milk. Blend well. Cook uncovered, stirring constantly, until thickened. Reduce heat and cook 5 minutes. Remove from heat and stir in vanilla. Spread small amount of custard on bottom of 1-1/2-quart bowl; cover with layers of 1/3 each of the vanilla wafers and sliced bananas. Pour about 1/3 of the remaining custard over bananas. Continue to layer wafers, bananas and custard to make a total of 3 layers of each, ending with custard. Garnish top with crumbled vanilla wafers.

"Keep calm and eat banana pudding." Unknown

LEMON BLUEBERRY BUNDT CAKE

Source: Author

Ingredients

2 ¾ cups cake flour

¼ tsp baking soda

1 cup butter flavor shortening

4 eggs

1 Tbsp lemon zest

1 cup buttermilk

1 Tbsp flour

1 ½ tsp baking powder

¼ tsp salt

1 ¾ cup sugar

2 Tbsp lemon juice

1 tsp vanilla extract

2 cups blueberries, tossed with

Glaze:

1 ½ cups confectioners' sugar

8-10 tsp lemon juice

1 Tbsp corn syrup

Lemon zest (to garnish)

Preparation

Heat oven to 350°F. Butter and flour a 12-cup Bundt pan. In a large bowl, whisk together flour, baking powder, baking soda and salt. Set aside. In a mixing bowl, beat shortening until smooth. Add sugar and beat until fluffy. Beat in eggs, one at a time, and beat well after each addition. Add lemon juice, lemon zest and vanilla and beat until combined. Beat in flour in three additions, alternating with buttermilk. Beat for 2 minutes. Fold in blueberries. Spoon into prepared pan. Bake at 350°F for one hour or until test wire comes out clean when inserted into center of cake. Cool on wire rack for 20 minutes. Turn cake out onto wire rack to cool then transfer to a cake plate. Mix glaze ingredients and drizzle over top of cake.

SACHERTORTE

Source: Rick Rodgers, November 2004 Kaffeehaus: The Best Desserts from the Classic Cafés of Vienna, Budapest, and Prague

In the past few years, bakers have been upping the ante with chocolate desserts (think of your local American bistro's "warm chocolate cakes with gooey chocolate centers"). The Sachertorte is a refined, elegant combination of chocolate flavors, complemented by a compulsory mound of Schlag. The whipped cream is an important part of the picture, as it moistens the frankly firm cake layers. Every bit of Sachertorte is supposed to be dipped in the whipped cream. This version is based on the recipe in Das Grosse Sacher Backbuch ("The Big Sacher Baking Cook"), which should be a reliable source.

Don't expect the cake layer to look perfect; sometimes the air bubbles are large and make holes in the top of the cake. If that happens, take some cake trimmings and mash them with a little of the apricot glaze to make a paste, and use a metal icing spatula to "spackle" the holes with the mixture.

Ingredients

Torte:

4 ounces semi sweet chocolate (chopped)

½ cup butter, softened   ¼ cup confectioners' sugar

2 tsp confectioners' sugar   6 eggs, separated

½ cup white sugar   2 Tbsp white sugar

1 cup cake flour

Icing:

9 oz. semisweet chocolate, chopped

3 oz. heavy cream

SACHERTORTE (CONTINUED)

Filling:

¼ cup water

¼ cup white sugar

3 Tbsp dark rum, divided

1 (12 oz.) jar apricot preserves

1 Tbsp water

Icing:

9 oz. semisweet chocolate, chopped

3 oz. heavy cream

Preheat oven to 350 degrees F (175 degrees C). Lightly butter a 9-inch springform pan; place a circle of parchment paper inside, and butter that as well.

Melt 4 ounces of chocolate in a metal bowl placed over gently simmering water. Stir frequently until melted, then remove from the heat and let cool slightly.

Beat the butter together with confectioners' sugar until creamy. Mix in the melted chocolate, then beat in the egg yolks, one at a time. In a clean bowl, beat egg whites with white sugar until stiff and glossy. Fold into chocolate mixture, then fold in cake flour, until incorporated. Pour into prepared springform pan, and smooth the top.

Bake in the preheated oven until the edges begin to pull away from the sides of the pan, and a toothpick inserted into the center comes out dry, about 45 minutes. Cool pan on a wire rack for 15 minutes, then run a small knife around the edge and remove the sides of the pan. Allow cake to cool completely on the base of the pan. When cool, remove from pan, and remove parchment paper; slice cake in half horizontally.

SACHERTORTE (CONTINUED)

Bring ¼ cup water and sugar to a boil in a small saucepan. When the sugar has dissolved and the syrup is clear, remove from heat and stir in 2 tablespoons rum. Brush 1/3 of the syrup onto the cut side of the cake bottom.

Puree the apricot preserves with 1 tablespoon of water until smooth. Bring to a simmer over medium heat in a small saucepan, and cook until thickened, about 2 minutes. Stir in remaining rum, then spread 1/3 of the jam mixture onto the cut side of the cake bottom. Place the top of the cake onto the bottom. Brush the outside of the cake with the remaining syrup, then spread remaining apricot preserves over the top and sides; refrigerate until the icing is ready.

To make the icing, melt 9 ounces of chocolate over a double boiler or in the microwave until smooth. Bring the cream to a simmer in a small saucepan, then stir into melted chocolate. Cool slightly, stirring often, until the chocolate reaches a spreadable consistency.

Set the cake on a cooling rack set over a cookie sheet or waxed paper to catch any drips. Pour the icing on top of the cake, and spread around the edges; allow excess icing to drip through the rack. Cool cake to room temperature, then carefully remove from the cooling rack using a spatula. Transfer to a dessert plate and store in the refigerator. Allow cake to come to room temperature before serving.

The cake can be prepared up to 2 days ahead and stored in an airtight cake container at room temperature.

Quality ingredients will really make a difference in this cake. Valhrona chocolate is perfect because of its dark, almost bitter flavor. For the most authenticity, look for the Austrian brand D'Arbo apricot preserves and Austrian Stroh rum for the glaze. For the best results, be generous with the apricot glaze — don't miss a spot, and let plenty sink into the cake before you pour on the chocolate.

FRUIT CRISP COBBLER

Source: My Mother; Mary Wilson Herriage

Place 1 to 1 ½ inches of fruit in a 9 X 13 inch baking dish. (Some fresh fruit may need sugar; berries, etc.)

Ingredients

Crust:

1 cup sugar

½ cup butter, softened

2 cups flour

2 tsp baking powder

½ tsp salt

1 cup milk

Directions

Cream sugar and butter. Mix dry ingredients and add alternately with by thirds.   Spoon mixture over the fruit, spreading evenly.

Ingredients

Topping:

½ cup sugar

1 Tbsp corn starch

1/4th tsp nutmeg (for apples and pears)

1 cup boiling water

Directions

Mix together dry ingredients and sprinkle over the batter. Drizzle boiling water evenly over the batter and the dry mix. Bake at 350° F for one hour or until golden brown.

Fried Pies

Source: Hazel Tyler

Ingredients

Dough:

1 cup flour

¼ cup + 1 Tbsp shortening

1 Tbsp sugar

¼ tsp salt

¼ tsp baking powder

¼ cup buttermilk

Directions

Combine dry ingredients. Cut in shortening until crumbly. Add buttermilk and mix well. Divide dough into golf ball size balls. Roll individual balls in flour, pat flat and roll out into a thin (approx. 1/8th inch thick) circle. Place two Tbsp of your favorite filling in the middle, wet edges, fold in half and press edges together using a fork to seal. Fry in hot oil at 375°F until golden brown.

FRESH APRICOT PIE

Source: My first x-wife; Audra White Wilson Jones

Ingredients

Filling:

¼ cup Tapioca

2 cups apricots, pitted and quartered

1 to 1 ½ cups sugar, depending upon how tart fruit is

2 - 3 Tbsp butter

Crust:

2 pie crusts

Beat together 1 Tbsp water and 1 egg yolk for glazing the crust

Instructions

Filling:

Mix together sugar, Tapioca and apricots. Set aside for 30 minutes to infuse and soften.

Pre-heat oven to 425°F. Roll out bottom crust and place in 9 inch pie plate with edges hanging over lip. Fill pastry with apricot mixture and top with dabs of butter. Carefully place top crust over fruit with edges hanging over lip of pan. Gently roll the edges of pastry together to form an ample ridge and crimp edges.

Brush top crust with beaten egg yolk and water and sprinkle liberally with sparkling sugar. Slash top crust to allow steam to escape. Place in hot oven, turn heat to 350°F after first 15 minutes and bake for another hour until bubbly and golden.

BANANA NUT BREAD

Source: Clara Wilson

Ingredients

Filling:

2 ½ cups flour

1 ¾ cups sugar

1 ¼ tsp baking powder

1 ¼ tsp baking soda

1 tsp salt

1 tsp cinnamon

2/3rd cup shortening

2/3rd cup buttermilk

1 ¼ cups mashed, medium ripe bananas

3 eggs

2/3rd cup chopped nuts

Directions

Preheat oven to 350°F. Combine first six ingredients and set aside. Cream sugar and shortening. Add mashed bananas and eggs and mix well. Add flour and buttermilk, alternating by thirds. Mix in the chopped nuts. Pour batter into prepared loaf pans (makes two loaves) and bake at 350°F for 1 ½ hours or until tester comes out clean.

SWEET POTATO PIE

Source: Clara Wilson

Ingredients

2 cups mashed sweet potatoes

2/3 cup sugar

½ cup butter, melted

½ tsp. orange extract

2 eggs, well beaten

1 cup heavy cream

½ tsp. salt

1 Tbsp. orange zest

Directions

Mix all ingredients together and pour into an unbaked pie shell. Bake at 350°F for 15 minutes. Reduce heat to 300°F and bake until set.

ORANGE DATE NUT CAKE

I grew up eating this cake. It was a Christmas favorite.

Source: My Mother; Mary Wilson Herriage

Ingredients

1 cup shortening	2 cups sugar
4 large eggs, separated (whites beaten)	4 cups all-purpose flour
2 tsp baking soda	2 cups buttermilk
1 (8 oz.) pkg chopped sugared dates	
2 cups pecans, chopped	2 Tbsp orange peel, grated

Directions

Dredge pecans and dates in flour. Beat the egg whites until stiff. Cream shortening until fluffy then mix in sugar and egg yolks. Combine flour and baking soda. Add flour and milk alternately by thirds. Fold in dates, nuts and egg whites.

Preheat oven to 350°F. Pour mix into a greased and floured Bundt pan. Reduce oven to 300°F and bake for 2 hours or until a wooden pick inserted in center comes out clean.

Icing:

1 cup orange juice

2 cups sugar

2 Tbsp orange peel, grated

Bring orange juice, sugar, and orange peel to a boil in a saucepan. Cook, stirring constantly until sugar has dissolved. Remove from heat.

Run a knife around edge of cake gently; punch holes in cake with a wooden pick (I use a chop stick). Drizzle glaze over warm cake until all is absorbed.

STRAWBERRY DELIGHT

Source: Dorothy Mullins

Ingredients

First layer:

1 cup flour

1 stick butter

1 cup pecans, chopped

Second layer:

8 oz. cream cheese

1 cup confectioners' sugar

12 oz. Cool Whip, less 1 cup

Third layer:

Large pkg. strawberry jello, mixed according to directions

2 (10 oz. pkg.) frozen strawberries

Fourth layer:

Cool Whip

Directions

Combine first thee ingredients. Press into 9x13 pan. Bake at 350°
F for 15 min.

Soften cheese, then blend in sugar and Cool whip. Spread over
cooled crust.

Make jello as directed. Mix with frozen strawberries. Let set until
partially congealed. Carefully spread over the second layer. Top
with remaining cool whip. Refrigerate.

PERFECT APPLE PIE

Source: McCall's Cooking School

Ingredients

1 pkg piecrust mix (or pastry for 2 crusts)	1 cup sugar
2 Tbsp all-purpose flour	¼ tsp salt
1 tsp cinnamon	1/8 tsp nutmeg
7 cups tart cooking apples, pealed & thinly sliced	
2 Tbsp lemon juice	2 Tbsp butter, cut in tiny pieces

Directions

Prepare pie crust as directed on package and line 9-inch glass pie plate. Reserve ½ mixture for top dough.

Preheat oven to 425°F. In small bowl, mix 1 cup sugar, flour, cinnamon, nutmeg and salt. In a large bowl, toss apple slices with lemon juice. Add sugar mixture into dough-lined pie plate. Dot with butter.

Trim overhanging edge of dough ½ inch form rim of pie plate. Fold reserved dough into quarters; cut slits to form steam vents. Place folded dough do that point is at the center of filling; gently unfold. Trim top crust 1 inch from rim of pie plate all around.

Moisten the edge of the bottom crust with a little water. Fold top crust under edge of bottom crust. With fingers, press edges together to form an upright edge, sealing so juices won't run out during baking. Decoratively crimp upright edge of crust: place thumb on edge of crust at an angle. Pinch dough between index finger and thumb. Repeat at the same angle all around. If desired, brush top crust with mild or cream and sprinkle with 2 tsp sugar.

Place pie on center rack of oven and bake for 45 minutes or until crust is golden brown. Let cool on wire rack at least 1 hour before serving with warm ice cream or cheddar cheese.

KING CAKE ORIGIN

The first "light" cakes in Europe made their way from medieval Moorish Spain to Renaissance Italy and from there eventually throughout Europe. The loose dough was baked in massive quantities in large wooden rings, each cake typically weighing six to twelve pounds. These treats were rich with white flour, butter, eggs, imported sugar, dried fruit, and spices. Because the ingredients were expensive, these cakes were reserved for very special occasions, notably weddings, christenings, and Epiphany.

The Roman Catholic Church chose the twelfth day from December 25th as the Feast of the Epiphany (Greek for "appearance"), commemorating the magi - magi were Zoroastrian priests (also the source of the word magic), but in Christian tradition came to mean "wise men" and sometimes mistakenly called "kings". January 6th marks Twelfth Day and the evening of January 5th is Twelfth Night. Twelfth Night was celebrated with a host of customs, many dating back to the Saturnalia, including masquerades, clowning, social satires, and rowdy, frequently bawdy games. Among the most beloved and enduring Epiphany traditions was the special sweet yeast cake. Ancient Romans, during the Saturnalia festival, baked a fava bean, a symbol of fertility and the underworld, inside a ritual round barley bread. Around the end of the 14th century, this practice was readopted in Italy for the new Twelfth Night cakes. Whoever found the bean in their portion was supposedly assured of good luck for the coming year. The notion of "king", derived from the token-finder and associated with the magi, gave rise to a special name for the bread – three king's cake or kings' cake.

LAYERED LEMON PIE

Source: Virginia Whitten courtesy of: Melvin and Virginia McConnell; Roseville B&B, Marshall, TX

Crust:

1 ½ cup flour

½ cup pecans, ground

1 ½ sticks butter

Melt butter in microwave. Mix with flour and pecans. Press in a 9 X 13 baking dish. Bake at 400°F for 20 minutes. Cool.

First layer:

1 (8 oz. pkg.) cream cheese

½ large Cool Whip

1 ½ cups powdered sugar

Mix all ingredients until creamy and spread over the crust.

Second layer:

2 eggs

1 cup lemon juice, freshly squeezed (it makes a difference)

2 cans sweetened condensed milk

Beat the eggs well. Mix in lemon juice and condensed milk. Pour evenly over cream cheese layer. Place in refrigerator until set. Before serving, spread remaining Cool Whip on top.

THE RAVE REVIEWS COCONUT CAKE

March 1978 Rave Reviews Coconut Cake from Bakers Coconut

Ingredients

1 pkg. yellow cake mix

1 pkg. (4-serving) Jello brand vanilla flavor instant pudding mix

2 cups Baker's Angel Flake Coconut

1 ½ cups water

4 eggs

¼ cup oil

1 cup chopped pecans

Frosting:

(And nothing says 'delicious' like fresher-tasting Baker's Coconut.)

4 Tbsp. butter or margarine	2 cups Baker's Angel Flake Coconut
1 (8 oz. pkg.) cream cheese	½ tsp. vanilla
3 tsp. milk	3 ½ cups confectioners' sugar

Instructions

Blend cake mix, pudding mix, water, eggs and oil in large mixer bowl. Beat at medium speed for 4 minutes. Stir in coconut and nuts. Pour mixture into 3 greased and floured 9-inch layer caked pans. Bake at 350 degrees for 35 minutes. Cool in pans for 15 minutes, remove and cool on wire rack. Fill and top cooled cake layers with Coconut Cream Cheese Frosting.

Coconut Cream Cheese Frosting:

Melt 2 tablespoons butter in skillet. Add coconut, stirring constantly over low heat until golden brown. Spread on absorbent paper to cool. Cream 2 tablespoons butter with cream cheese. Add milk. Beat in sugar gradually. Blend in vanilla. Stir in 1¾ cups coconut. Spread on top of cooled cake layers. Stack and sprinkle with remaining coconut.

FUDGE CAKE

Source: Farm Journal Kitchens, 1959

Ingredients

¾ cup butter, softened

2 ¼ cups sugar

1 ½ tsp. vanilla

3 eggs

3 squares (1 oz. each) unsweetened chocolate, melted

3 cups sifted cake flour

1 ½ tsp. baking soda

¾ tsp. salt

1 ½ cups ice water

Date Cream Filling (recipe follows)

Fudge frosting (recipe follows)

Directions

Cream together butter, sugar, and vanilla. Add eggs and beat until light and fluffy. Add melted chocolate blend well. Sift together dry ingredients; add alternately with water to chocolate mixture. Pour batter into three 8" round layer cake pans which have been waxed and greased and lined with waxed paper. Bake in a 350 degree F oven for 30-35 minutes. Cool on racks. Put layers together with date cream filling. Frost sides and top with fudge frosting.

Date Cream Filling:

Combine 1 cup milk and ½ cup chopped dates in top of double boiler. Combine 1 Tbsp. flour and ¼ cup sugar; add 1 beaten egg, blending until smooth. Add to hot milk mixture. Cook, stirring, until thick. Cool. Stir in ½ cup chopped nuts and 1 tsp. vanilla. Spread between layers.

Fudge Cake

Fudge frosting (the original 1959 version):

2 cups sugar

1 cup light cream

2 (1 oz.) squares unsweetened chocolate, grated

Combine all ingredients in a heavy saucepan. Boil over high heat 3 minutes without stirring. Reduce heat and continue cooking until it reaches soft ball stage (238°F). Cool. Beat until creamy and spreading consistency. Add cream if too thick.

Fudge frosting (the easier 1972 version):

2 cups sugar

¼ tsp. salt

1 cup light cream

2 Tbsp. light corn syrup

2 squares unsweetened chocolate

Combine sugar, salt, cream, corn syrup, and chocolate. Cook over low heat, stirring until sugar dissolves. Cover saucepan for 2-3 minutes. Remove lid and cook to the soft ball stage (234°F). Beat until spreading consistency. Add a little hot water if too stiff, sifted confectioners' sugar if too thin.

GERMAN'S SWEET CHOCOLATE CAKE

Ingredients

1 pkg. (4 oz.) Baker's German's Sweet Baking Chocolate

½ cup water

2 cups flour

1 tsp baking soda

¼ tsp salt

1 cup butter, softened (2 sticks)

2 cups sugar

4 eggs, separated (reserving the whites)

1 tsp vanilla

1 cup buttermilk

Directions

Preheat oven to 350°F. Grease and flour three 9-in. round baking pans. In small saucepan, melt chocolate with water over low heat; cool. Combine flour, baking soda and salt. Set aside.

In a large bowl, cream butter and sugar until light and fluffy. Add egg yolks, one at a time, beating well after each addition. Stir in melted chocolate and vanilla. Add flour mixture alternately with buttermilk, beating after each addition until smooth.

In a small bowl, beat the 4 egg whites until stiff peaks form. Gently stir into batter. Pour into prepared pans. Bake 30 minutes or until cake springs back when lightly touched. Immediately run spatula between cakes and sides of pans. Cool 15 minutes; remove from pans. Cool completely on wire racks. Spread Coconut-Pecan Filling and Frosting between layers and over top of cake. Note: This delicate cake will have a flat slightly sugary top crust which tends to crack.

GERMAN'S SWEET CHOCOLATE CAKE

Coconut-Pecan Filling and Frosting:

1 (12 oz. can) evaporated milk

1 ½ cups sugar

¾ cup butter (1 ½ sticks)

4 egg yolks, slightly beaten

1 ½ tsp vanilla

1 pkg. (7 oz.) Baker's Angel Flake Coconut (about 1 1/3 cups)

1 ½ cups pecans, chopped

In a large saucepan, stir milk, sugar, butter egg yolks and vanilla. Stirring constantly, cook on medium heat 12 minutes or until thickened and golden brown. Remove from heat. Stir in coconut and pecans. Cool to room temperature and of spreading consistency. Makes about 4 ½ cups.

RICE PUDDING

Source: My Mother; Mary Wilson Herriage

Ingredients

6 eggs, lightly beaten

3 cups milk

1 cup sugar

1 tsp vanilla

1 tsp cinnamon

Pinch of nutmeg

½ tsp salt

1 ½ cups cooked rice

1 cup dried apricots, chopped

Directions

Beat eggs in a medium mixing bowl. Add milk, sugar, vanilla, cinnamon, nutmeg and salt. Blend well. Stir in rice and apricots. Pour into a 2-quart buttered casserole. Set casserole in pan of water.

Bake in 350°F oven for 40-45 minutes, stirring once half way through baking. Custard is done when the tip of a small knife inserted into the center comes out clean. Remove the dish from the pan of water and set aside for 1 hour to cool.

"I don't know -- maybe the world has two different kinds of people, and for one kind the world is this completely logical, rice pudding place, and for the other it's all hit-or-miss macaroni gratin."

Haruki Murakami

EAGLE BRAND CHERRY CHEESE PIE

My son grew up eating this cheese pie. He prefers it over baked cheesecakes and calls it "normal" cheesecake.

Source: Eagle Brand

Ingredients

1 (8 oz.) package cream cheese, softened.

1 (14 oz.) can Eagle Brand sweetened condensed milk

1/3 cup fresh lemon juice

1 teaspoon vanilla extract

1 9 ounce graham cracker crust

1 (21 oz.) can cherry pie filling

Instructions

In large mixing bowl, beat cream cheese until fluffy. Gradually beat in Eagle Brand sweetened condensed milk until smooth. Stir in lemon juice and vanilla.

Pour into graham cracker crust. Chill 4 hours or until set. Top with desired amount of cherry pie filling before serving.

Note: Crushed pineapple (or fresh blueberries) cooked with a little cornstarch, to thicken, are delicious toppings also.

TIRAMISU

Source: Olive Garden™

Ingredients

3 egg yolks	¼ cup whole milk
¾ cup granulated sugar	3 cups mascarpone cheese
8 oz. cream cheese	¼ tsp vanilla extract
20 - 24 lady finger cookies	¼ cup cold espresso
¼ cup Kahlua coffee liqueur	2 tsp cocoa powder

Directions

Fill a medium saucepan halfway with water and bring it to a boil over medium/high heat, then reduce heat so that the water is simmering.

Whisk egg yolks, milk and sugar together in a double boiler. Stir the mixture often for ten minutes. After the sugar dissolves the mixture should begin to thicken and turn light yellow. Remove it from the heat to cool.

Use an electric mixer to combine mascarpone, cream cheese and vanilla in a large bowl. Mix until mostly creamy, with a few small chunks remaining. Add egg yolk mixture to the cheese mixture and combine well.

Combine espresso and Kahlua in a small bowl pour this mixture onto a dinner plate. One-by-one touch the bottom of each lady finger in the espresso. The lady finger will quickly soak up the espresso/Kahlua mixture, but you don't want the lady finger soaked -- just a dab will do ya. The top half of each lady finger should still be dry. Arrange the soaked lady fingers side-by-side on the bottom of an 8x8-inch serving dish or baking pan.

Spoon about half of the cheese mixture over the lady fingers, then add another layer of soaked lady fingers on top of the cheese mixture. Spoon the remaining cheese mixture over the second layer of lady fingers spreading it evenly.

Put two teaspoons of cocoa powder in a tight-mesh strainer and gently tap the side of the strainer to add an even dusting of cocoa powder over the top of the dessert. Cover and chill for several hours. To serve, slice the dessert twice across and twice down, creating 9 even portions (the first serving is always the hardest to get out).

SHERRY CAKE

Source: Cheryl Kitchens

Ingredients

½ cup pecans, chopped

1 pkg. butter cake mix

1 small pkg. instant vanilla pudding

½ cup sherry

½ cup Wesson oil

4 eggs

Glaze:

1 cup sugar

1 stick butter

¼ cup sherry

¼ cup water

Directions

Crumble nuts into bottom of well-greased Bundt pan. Place all other ingredients in a large mixing bowl and beat 2 minutes. Pour into Bundt pan and bake at 325°F for 1 hour.

While cake is baking, make the sauce. Combine sugar, water, cream sherry and butter in a saucepan. Boil 3 minutes, stirring continuously. Remove from heat.

Remove cake from oven and let cool 10 minutes. Pour ½ of hot glaze over the hot cake and let stand for 30 minutes, still in the pan. Remove to a serving platter and pour remaining glaze on top.

"If God had not made Sherry, how imperfect his work would have been." Benito Perez Galdos

CREAM SHERRY BUNDT CAKE

Source: Author

Ingredients

1 pkg. yellow cake mix

2 (3 oz.) boxes instant vanilla pudding

¾ cup canola oil

¾ cup cream sherry

4 eggs

¾ cup pecans, chopped

½ tsp allspice

½ tsp cardamom

Glaze:

1 cup sugar

1 stick butter

¼ cup cream sherry

¼ cup water

Preparation

Mix all cake ingredients on medium speed for 2 minutes. Pour into well-greased Bundt pan and bake at 325°F for 1 hour.

While cake is baking, make the sauce. Combine sugar, water, cream sherry and butter in a saucepan. Boil 3 minutes, stirring continuously. Remove from heat.

Immediately after removing cake from the oven, use a thin, non-metal utensil to gently separate cake from edge of pan. Slowly pour ½ of the glaze over the hot cake. Let cool for 30 minutes. Remove to a serving platter and pour remaining glaze on top. Lightly dust with powdered sugar.

SWEET POTATO CRUNCH

Although this is listed under desserts, we usually serve it as a main dish on Thanksgiving and Christmas.

Source: My Mother; Mary Wilson Herriage

Ingredients

1 stick butter

6 cups potatoes, mashed

1 cup sugar

4 eggs, beaten

1 cup milk

1 tsp vanilla

Crunch Topping:

2 cups brown sugar

2/3 cup all-purpose flour

2 cups pecans, chopped

2/3 stick butter, melted

Directions

Preheat oven to 350°F.

Bake sweet potatoes until tender, 20 to 30 minutes. Peel and mash.

Blend all filling ingredients well in a mixer. Pour into a 9 X 13 casserole dish.

Mix and crumble crunch topping evenly on top of potato mixture.

Bake in the preheated oven until cooked through and topping is lightly browned, about 35 minutes.

PEANUT BUTTER PIE

Source: Author

Ingredients

Crust:

25 whole chocolate sandwich cookies, such as Oreos (or

1 (9 inch) graham cracker crust)

4 Tbsp butter, melted

Filling:

1 cup creamy peanut butter

1 (8 oz.) pkg cream cheese, softened

1 (14 oz.) can Eagle Brand sweetened condensed milk

1 (8 oz.) pkg. Cool Whip, thawed

Salted chopped peanuts

Directions

For the crust: Preheat the oven to 350°F. Crush the cookies until they're fine crumbs. Pour the melted butter over the top and stir with a fork to combine. Press into a 9 inch pie pan and bake until set, 5 to 7 minutes (or use a prepared 9 inch graham cracker crust). Remove from the oven and allow to cool completely.

For the filling: Beat the peanut butter with the cream cheese until smooth. Add the sweetened condensed milk and beat until smooth. Add the thawed Cool Whip and beat until smooth, scraping the sides as needed.

Pour the filling into the crust, evening out the top with a knife or spatula. Sprinkle top with chopped peanuts. Chill for at least an hour before serving.

ROBERT E. LEE BUNDT

Legend has it that this was Robert E. Lee's favorite cake. Given its moist texture and light citrus notes, it will likely become a favorite of yours, as well.

Source: Southern Living

Ingredients

1 cup butter, softened

3 cups sugar

3 cups all-purpose flour

1/8 tsp salt

4 tsp orange zest, divided

¼ cup fresh lemon juice

2 to 3 Tbsp fresh orange juice

½ cup shortening

6 large eggs

½ tsp baking powder

1 cup milk

2 tsp lemon zest, divided

2 cups powdered sugar

Directions

Preheat oven to 325°F. Beat butter and shortening at medium speed with a heavy-duty electric stand mixer until creamy. Gradually add granulated sugar, beating at medium speed until light and fluffy. Add eggs, 1 at a time, beating just until blended after each addition.

Stir together flour, baking powder, and salt. Add to butter mixture alternately with milk. Beat at low speed just until blended after each addition. Stir in 2 tsp orange zest, 1 tsp lemon zest, and ¼ cup fresh lemon juice. Pour batter into a greased and floured 10-inch (12-cup) Bundt pan.

Bake at 325°F for 1 hour and 5 minutes to 1 hour and 15 minutes or until a long wooden pick inserted in center comes out clean. Cool in pan on a wire rack 10 minutes; remove from pan to wire rack, and cool completely (about 1 hour). Garnish with fresh raspberries, orange peel curls and mint sprigs.

APRICOT (NUT) MUFFINS

Source: Valeria (Val) Corley

Ingredients

1 cup boiling water

1 cup dried apricots, chopped

1 cup sugar

1 stick butter, softened

1 cup sour cream

2 cups all-purpose flour

1 tsp soda

½ tsp salt

1 cup nuts, chopped (optional)

1 Tbsp orange zest

Directions

Preheat oven to 350°F. Pour boiling water over apricots and set aside for at least 5 minutes then drain. In a large bowl, cream butter and sugar until fluffy. Add sour cream and mix well. Combine dry ingredients and add to butter mixture, mixing on low until just combined. Fold in orange zest, nuts and apricots. Batter will be very stiff. One to two Tbsp of the water drained from the apricots can be added if necessary. Spoon into well-greased muffin tins, filling each cup almost to the top. Bake at 350°F for 18-20 minutes or until done. Makes 18 muffins.

"Five tender apricots in a blue bowl, a brief and exact promise of things to come."

Frances Mayes

ROBERT REDFORD DESSERT

Source: Ruth Hanson

Ingredients

1 stick butter, softened

1 cup all-purpose flour

1 cup pecans, chopped

8 oz. cream cheese, softened

1 cup sugar

1 (10 oz.) container Cool Whip, thawed

2 small instant chocolate fudge pudding mixes

1 large instant vanilla pudding mix

3 cups milk

Chopped pecans and grated chocolate, for garnish

Directions

Preheat oven to 350 degrees. On medium speed in a large mixing bowl cream butter. On low speed gradually add the flour and mix just until blended. Stir in pecans. Press into the bottom of a 13 X 9 inch pan and bake for 15 to 20 minutes. Cool.

In a medium mixing bowl on medium speed, beat cream cheese, sugar and ½ of the Cool Whip until smooth. Spread cream cheese mixture over cooled crust.

Combine pudding mixes with 3 cups cold milk. Whip by hand until well blended and smooth. Spread pudding mix over cream cheese mixture. Top with remaining Cool Whip. Chill for several hours before serving. Garnish with chopped pecans and grated chocolate.

CHOCOLATE DOBERGE CAKE

This cake seems typically New Orleanian to me, having grown up seeing it impressively displayed in local bakeries, but never anywhere else. I'm unsure as to its origin, what "Doberge" means, or if it's a corruption of "D'Auberge", which someone suggested, or if it's related to the Hungarian dobostorte (unlikely, since it lacks the hard caramel topping). In any case, it's great. Here's a recipe submitted by New Orleanian expat Greg Beron. It's a "beginner's" Doberge cake, in that it only has four layers. If you like, double the batter and filling recipes and try making it with eight!

Source: Greg Beron

Ingredients

For the batter:

2 cups cake flour, sifted	1 tsp baking soda
1 tsp salt	10 Tbsp butter
1 ½ cups sugar	3 eggs, separated, whites beaten until stiff
1 cup buttermilk	1 ½ squares unsweetened chocolate, melted
1 ¼ tsp vanilla	1 tsp almond extract

For the filling:

2 ½ cups evaporated milk	2 squares semi-sweet chocolate
1 ¼ cups sugar	5 Tbsp flour
4 egg yolks	2 Tbsp butter
1 ¼ tsp vanilla	¼ tsp almond extract

For the frosting:

3 cups sugar	1 cup evaporated milk
2 oz. bittersweet or unsweetened chocolate	
4 Tbsp butter	1 tsp vanilla

CHOCOLATE DOBERGE CAKE

Directions

Preheat oven to 300°F. Grease and flour 2 nine-inch round cake pans. In a medium bowl, sift the flour, soda, and salt 3 times. Cream the butter and sugar in a large mixing bowl, and add egg yolks, one at a time. Gradually alternate adding the flour mixture and buttermilk, then add chocolate and mix well by beating about 3 minutes. Fold in the 3 beaten egg whites, vanilla, and almond extracts. Bake for 45 minutes or until done. After the cake cools, carefully split each layer into thirds to make 6 thin layers.

To make the filling, put milk and chocolate in a saucepan and heat until chocolate is melted. In a bowl, combine sugar and flour. Make a paste by adding hot milk chocolate by Tablespoons to the sugar and flour, then return to saucepan. Stir over medium heat until thick. Add 4 egg yolks all at once and stir rapidly to completely blend. Cook 2 or 3 minutes more. Remove from heat, and add butter, vanilla, and almond extract. Cool and spread on cake, layering as you go. Do not spread on top layer.

For frosting, combine sugar and milk in a heavy saucepan, and bring to a boil, stirring constantly. Reduce heat and simmer for 6 minutes without stirring. Remove from heat and blend in chocolate. Add butter and vanilla and return to medium-low heat, cooking 1 or 2 minutes. Place in refrigerator to cool. Beat well, then spread on top and the sides of the cake.

A "must" for chocolate lovers! A special dessert of Louisiana that's worth every minute of time and effort.

CATAHOULA'S KEY LIME PIE

This key lime pie is just amazing. It comes from Catahoula's Restaurant in Louisiana's Cajun Country. Serve it garnished with lime zest, as they do, below, or over our mango purée, shown above.

Ingredients

Crust:

3 Tbsp butter, melted

3 tsp sugar

6 oz. graham cracker crumbs (15 full crackers)

Filling:

1 cup Key Lime juice (20 - 40 key limes, depending on size and juiciness)

2 (14 oz. cans) sweetened condensed milk

2 egg yolks

2 whole eggs

Zest of 2 limes

Directions

Mix all crust ingredients thoroughly. Press into bottom and sides of a 10" pie tin to with fingertips. Bake at 350°F degrees for 8-10 minutes. Do not let burn. Remove from oven.

Combine filling ingredients and blend until smooth and creamy. Pour into pie crust. Bake at 350°F degrees for 35 minutes or until firm.

Remove and let cool. Refrigerate. Serve with dollop of whipped cream and fresh lime zest. Serving plate may be sauced with mango purée.

RAISIN CARAMEL PUDDING

I grew eating this dessert. It is delicious, but I don't like raisins, so I would ask my mother to leave them out. Sometimes, she would. When she wouldn't, I would pick them out!

Source: My Mother; Mary Wilson Herriage

Ingredients

½ cup sugar

½ cup shortening

½ cup milk

½ cup raisins or apples

1 ½ cup flour

1 tsp baking powder, rounded

Directions

Preheat oven to 350°F. Mix first 6 ingredients and pour into a greased 9X9 baking dish.

Pour on top of this mixture:

2 cups water

1 cup brown sugar

Dot with butter. Bake for 30 to 40 minutes at 350°F.

"I'd like to meet the idiot who came up with these. Take a grape, let it shrivel into a disgusting little wart and cover it with perfectly good chocolate. Ah, what the heck, I'll just suck off the chocolate."

Roz Doyle; from the Sitcom, Frasier

APPLE TART WITH ALMOND CUSTARD

Source: Seasons of the Vineyard; Robert Mondavi Winery

Ingredients

For the crust:

2 cups all-purpose flour

1 tsp salt

2 Tbsp milk

2 sticks butter, cut into pieces

1 large egg, lightly beaten

For the filling:

2 lbs. Granny Smith apples, peeled, cored, and cut in ½ inch cubes

½ stick butter, room temperature

¼ cup plus 1/3 cup sugar

1 large egg, lightly beaten

¼ cup dark rum

1/3 cup crème fraiche

½ cup almonds, ground

Directions

To make the crust, combine all the ingredients in a food processer and process until dough gathers and just begins to turn over the top, about a minute. Remove the dough to a work surface and divide into half and roll one portion to fit a 9 ½ inch tart pan. Reserve the remaining portion for another use. After rolling and fitting, chill the tart shell in the freezer for at least 15 minutes. Preheat oven to 400°F, and make filling.

Line tart shell with foil and beans or pie weights, and place it on a baking sheet. Bake for 10 minutes. Remove the foil and beans, reduce the heat to 375°F, and bake for 10 minutes longer. Cover the edges with foil to prevent them from browning too much. Remove the shell to a rack to cool to room temperature. Reset oven to 400° F.

Combine the butter, rum and ¼ cup sugar in a nonreactive sauté pan. Place over high heat and add the apples. Toss or stir the butter-

APPLE TART WITH ALMOND CUSTARD

rum mixture to coat the apples well. Cook until apples are golden brown and slightly caramelized, 10 to 15 minutes, stirring frequently. The apples should be tender, yet still hold their shape. Remove from heat and let the apples cool slightly.

Combine crème fraiche with the egg, almonds and 1/3 cup sugar. Distribute the apples in the baked tart shell. Pour the custard over the apples and bake the tart for 25 to 30 minutes, until the custard is firm in the center and the top is golden brown. Remove to a rack to cool. Serve slightly warm or at room temperature.

"I've always wanted to improve on the idea of living well. In moderation, wine is good for you - mentally, physically, and spiritually." Robert Mondavi

"I always knew that food and wine were vital, with my mother being Italian and a good cook." Robert Mondavi

PEARS EN CROUTE

Source: Café Nervosa; from the Sitcom, Frasier

Ingredients

2 (15 oz.) pkgs. refrigerated piecrusts

5 pears, washed and dried

1 egg yolk

1 Tbsp water

Caramel sauce:

12 oz. caramel ice cream topping

14 oz. condensed milk

2 Tbsp lemon juice

¼ cup Cointreau liqueur or other orange-flavored liqueur

Directions

Preheat oven to 350°F.

Unfold piecrusts, one at a time and place on a floured surface. Roll each into a 10 inch square. Cut each square into 1 inch strips. Starting at the bottom of 1 pear, begin wrapping with 1 pastry strip, overlapping ¼ inch as you go. Continue wrapping by moistening ends of strips with water and joining to previous strip until pear is covered. Repeat with remaining pears and pastry strips. Combine egg yolk and water and brush on pastry. Bake at 350°F for 1 hour or until tender. Spoon caramel sauce onto each serving plate and top with a pear. Garnish, if desired.

Carmel Sauce:

Combine caramel topping and condensed milk in top of double boiler. Bring water to a boil. Reduce heat to low and cook, stirring constantly, until smooth. Stir in lemon juice and Cointreau.

IRISH CREAM-AND-COFFEE POUND CAKE

Source: Café Nervosa; from the Sitcom, Frasier

Ingredients

1 ½ cups butter (3 sticks), softened	3 cups granulated sugar
6 large eggs	1 ½ Tbsp instant coffee granules
¼ cup boiling water	½ cup Irish cream liqueur
4 cups all-purpose flour	1 tsp vanilla
1 tsp almond extract	3 Tbsp sliced almonds, toasted

Irish Cream Glaze:

1 tsp instant coffee granules	2 Tbsp boiling water
1 ½ Tbsp Irish cream liqueur	2/3 cup powdered sugar, sifted

Instructions

Beat butter at medium speed with an electric mixer about 2 minutes or until soft and creamy. Gradually add sugar, beating at medium speed 5 to 7 minutes. Add eggs, one at a time, beating just until yellow disappears.

Dissolve coffee granules in boiling water; stir in liqueur. Add flour to butter mixture alternately with coffee mixture, beginning and ending with flour mixture. Mix at low speed just until blended after each addition. Stir in flavorings.

Pour batter into a greased and floured 13-cup Bundt pan. Bake at 300°F for 1 hour and 40 minutes or until a wooden pick inserted in center of cake comes out clean. Let cool in pan on a wire rack 10 to 15 minutes; remove from pan and let cool 30 minutes on wire rack. Brush with Irish Cream Glaze, and sprinkle with toasted almonds. Let cool completely.

Irish Cream Glaze: Dissolve coffee granules in water; add liqueur and powdered sugar, stirring until blended.

CHOCOLATE PIE

Source: Author

Ingredients

1 pie crust, baked and cooled (in a deep dish pie plate)

1 ½ cup sugar

¼ tsp salt

¼ cup cornstarch

1 Tbsp flour

2 ½ cups whole milk

½ cup heavy cream

4 egg yolks

6 ½ oz. dark chocolate, finely chopped

2 tsp vanilla extract

2 Tbsp butter

Whipped cream, optional

Preparation

Combine the sugar, salt, cornstarch and flour in a medium sauce-pan. Stir or whisk together. Pour in milk, heavy cream and egg yolks, mixing well. Cook over medium heat, stirring constantly, until the mixture reaches a boil and becomes thick, about 6 to 8 minutes. Continue to cook an additional minute, stirring constant-ly. The second it starts to bubble and thicken and looks like pud-ding, remove it from the heat. Add the chocolate, vanilla, and but-ter, and stir until combined and smooth.

Pour the filling into the pie crust and cover with clear wrap, making sure that the clear wrap is pressed against the surface of the choco-late to prevent a skin from forming. place in the fridge to chill for 4 hours uncovered.

GRAND MARNIER CAKE

Source: Gateau Grand Marnier; A Treasury of Great Recipes by Mary and Vincent Price 1965

Ingredients

1 cup butter

3 eggs, separated

2 cups all-purpose flour

1 tsp baking soda

Zest of 1 orange

Topping:

½ cup sugar

1/3 cup Grand Marnier

1 cup sugar

1 tsp Grand Marnier

1 tsp baking powder

1 ¼ cup sour cream

1 cup walnuts, chopped

1 cup orange juice

½ cup slivered almonds

Instructions

Preheat oven to moderate 350°F.

Cream butter with sugar until pale and fluffy. Beat in egg yolks, one at the time. Add Grand Marnier.

Sift together flour, baking powder, and baking soda. Add dry ingredients to butter, alternating with sour cream, beginning and ending with dry ingredients and mixing until smooth. Stir in grated rind of orange and chopped walnuts.

Beat until stiff the egg whites and fold into batter. Pour batter into a greased 9-inch cake pan. Bake in the moderate oven for 50 to 55 minutes, or until cake tests done.

Topping:

Combine sugar, orange juice, and Grand Marnier. Pour over hot cake while it is in the pan. Sprinkle with almonds and let cake cool before removing from the pan.

FRANGELICO PIE

Source: Mountain Top Inn; Rutland, Vermont, courtesy of Betty Parks

Ingredients

1 cup graham cracker crumbs

2 oz. butter, melted

2 cups (12 oz.) chocolate chips

2 Tbsp water

3 cups heavy cream

2 shots Frangelico liqueur

Sliced almonds

Directions

Mix graham crackers and butter and press into the bottom of an 8 or 9 inch springform pan.

In a double boiler, melt chocolate chips and 2 Tbsp water. Remove from heat and stir in 2 shots of Frangelico liqueur. Cool mixture to room temperature.

Using a chilled mixing bowl, whip heavy cream until fluffy. Fold into the chocolate mix. Spread evenly on top of the graham cracker mixture in the springform pan. Chill until firm. Garnish with the almonds.

BLUEBERRY CRUMB BARS

Source: Clara Wilson

Ingredients

Crust:

3 cups all-purpose flour	1 cup granulated sugar
2 cups old-fashioned rolled oats	½ cup brown sugar
1 tsp baking powder	¼ tsp salt
1 Tbsp lemon zest	1 cup cold butter, cut in pieces

Filling:

4 cups fresh blueberries	1 cup sugar
2 Tbsp lemon juice	4 Tbsp cornstarch

Instructions

Preheat oven to 375°F.

In a large mixing bowl, mix together the flour, granulated sugar, oats, brown sugar, baking powder and salt until well combined. Cut butter into the mixture until it resembles coarse crumbs. Remove ½ of the crumb mixture and set aside for the topping. Press remaining ½ of crust mixture into the bottom of a greased 9x13 inch baking dish.

In a large bowl, combine the blueberries, sugar, lemon juice, and cornstarch. Spread the blueberry filling evenly onto the prepared crust. Sprinkle the remaining crust mixture on top of the blueberries.

Bake at 375°F for 40-50 minutes or until the topping is lightly golden brown. Remove from the oven and transfer to a wire rack to cool completely. Once cooled, slice into desired size bars.

BLUEBERRY SOUR CREAM PIE

Source: Valeria (Val) Corley

Ingredients

1 pie shell

1 ½ cups fresh or frozen blueberries

1 ½ cups sugar

½ cup flour

½ cup sour cream

Pinch of salt

2 eggs, lightly beaten

Topping:

4 Tbsp flour

4 Tbsp sugar

2 Tbsp butter

Directions

Preheat oven to 325°F.

Spread blueberries in pie shell. Combine sugar, flour and salt. Mix in eggs and sour cream and spread evenly over the berries.

For the topping, cut butter into the flour and sugar until crumbly. Sprinkle over the pie filling. Bake in the preheated oven for 1 hour.

"Blueberries, strawberries and blackberries are true super foods. Naturally sweet and juicy, berries are low in sugar and high in nutrients - they are among the best foods you can eat." **Joel Fuhrman**

"I found my thrill on Blueberry Hill." **Fats Domino**

BASIC RECIPE FOR ANY CREAM PIE

I grew up eating pies with a pastry pie crust, this cream filling as the first layer and cherry pie filling on top. No Cool Whip (it didn't exist back then) or any other "filler" was mixed into the cream. It is simple and good!

Source: My Mother; Mary Wilson Herriage

Ingredients

2/3 cup sugar   1/3 cup flour

2 cups milk   2 or 3 eggs

1 tsp vanilla

Directions

Mix together flour and sugar. Stir in eggs, milk and vanilla and mix well. Cook on stove top or in microwave, stirring frequently, until smooth and creamy.

Shown is my favorite; Cherry Cream Pie

CALLOWAY CORNERS MUD PIE

Source: Author

Ingredients

1 prepared 9-inch chocolate crumb crust

2 pints coffee ice cream, slightly softened*

Hershey's chocolate syrup

Chopped walnuts

Kool Whip (optional)

Preparation

Spread ice cream into the prepared crust, scooping thin slices with a large spoon to help it spread easier. Drizzle chocolate syrup over the mixture. Top with walnuts (optional). Freeze for 2 hours or until firm. Top with Kool Whip (optional) before serving.

*Do not soften too much; just barely soft enough to spread.

"MUDDY BOTTOMS" PIE

Muddy Bottoms ATV & Recreation Park was created to provide northwest Louisiana and surrounding areas with a recreational escape for people of all ages. It is a scenic area where you can experience the outdoors by pitching tents, building campfires and riding through the mud, then wash off and relax in a bed. Complete with a welcome center, bathhouse, pro shop, eating pavilion, amphitheater, cabins, RV hookups and Sprinkler Park, you're sure to feel right at home. With that said, the main focus is the mud. I have developed this simple, refreshing and delicious recipe in celebration of Muddy Bottoms.

Source: Author

Ingredients

1 prepared 9-inch chocolate crumb crust

1 pint Dutch chocolate ice cream, slightly softened*

1 pint pistachio almond ice cream, slightly softened*

Hershey's chocolate syrup

¼ cup walnuts, chopped

Preparation

Spread 1 pint Dutch chocolate ice cream into the prepared crust, scooping thin slices with a large spoon to help it spread easier. Freeze for 1 hour. Carefully spread 1 pint pistachio almond ice cream over the chocolate layer. Drizzle chocolate syrup over the mixture. Sprinkle with walnuts. Freeze for 2 hours or until firm.

*Do not soften too much; just barely soft enough to spread.

BLUEBERRY STREUSEL MUFFINS

Source: Southern Living 5-Star Recipe Collection

Ingredients

1 ¾ cups all-purpose flour

½ cup sugar

2 ¾ tsp baking powder

2 tsp fresh lemon zest

½ tsp salt

1 egg, lightly beaten

¾ cup milk

1/3 cup vegetable oil

1 cup fresh or frozen blueberries (if frozen, thaw and drain well)

1 Tbsp all-purpose flour	1 Tbsp sugar
2 ½ Tbsp all-purpose flour	½ tsp cinnamon
1 ½ Tbsp butter	

Directions

Combine first 5 ingredients in a large bowl; make a well in center of mixture. Combine milk, oil, and eggs in a small bowl; add to dry ingredients, stirring just until moistened.

Combine blueberries, 1 Tbsp flour and 1 Tbsp sugar, tossing gently to coat. Fold blueberry mixture into batter. Spoon batter into 6 large (3 1/2inch) greased muffin pans, filling 2/3 full.

Combine ¼ cup sugar, 2 ½ Tbsp flour and cinnamon. Cut in 1 ½ Tbsp butter until mixture resembles coarse meal. Sprinkle over batter. Bake at 400°F for 20 minutes or until golden and a wooden pick inserted in center comes out clean. Remove from pan immediately.

HUMMINGBIRD CAKE

In February, 1978 we shared a recipe for Hummingbird Cake submitted by one of our readers, Mrs. L.H. Wiggins of Greensboro, North Carolina. That layer cake turned out to be Southern Living's most requested recipe in our 51 years, elevating it to the echelon of classic Southern Cakes.

Source: Southern Living 5-Star Recipe Collection

Ingredients

3 cups all-purpose flour

½ tsp salt

1 tsp ground cinnamon

¾ cup vegetable oil

1 (8 oz.) can crushed pineapple, undrained

1 ¾ cups bananas, mashed

½ cup pecans, chopped

1 tsp baking soda

2 cups sugar

3 eggs, beaten

1 ½ tsp vanilla extract

1 cup pecans, chopped

Cream cheese frosting

Directions

Preheat the oven to 350°F. Grease and flour three 9 inch pans.

Combine the first 5 ingredients in a large bowl. Add eggs and oil, stirring with until dry ingredients are moistened. Do not beat. Stir in vanilla, pineapple, 1 cup pecans and bananas.

Pour batter into three greased and floured 9 inch round cake pans. Bake at 350°F for 23 to 28 minutes or until a toothpick inserted in the center comes out clean. Cool in pans 10 minutes, remove from pans and let cool completely on wire racks.

Spread cream cheese frosting between layers and on top and sides of cake. Sprinkle ½ cup chopped pecans over top.

MOCHA-APPLE CAKE WITH BROWNED BUTTER FROSTING

Source: Southern Living 5-Star Recipe Collection

Ingredients

1 cup chopped pecans	1 cup sugar
1 cup canola oil	2 large eggs
1 Tbsp instant coffee granules	1 tsp vanilla extract
3 cups all-purpose flour	2 tsp baking powder
1 tsp ground cinnamon	1 tsp ground nutmeg

½ tsp salt

4 cups Granny Smith apples, cored, peeled and diced

2 (2.6-oz.) milk chocolate candy bars, chopped

Browned Butter Frosting

Directions

Preheat oven to 350°F. Bake pecans in a single layer in a shallow pan 8 to 10 minutes or until toasted and fragrant, stirring halfway through.

Beat sugar and next 4 ingredients at high speed with a heavy-duty electric stand mixer 5 minutes. Stir together flour and next 4 ingredients. Gradually add flour mixture to sugar mixture, beating at low speed just until blended. Add apples, chocolate, and pecans. Beat just until blended. Spoon into 2 greased and floured 9-inch round cake pans.

Bake at 350°F for 28 to 32 minutes or until a wooden pick inserted in center comes out clean. Cool in pans on a wire rack 10 minutes; remove from pans to wire rack, and cool completely (about 1 hour). Spread Browned Butter Frosting between layers and on top and sides of cake.

Mocha-Apple Bundt Cake: Prepare batter as directed; spoon into a greased and floured 12-cup Bundt pan. Bake at 350° for 1 hour to 1 hour and 10 minutes or until a long wooden pick inserted in center comes out clean. Cool in pan on a wire rack 15 minutes; remove from pan to wire rack, and cool completely (about 2 hours). Transfer to a serving platter and drizzle Browned Butter Frosting over the top.

Traditional Apple Dumplings

Source: Southern Living 5-Star Recipe Collection

Ingredients

3 cups all-purpose flour	2 tsp baking powder
½ tsp salt	1 cup shortening
¾ cup milk	2 Tbsp butter

3 large Granny Smith or other cooking apples

1 Tbsp sugar	1 ½ tsp ground cinnamon

Sauce:

1 ½ cups sugar	1 cup orange juice
½ cup water	1 Tbsp butter
¼ tsp ground cinnamon	¼ tsp ground nutmeg

Directions

Preheat oven to 375°.

Combine flour, baking powder and salt. Cut in shortening with a pastry blender until crumbly. Gradually add milk, stirring with a fork until dry ingredients are moistened.

Turn out onto a lightly floured surface, and knead 3 to 4 times. Roll pastry to ¼ inch thickness. Shape into a 21 X 14 inch rectangle. Cut pastry into 6 (7 inch) squares with a fluted wheel. Place 1 apple half in center of each square, cut side down. Dot each apple with 1 tsp butter. Sprinkle each with ½ tsp sugar and ¼ tsp cinnamon. Moisten edges of each pastry square with water and bring corners to center, pressing edges to seal. Place dumplings in a lightly greased 13 x 9 inch baking dish. Bake at 375° F for 35 minutes apples are tender and pastry is golden brown.

Sauce: Combine 1 ½ cups sugar, orange juice, water, 1 Tbsp butter, ¼ tsp cinnamon and nutmeg in a medium saucepan. Bring to a boil, reduce heat and simmer, uncovered, 4 minutes or until butter melts and sugar dissolves, stirring occasionally. Pour syrup over dumplings and serve immediately. Yield: 6 servings.

CUESTA ENCANTADA CAKE

I visited Hearst Castle several times during the 20 years that I lived in California, usually accompanied by my family, friends or guests visiting from such faraway "countries" as Louisiana. William Randolph Hearst formally named the estate "La Cuesta Encantada" (The Enchanted Hill), but usually called it "the Ranch". It is located near San Simeon and is now a state historical monument.

Source: Castle Fare; Hearst Castle, California

Ingredients

1 cup butter	1 cup sugar
1 cup sour cream	3 eggs, separated
1 tsp baking powder	¼ tsp salt
2 cups flour, sifted	1 tsp soda

Topping:

½ cup sugar	¾ cup orange juice
¼ cup rum	1 Tbsp Curacao

Instructions

Preheat oven to 350°F.

Beat egg whites until stiff. Cream butter and sugar together until light. Add egg yolks, one at a time, beating well after each addition. Sift flour, salt baking powder and soda together several times. Add dry ingredients to the mixture alternately with sour cream. Fold in beaten egg whites. Pour batter into a 9 inch tube pan that has been greased. Bake at 350°F for 55 minutes, or until done.

Topping:

Combine and stir until sugar is dissolved. Pour over the cake while cake is still hot. Let cake cool in the pan then remove to a serving dish.

LA MAISON ENCHANTE BUNDT CAKE

Source: Author

Ingredients

1 pkg. butter cake mix

2 (3 oz.) boxes instant vanilla pudding

¾ cup canola oil

¾ cup Grand Marnier

4 eggs

¾ cup pecans, chopped

½ tsp allspice

½ tsp cardamom

Topping:

1 cup sugar	1 stick butter
¾ cup orange juice	¼ cup rum
1 Tbsp Grand Marnier	

Preparation

In a stand mixer, mix all cake ingredients on medium speed for 2 minutes. Pour into well-greased Bundt pan and bake at 325°F for 1 hour.

While cake is baking, combine all topping ingredients in a medium saucepan. Bring to a boil, stirring continuously, until sugar is dissolved. Remove from heat.

Immediately after removing cake from the oven, use a thin, non-metal utensil to gently separate cake from edge of pan. Slowly pour ½ of the hot glaze over the hot cake. Let cool for 30 minutes. Remove to a serving platter and pour remaining glaze on top. Lightly dust with powdered sugar.

BROWNIE PIE

Source: Valeria (Val) Corley

Ingredients

Cookie crust:

1 stick butter, softened

1 cup all-purpose flour

1 Tbsp sugar

¼ tsp salt

1 cup nuts, chopped

Filling:

1 stick butter, softened

1 cup sugar

2 eggs

5 Tbsp cocoa powder

½ cup self-rising flour

½ cup nuts, chopped

Directions

Preheat oven to 325°F.

Cookie crust: Using a pastry blender, mix together all ingredients except the nuts. Blend in nuts and press into a lightly greased 9 inch pie plate.

Filling: Mix together all ingredients except nuts. Stir in nuts and pour into the pie crust. Bake at 325°F for 30 minutes. Serve with ice cream, whipped cream or both. Drizzle a little chocolate syrup over top.

MOE'S BANANA PUDDING

Source: Marilyn Thomas

Ingredients

2 ½ cups milk

2 small boxes instant vanilla pudding

1 can sweetened condensed milk

1 (8 oz.) container Cool Whip

1 box vanilla wafers

5 bananas, sliced

Directions

Pour milk into a medium sized bowl. Add instant pudding and mix well. Add condensed milk and Cool Whip, mixing well. In a large bowl, layer vanilla wafers, sliced bananas and pudding mixture, finishing with pudding. Refrigerate until ready to serve.

NOTES

NOTES

DRINKS

CHAI LATTE MIX

Source: Author

Ingredients

1 cup nonfat dry milk powder

1 cup powdered non-dairy creamer

1 cup French vanilla flavored powdered non-dairy creamer

2 ½ cups Organic Sucanat

1 ½ cups unsweetened instant tea

2 tsp ground ginger

2 tsp ground cinnamon

1 tsp ground cloves

1 tsp ground cardamom

Preparation

Mix all ingredients together in a large bowl. Working with about half the mixture at a time, process in a food processor until fine and smooth. Store in a cool, dry place, in an airtight container.

To use, stir two heaping tablespoons into 6-8 oz. of hot water.

"I cook with wine; sometimes I even add it to the food." W.C. Fields

"I rather like bad wine; one gets so bored with good wine." – Benjamin Disraeli

"Wine can be considered, with good reason, as the most healthful and hygienic of all beverages." – Louis Pasteur

SCANDINAVIAN COFFEE

If your family's from the Midwest (especially Wisconsin or Minnesota, both of which have a significant Scandinavian-rooted population), you might remember your grandma boiling up big, big batches of what she called Scandinavian coffee (or perhaps Norwegian or Swedish coffee, if she wanted to get specific). If she was making it for a church get-together, she might have called it church basement coffee and brought along one of those heavenly potluck dishes.

But what was that secret-ingredient coffee that Gran made? If you peeked in the percolator, you might have seen it.

The secret ingredient in Scandinavian coffee...Eggs!

They are what make Scandinavian coffee the richly-flavored, amber-hued, perfectly-balanced perfect brew that it is. Or more specifically, a raw egg—shell and all—which you crack over and mix it into your coffee grounds to form a thick slurry, which you then boil for three minutes in a pot of water (we'll get to the how-to just below).

Not everyone knows this, but eggs have a seemingly magical power to "clarify" liquids from broth to wine to...yes, coffee. As the liquid is heated, the egg coagulates, drawing impurities out of the liquid and into itself. In the case of coffee, those impurities include substances that can cause coffee to taste bitter or burnt. Ultimately, the impurities also include the grounds, themselves. In other words, the egg acts as an "ick" magnet, filtering your coffee without the need for a paper or mesh filter (yay!). After a mere three minutes, the egg and grounds have formed a unified lump that you can easily strain as you pour yourself a cup.

Here's how to make Scandinavian coffee

3 tablespoons ground coffee (I used a dark roast from Folgers 1850, the new Folgers coffee line aimed at millennials....ahem, no, I'm not a millennial, but gosh darn it, this coffee is awesome)

SCANDINAVIAN COFFEE

1 egg, including the shell

4 cups plus 3 Tbsp of water

Set three cups of water to boil in a pot. Set aside one cup of cold water.

In a small bowl, combine coffee grounds, egg (crush the shell as you mix it up), and the remaining 3 Tbsp of water. This is your slurry.

When the water is boiling, add the slurry to the water and set a timer for three minutes.

When the timer goes off, remove the pot from the heat source and pour in the cold water.

Strain into a pitcher (you'll leave behind a large clump of egg and grounds) and serve

Peach Tea

This makes a wonderful non-alcoholic party drink!

Source: Deena Coyle

Ingredients

2 liter Sprite

1 pkg Crystal Lite Peach Tea powder

2 liter Ginger Ale

1 lemon, sliced

1 orange, sliced

Crushed Ice

Directions

Pour sprite in a 2 gallon container. Very slowly stir in Crystal Lite Peach Tea powder (it will initially foam up). Slowly add Ginger Ale. Add lemon and orange slices and crushed ice.

SANGRIA

Source: Seasons of the Vineyard; Robert Mondavi Winery

This sangria relies on the natural sugars in the wine and fruit for its sweetness. Some palates may prefer a little sugar in their sangria.

Ingredients

1 (750 ml.) bottle zinfandel or other full-bodied red wine

1 cup orange juice, freshly squeezed

1 lemon, squeezed

½ orange, sliced very thin

½ lime, sliced very thin

½ lemon, sliced very thin

Instructions

Pour the wine into a pitcher or serving bowl. Stir in the orange and lemon juice. Chill the sangria for at least an hour before serving. When ready to serve, float the orange, lime and lemon slices on top.

NEARLY CHAMPAGNE

Source: Castle Fare; Hearst Castle, California

Ingredients

2 quarts apple juice

2 cups light corn syrup

2 cups lime juice

2 cups sparkling water

Maraschino cherries

Lime, thinly sliced

Instructions

Combine juices and corn syrup. Pour over ice in a large bowl. Just before serving, add sparkling water. Garnish with lime slices and cherries.

LEMONY FRUIT COOLER

This punch looks so pretty with all the colorful fruit floating in the bowl. It has a refreshing taste and is easy to put together. —Dawn Shackelford, Fort Worth, Texas

Source: Taste of Home

Ingredients

½ cup sugar

½ cup lemon juice

4 cups cold white grape juice

1 liter club soda, chilled

1 medium orange, halved and sliced

½ cup sliced strawberries

½ cup sliced fresh peaches

Ice cubes, optional

Directions

In a punch bowl or pitcher, mix sugar and lemon juice until sugar is dissolved. Stir in grape juice.

To serve, stir in club soda and fruit. If desired, serve with ice.

TOMATO-LIME SIPPER

It's easy to make lots of this in advance. Everybody loves a bloody Mary—and this virgin version's not too spicy, either.—Bonnie Hawkins, Elkhorn, Wisconsin

Source: Taste of Home

Ingredients

¼ tsp beef bouillon granules

¾ cup boiling water

3 cups tomato juice

¼ cup lime juice

1 tsp Worcestershire sauce

¼ tsp celery salt

¼ tsp dried basil

4 celery ribs, with leaves

Directions

Dissolve bouillon in boiling water. Add next five ingredients. Cover and chill.

To serve, pour into glasses; add celery rib to each glass.

"I pray you, do not fall in love with me, for I am falser than vows made in wine."
William Shakespeare, As You Like It

"Age appears best in four things: old wood to burn, old wine to drink, old friends to trust and old authors to read."
Francis Bacon

"High and fine literature is wine, and mine is only water; but everybody likes water." Mark Twain

RASPBERRY FIZZ

As a festive, non-alcoholic beverage for adults, our Test Kitchen staff came up with this pretty pink drink. It has a mild raspberry flavor and isn't overly sweet.

Source: Taste of Home

Ingredients

2 oz. ruby red grapefruit juice

½ to 1 oz. raspberry flavoring syrup

½ to ¾ cup ice cubes

6 oz. club soda, chilled

Directions

In a mixing glass or tumbler, combine grapefruit juice and syrup. Place ice in a highball glass; add juice mixture. Top with club soda.

Editor's Note:

This recipe was tested with Torani brand flavoring syrup. Look for it in the coffee section.

KAHLUA

Source: Author

Origin of Kahlua

Pedro Domecq first produced Kahlua in 1936 in Veracruz, Mexico. The name Kahlua carries the meaning, "House of the Acolhua people" in the Veracruz Nahuatl language, which was spoken in the area before the conquest of the Spanish. Kahlua became available in the US only from 1962 onward.

The base spirit used for making Kahlua has similarities with rum. Primarily made from coffee beans, Kahlua contains high amounts of caffeine. Besides its blend of fine Mexican coffee, this drink contains other ingredients like rum, corn syrup, vodka, and sugar. It takes about seven years when making one bottle of Kahlua.

Ingredients

4 cups strong brewed Mexican coffee

3 cups sugar

1 cup corn syrup

3 Tbsp vanilla

4 cups good quality white rum

Preparation

In a saucepan, bring the coffee and sugar to a boil. Reduce heat and simmer for 10 minutes. Remove from heat and allow to cool completely.

Stir the vanilla, corn syrup and rum into the cooled coffee syrup until combined.

Pour into clean bottles, cap tightly and store in a cool, dry place. If stored properly, your homemade Kahlua will maintain its flavor and potency for about three to four years.

Layered Blueberry Mango Smoothie

Source: Author

Ingredients

For the mango smoothie:

1 (16 oz.) bag frozen mangos

1 small banana, frozen

½ cup vanilla yogurt

3 Tbsp honey

1 ½ cups orange juice (don't pour

into blender until ready to blend)

For the blueberry smoothie:

16 oz. frozen blueberries

1 small banana, frozen

½ cup vanilla yogurt

3 Tbsp honey

1 ½ cups cranberry juice (don't pour into blender until ready to blend)

Preparation

For the mango smoothie: Blend, on lowest speed, all ingredients together well. Pour into bottom half of glasses.

For the blueberry smoothie: Blend, on lowest speed, all ingredients together well. Gently pour into top half of glasses.

SPICED CARAMEL APPLE CIDER

It's better than Starbucks!

Source: Author

Ingredients

5 cups Simply Apple 100% pressed cider

1 cup Cinnamon Syrup

5 whole cloves

5 allspice berries

Whipped cream

Caramel syrup

Preparation

Combine and heat the apple cider, cinnamon syrup, cloves and allspice over medium heat for 5 minutes. Let steep longer if desired. Strain and pour into mugs. Top with whipped cream and drizzle with caramel syrup.

NON-ALCOHOLIC PARTY PUNCH

Source: Author

Ingredients

2 (3 oz.) pkg. raspberry Jell-O® mix

1 (3 oz.) pkg. strawberry Jell-O® mix

4 cups sugar

13 cups boiling water

1 (5.4 oz.) can cream of coconut

2 (46 oz.) cans pineapple juice

1 (16 oz.) bottle lemon juice concentrate

2 (2 liter) bottles ginger ale, chilled

Preparation

In a large bowl, combine gelatin and sugar. Stir in boiling water until mixture is dissolved. Stir in cream of coconut, pineapple juice and lemon juice concentrate. Divide into 2 containers, and freeze until solid.

To serve, place frozen mixture in punch bowl, and chop into pieces. Pour in ginger ale.

NOTES

FOR RESERVATIONS CALL: 1-318-371-1331

NOTES

FRUITS & SALADS

Strawberry Spinach Salad

Source: Valeria (Val) Corley

Ingredients

1 ½ lbs. fresh baby spinach

Red onion, thinly sliced (just enough for garnish)

2 cups fresh strawberries, sliced

1 cup walnuts, chopped

½ cup feta cheese, crumbled

Dressing: (Or use Brianna Blush Dressing)

¼ cup apple cider vinegar

1/3 cup sugar

½ tsp salt

½ cup EVOO (extra virgin olive oil)

2 Tbsp poppy seeds   .

Red onion, grated (to taste)

1 tsp dried mustard

Directions

Mix salad ingredients together. Toss with dressing just before serving.

GUMBO POTATO SALAD

The second you saw Gumbo Potato Salad as the title of this post you probably thought one of two things. You knew exactly what I was talking about or you thought I'd gone and lost my mind. Don't worry. I had the same thought the first time I was served a side of potato salad with my gumbo at "Mama's House" in Morgan City, Louisiana. Being from West Texas by way of North Louisiana, I was wondering if someone hadn't made a mistake.

This "gumbo" potato salad, unlike the more common and chunkier Southern Style Potato Salad, has no mustard, pickles or onions and is mostly mashed. It's perfect for eating with gumbo, whether you scoop it right into the gumbo bowl, or serve it on the side.

Source: Ruth Mire Hanson

Ingredients

6 medium potatoes, peeled and diced

3 large hard-boiled eggs

1 cup BLUE PLATE Mayonnaise

Salt to taste

White pepper to taste

Directions

Boil potatoes until tender and crumbly, about 20 minutes. Drain and set aside to cool. Place into serving bowl and use a masher to partially mash them, leaving some chunks.

In a separate small bowl, mix together the ¾ cup of BLUE PLATE mayonnaise and salt; spoon over the potatoes. Stir in until mixed well, adding additional mayonnaise to reached desired consistency. Taste and adjust seasonings as desired. To serve with gumbo, spoon gumbo into individual serving bowls, with or without rice, and use a cookie scoop to place a scoop of the potato salad right into the bowl, or serve it on the side. Refrigerate leftovers.

CREAMY COLESLAW

Source: Author

Ingredients

16 ounces shredded cabbage/carrot blend

Coleslaw Dressing:

1 cup Blue Plate mayonnaise

¼ cup sour cream

1 ½ tsp mustard

2 Tbsp apple cider vinegar

2 Tbsp sugar

½ tsp celery salt

½ tsp onion powder

¼ tsp salt

½ tsp black pepper

1 tsp smoked paprika

Preparation

Place the shredded cabbage and carrots in a large bowl and sprinkle a teaspoon of salt over them. Toss to combine. Let this sit for at least an hour to draw out excess water. Rinse and drain.

Combine the dressing ingredients in a small bowl. Pour it over the cabbage mixture and stir until combined. Cover and refrigerate for at least 2 hours before serving.

"Well, we became a vegetarian. But that didn't last very long, because, um, I don't like vegetables. Or salad, nothing like that!"
-- Dakota Fanning

Smoked Turkey Bacon, Vegetable and Rice Bowl

Source: Author

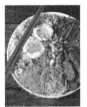

Ingredients

4 slices Smoked Turkey Bacon, halved

For rice:

2 cups vegetable broth	1 cup brown rice, uncooked
1 tsp lime juice	½ tsp ground coriander
¼ tsp black pepper	1 tsp fresh cilantro, chopped

For salad:

1 cup sprouts	1 cup carrots, coarsely grated
1 cup beets, julienned	2 green onions, sliced diagonally
2 eggs, soft boiled	1 Tbsp fresh cilantro, chopped

Tamari sauce and/or water-thinned oyster sauce for dressing (optional)

Preparation

Cook the bacon.

To cook the rice, bring the broth to a boil in a medium sauce pan. Add the rice and lime juice, reduce heat to an active simmer, and cover. Cook the rice for the time indicated on the package directions.

Divide the rice between two serving bowls, layering each with half of the turkey bacon, sprouts, carrots, and beets. Gently peel and slice the eggs in half, and nestle two halves in each bowl.

Top with green onions and a sprinkle of cilantro. If desired, add a dash or two of tamari sauce or a drizzle of water-thinned oyster sauce over the bowls.

MARINATED VEGETABLE-BACON BOWL

Source: Sandra Owens

Ingredients

1 (8 ½ oz. can) English peas, drained

1 medium onion, sliced

2/3 cup vegetable oil

1 ¼ tsp salt

Dash cayenne pepper

1 lb. fresh mushrooms, sliced

1 small cauliflower, broken into flowerets

¼ cup lemon juice

½ tsp dry mustard

¼ cup bacon, cooked and crumbled

Directions

Combine vegetables, tossing lightly. Combine the remaining ingredients, except bacon, and mix well. Pour dressing over vegetables and toss lightly. Cover and chill, at least 3 hours, stirring occasionally. Sprinkle bacon over salad just before serving.

Tomatoes Caprese

Source: Carrabba's

Ingredients

1 lb. Cherry/Grape tomatoes

½ cup fresh Basil leaves

1 small red onion, diced fine

4 ounces of Mozzarella cheese

¼ cup of extra virgin olive oil

2 tsp of Red Wine Vinegar

½ tsp Sea Salt

¼ tsp fresh cracked pepper

NOTE: Sea Salt and Cracked Pepper are essential to this recipe. This will not taste the same if using regular salt and pepper.

Directions

Cut tomatoes in half and place in a medium bowl.

Chiffonade the Basil (take leaves of basil and roll into a log and cut into thin strips). Add basil and diced onions to the tomatoes.

Either cut or break the mozzarella into small pieces and add it to the bowl.

Whisk the Red Wine Vinegar and the olive oil together and pour over the tomato mixture.

Allow to set for 10 minutes to bring to room temp and all the flavors to blend.

Sprinkle with the Sea Salt and cracked pepper right before serving (the salt brings out the moisture in the tomatoes).

FRENCH COUNTRY SALAD WITH LEMON DIJON VINAIGRETTE

A light and tasty salad.

Source: Mon Petit Four; The French Lifestyle

Ingredients

For the salad:

1 (5 oz.) bag of arugula

Olive oil to drizzle over asparagus

Sea salt to sprinkle over asparagus

¼ cup goat cheese, crumbled

½ lb. asparagus, trimmed

½ cup cooked beets, sliced

½ cup whole walnuts

For the vinaigrette:

2 Tbsp Dijon mustard

2 Tbsp olive oil

½ tsp sea salt

Juice of ½ lemon

3 Tbsp balsamic vinegar

2 cloves garlic, minced

Pinch of freshly ground black pepper

Zest of ½ lemon

Instructions

Preheat the oven to 400°F. Line a baking sheet with a piece of parchment paper. Cut the asparagus into 1 1/2" long pieces. Spread the asparagus out onto the prepared baking sheet. Drizzle olive oil over the asparagus along with a sprinkle of sea salt. Roast for 4 to 5 minutes, until the asparagus is tender but still has a bite. Allow the asparagus to cool before using.

Toss the arugula with the asparagus in a large bowl; temporarily set aside.

Whisk all of the vinaigrette ingredients together in a small measuring cup. Toss the salad with the vinaigrette until everything is lightly coated in the dressing. Garnish the salad with the sliced beets, toasted nuts, and crumbled goat cheese.

TACO SALAD

Source: Frances Garrett

Ingredients

8 to 10 cups of romaine or iceberg lettuce, chopped.

1 lb. ground beef (or turkey)

1 pkg. taco seasoning

1 (14.5 oz. can) pinto beans, drained

2 tomatoes, chopped

1 ½ cups cheddar cheese, shredded

1 (12 oz. pkg.) corn chips (doesn't have to be Fritos)

Catalina Dressing

Green onions, chopped (optional)

Black olives (optional)

Instructions

Brown the ground meat, adding the taco seasoning in towards the end. Remove from heat and drain if needed. Add the beans to the meat, mix well.

In a large bowl, mix lettuce, tomatoes, green onions and (optional) olives. Top with corn chips and cheese. Add meat and beans. Last, pour on the dressing and gently mix to coat well. Serve immediately.

"To make a good salad is to be a brilliant diplomatist - the problem is entirely the same in both cases. To know exactly how much oil one must put with one's vinegar."

Oscar Wilde

ITALIAN LINGUINE SALAD

Source: Taste of Home

Ingredients

8 oz. uncooked linguine

1 medium cucumber, quartered and sliced

2 medium tomatoes, seeded and chopped

½ cup thinly sliced green onions

¾ cup Italian salad dressing

Directions

Cook linguine according to package directions. Meanwhile, in a large bowl, combine the cucumber, tomatoes and onions. Drain linguine; rinse under cold water. Add linguine to vegetable mixture. Drizzle with dressing; toss to coat. Refrigerate until serving.

CLASSIC CRANBERRY SALAD

"Not only is this cranberry salad delicious on its own, it will taste amazing over turkey, ham, pork chops, or chicken. Leftovers of this crunchy cranberry salad would be "great over vanilla ice cream for dessert or with Greek yogurt for breakfast." We love the idea of making your Thanksgiving leftovers into something more than a sandwich. If you'll be overwhelmed the day you're serving, you can prepare this salad up to three days in advance, just cover and store it in the refrigerator. Cranberries are often thought of only around Thanksgiving or Christmas, but you can make this recipe any time to serve with a great protein or eat as snack during the later fall and winter months."

Source: Southern Living

Ingredients

4 cups (14 oz.) fresh or frozen cranberries

¾ cup light brown sugar, packed

½ cup fresh orange juice (from 2 oranges)

1 cup Bartlett pears, peeled and chopped (about 2 small pears)

1 cup fresh pineapple, chopped

½ cup celery, thinly sliced (from 2 stalks)

½ cup toasted pecans, chopped

Instructions

Bring the cranberries, brown sugar, and orange juice to a boil in a large saucepan over medium-high, stirring often. Reduce heat to medium-low, and simmer, stirring occasionally, until cranberries pop and mixture thickens, 12 to 15 minutes. Remove from heat, and cool to room temperature, about 30 minutes.

Stir in the Bartlett pears, pineapple, celery, and pecans. Transfer to a serving bowl; cover and chill salad 4 to 24 hours.

WALDORF SALAD

"The Waldorf Salad was created in New York City at the Waldorf Hotel (which later merged with the Astoria Hotel and is now the Waldorf-Astoria Hotel). Oscar Tschirky was the maître d'hôtel, or head waiter, at the Waldorf Hotel and he is credited with creating the recipe.

The original Waldorf Salad recipe contained only apples, celery, and mayonnaise. Many variations on this salad have been developed over the years by adding turkey, chicken, raisins, dates, walnuts, and even cauliflower, but I prefer this version with grapes."

Source: Oscar Tschirky, Waldorf Hotel

Ingredients

3 crisp red apples; Pink Lady, Fuji, or Gala

3 crisp Granny Smith apples

1 Tbsp lemon juice

2 cups red grapes cut in half

1 cup celery chopped (about 3 stalks)

1 cup walnuts halves

¾ cup mayonnaise or plain yogurt

Green leaf lettuce or mixed greens

Instructions

Slice apples then chop into bite-size pieces. Place apple chunks in a bowl and toss in lemon juice. Mix celery, grapes, and walnuts in with the apples. Add mayonnaise or yogurt and stir until the fruit and nuts are well-coated. Refrigerate salad until ready to serve.

Serve on a bed of green leaf lettuce or mixed greens.

SHRIMP AND JICAMA SALAD

Source: Seasons of the Vineyard; Robert Mondavi Winery

Marinade and shrimp:

Ingredients

2 tsp lemon zest   1 large clove garlic, minced

1 jalapeno pepper, seeded & diced fine   ¼ cup olive oil

1 Tbsp fresh cilantro leaves, minced

1 ½ lbs. medium shrimp, shelled and deveined

Directions

Mix lemon zest, jalapenos, cilantro and olive oil together in a bowl. Add the shrimp and marinate in the refrigerator for 2 to 8 hours, stirring occasionally.

Vinaigrette and salad:

Ingredients

½ red onion, minced   1 Tbsp fresh cilantro leaves, chopped

2 Tbsp champagne vinegar or white wine vinegar

1 Tbsp lime juice   ½ cup olive oil

½ tsp salt   1 head Romaine lettuce, about 12 oz.

6 oz. plum tomatoes, cut small   6 oz. jicama, pealed & julienned

Directions

Combine the onion, cilantro, vinegar, salt and lime juice in a bowl. Whisk in the olive oil to make an emulsion. Trim and clean the lettuce, reserving the large outer leaves for another use. Dry the lettuce and arrange it on a serving platter.

Remove the shrimp from the refrigerator about 30 minutes before you're ready to cook it. Let stand while you prepare a medium-hot grill. Thread the shrimp loosely on skewers and grill until they are

SHRIMP AND JICAMA SALAD

just done, about 1 ½ minutes on each side. Remove the shrimp from the skewers to a dish and drizzle them with about 2 Tbsp of the vinaigrette. Drizzle about 2 Tbsp of the vinaigrette over the lettuce. Toss the remaining vinaigrette with the tomatoes and jicama. Mound the tomatoes and jicama on the lettuce and arrange the shrimp on the salad. Serve immediately.

"Anyway, like I was sayin', shrimp is the fruit of the sea. You can barbecue it, boil it, broil it, bake it, sauté it. There's shrimp-kabobs, shrimp creole, shrimp gumbo. Pan fried, deep fried, stir-fried. There's pineapple shrimp, lemon shrimp, coconut shrimp, pepper shrimp, shrimp soup, shrimp stew, shrimp salad, shrimp and potatoes, shrimp burger, shrimp sandwich. That, that's about it." Bubba; from the movie Forrest Gump

"It specifically says in the Torah that you can eat shrimp and bacon in a Chinese restaurant. " Jason Alexander

CHICKEN SALAD AU VIN

Source: Café Nervosa; from the Sitcom, Frasier

Ingredients

6 cups chicken breasts, cooked and chopped

1 ¼ cups celery, diced

1 (8 oz.) can pineapple tidbits, drained

1 ¼ cups BLUEPLATE mayonnaise

2 ½ tsp dry white wine

½ tsp salt

½ tsp curry powder

2 Gala apples, seeded and thinly sliced

1 cantaloupe, peeled, seeded and thinly sliced (must be perfectly ripe)

½ lb. green seedless grapes

1 pint fresh strawberries

1 cup fresh blackberries

1 cup walnuts, toasted and coarsely chopped

Curly leaf lettuce leaves

Preparation

Combine first 3 ingredients in a large bowl and set aside.

Combine mayonnaise and next 3 ingredients. Add to chicken mixture, tossing to coat. Cover and chill 1 to 2 hours.

Arrange apple and next 4 ingredients on a lettuce lined platter and top with chicken mixture. Sprinkle with walnuts. Garnish, if desired.

CRANBERRY BROCCOLI SALAD

"For 20 years, the Austin American-Statesman held an annual Christmas Cookin' Contest, with readers bringing their favorite holiday dishes to a taste-off. Cranberry Broccoli Salad won the side dish category in 1993. I have made it once or twice a year ever since, usually by request, for a holiday potluck. If you double the amount of broccoli and cabbage, which I prefer, the salad will serve at least a dozen people." Kitty Crider

Source: Donna Alexander-Grabs; "A Christmas to be remembered"

Ingredients

1 ¼ cups fresh or dried cranberries, halved or whole (See note.)

2 cups broccoli florets or more

4 cups shredded cabbage or more

1 cup coarsely chopped walnuts

1 cup raisins

1 small onion, finely minced

1 cup mayonnaise

1/3 cup sugar

2 Tbsp. cider vinegar

8 slices bacon, cooked and crumbled

Directions

In a large bowl, combine cranberries, broccoli, cabbage, walnuts, raisins and onion. Combine remaining ingredients except bacon and pour over cranberry mixture. Toss well. Cover and refrigerate for up to 24 hours. Sprinkle bacon on just before serving. Serves 6-8.

Note: Dried cranberries are better (sweeter). Look for them in bags or bulk bins at places such as Whole Foods and H-E-B. About ¼ to 1/3 lb. is plenty.

CRAB LOUIE

"After at least 100 and possibly more than 300 years, the salad's preparation has developed in many varied ways. There are constants, of course: the crabmeat, lettuce, tomato and a so-called Louie dressing, which is a variation on mayonnaise-based Russian or Thousand Island dressing. Some versions may include hardboiled egg or asparagus, chopped cucumber or other vegetables.

Over time, I've developed my own favorite version. In place of the usual Romaine or iceberg lettuce, I like to use spears of Belgian endive. In place of plain tomato, I make a relish-like chopped tomato salad. And rather than spooning prepared dressing from a bottle, I make my own simple version, which I also share with you here.

Now, be creative and come up with your own version."

Source: Wolfgang Puck

Ingredients

1 pound jumbo lump crabmeat

6 Tbsp Thousand Island dressing (recipe on page 256)

4 Tbsp fresh chives, finely chopped

32 Belgian endive leaves

6 cups mixed baby salad leaves, well chilled

2 ripe but firm Hass avocados, cut into ½ inch dice

To make Crab Louie: Shortly before serving, thoroughly pick through crabmeat, removing any traces of shell or cartilage. Put crabmeat in mixing bowl. Gently fold in Thousand Island dressing and chives. (Note: Take care to leave lumps of crab.) Arrange individual endive leaves in flower patterns on chilled serving plates. Arrange bed of baby salad leaves in center of each plate. Distribute crabmeat mixture evenly among plates, mounding it on top of salad leaves. Spoon diced avocado and Tomato Relish (recipe on page 257) on top of crabmeat. Serve immediately.

LIME CHICKEN AND PASTA SALAD WITH CILANTRO PESTO

"Back in the '90s, the American-Statesman did a story on chicken salads. Food stylist Carol Johnson created this salad, which can be served warm or cold. The cilantro pesto is a snap to make in a food processor." Kitty Crider

Source: Carol Johnson

Ingredients

4 boneless chicken breast halves

Marinade:

Juice of 2 limes

¼ cup olive oil

¼ tsp cayenne pepper

¼ tsp paprika

Salt to taste

1 Tbsp brown sugar

Cilantro pesto:

1 large bunch cilantro

¼ cup walnuts, chopped

½ tsp fresh ground pepper

3 cloves garlic

¾ cup olive oil

Salt to taste

½ cup fresh Parmesan cheese, grated

4 to 8 oz. bow-tie pasta

Tomato halves, grilled

Instructions

To make marinade: Combine the lime juice, olive oil, cayenne pepper, paprika, salt and brown sugar in a glass bowl or casserole. Add the chicken, cover with plastic wrap and refrigerate 2 hours, turning once during that time.

To make pesto: Combine cilantro, walnuts, ground pepper, garlic, olive oil and salt in a food processor and process to a smooth paste. Stir in the Parmesan cheese. Cook pasta to al dente stage. While pasta is cooking, grill or broil chicken until done, about 10 minutes. Slice into short strips.

Combine the warm pasta and warm chicken with the pesto. Toss until well coated. Serve with grilled tomato halves, and crusty bread.

THOUSAND ISLAND DRESSING

Source: Wolfgang puck

Ingredients

Makes about 1 ¼ cups.

¾ cup BLUEPLATE mayonnaise

¼ cup tomato ketchup

2 Tbsp barbecue sauce, bottled-tomato-based

2 Tbsp red onion, finely chopped

1 Tbsp dill pickle or sweet pickle, finely chopped (or bottled cucumber relish)

½ Tbsp fresh Italian parsley, finely chopped

½ Tbsp fresh chives, finely chopped

Preparation

In nonreactive mixing bowl, combine all ingredients. Stir thoroughly. Cover with plastic wrap. Store in refrigerator.

FRESH TOMATO RELISH

Source: Wolfgang Puck

Ingredients

2 medium-sized sun-ripened tomatoes, halved, stemmed, seeded and cut into ¼ inch dice

½ medium-sized red onion, finely diced

4 Tbsp extra-virgin olive oil

2 tsp fresh Italian parsley, finely chopped

1/8 tsp sugar

Salt, to taste

Freshly ground black pepper, to taste

Preparation

To make tomato relish: In mixing bowl, combine tomato, onion, olive oil, parsley, sugar, salt and pepper. Stir thoroughly. Cover with plastic wrap. Refrigerate until serving time.

NOTES

NOTES

_____

_____

_____

_____

_____

_____

_____

_____

_____

_____

_____

_____

_____

_____

GLOBE TROTTING

International Cuisine

"The secret of success in life is to eat what you like and let the food fight it out inside." -Mark Twain

ARROZ CON POLLO (CHICKEN AND RICE)

Although chicken and rice is a classic Puerto Rican comfort food, many Latin countries have their own versions of arroz con pollo.

Ingredients

1 whole chicken, cut into 8 pieces, skin removed (or 4 boneless chicken breasts, skin removed)

½ cup olive oil   2 large bay leaves

1 large onion, chopped   1 clove garlic, minced

½ tsp crushed red pepper   1 tablespoon capers

2 ½ tsp salt   ½ tsp black pepper

2 cups medium-grain rice, rinsed   ¼ tsp saffron threads

2 (14.5 oz. cans) diced tomatoes, undrained

1 (4 oz. can) green chiles, diced   10 ½ oz. chicken broth

1 teaspoon ground cumin   1 teaspoon ground coriander

5 oz. frozen English peas   12 black olives, chopped

Directions

Wipe chicken pieces with paper towels. In a heavy, 6 quart Dutch oven, heat olive oil. Brown chicken until golden brown all over. Remove chicken, debone, cut into bite size chunks and set aside.

Preheat oven to 325°F. Add onion, garlic and red pepper to the Dutch oven. Sauté, stirring occasionally, over medium heat until golden; about 3 minutes. Add rice, salt, black pepper, capers and saffron and cook, stirring until rice is lightly browned; about 10 minutes. Add tomatoes, green chiles and chicken broth to the mixture. Add chicken and bring just to boiling. Stir in cumin and coriander. Bake, covered, 1 hour. Add ½ cup water, sprinkle peas and olives over the top; do not stir. Bake, covered, 20 minutes longer. Serve hot right from the Dutch oven.

ARROZ CENTRAL CAFÉ

Modern Mexican cooking is considered by culinary historians to be a fusion of three cuisines - indigenous, Spanish and French, but the strength and ongoing force of the pre-Hispanic cooking system is clearly demonstrated by its dominate influence on the cuisine of contemporary Mexico.

Source: Café Central, El Paso, TX

Ingredients

1 cup long grain rice, rinsed well

½ onion, chopped

1 (4 oz. can) green chiles, chopped and drained

1 garlic clove, minced

1 Tbsp butter, melted

1 Tbsp olive oil

2 cups chicken stock

Directions

Preheat oven to 350°F. Saute rice, onion, chiles and garlic in butter and olive oil. Add chicken stock. Place in 1 ½ quart baking dish. Cover and bake 30 minutes.

PUERCO DE ADOBADO

Source: Puerto Vallarta

Ingredients

2 lbs. pork ribs or tenderloin

4 Tbsp chili powder

2 Tbsp chocolate powder, unsweetened

½ tsp cinnamon

½ tsp ground cloves

2 tsp garlic powder

½ tsp ground cumin

½ tsp salt

½ tsp black pepper

1 tsp dried oregano

½ cup Kahlua

½ cup cider vinegar

Directions

Mix together all ingredients except meat. Marinate overnight. Cook on a grill, basting with sauce until tender.

"Mexican food is one of the best culinary experiences that people can have." Karla Souza

"I've seen zero evidence of any nation on Earth other than Mexico even remotely having the slightest clue what Mexican food is about or even come close to reproducing it. It is perhaps the most misunderstood country and cuisine on Earth."

Anthony Bourdain

CARNÉ ASADA

Source: Lisa Bryan; Downshiftology

Ingredients

1 ½ lbs. flank steak

1/3 cup olive oil

3 limes, juiced

½ cup fresh cilantro, chopped

4 garlic cloves, minced

1 tsp cumin powder

½ tsp chili powder

Salt and pepper, to taste

Directions

Whisk all of the marinade ingredients together in a small bowl. Add the steak to glass baking tray and pour the marinade on top. Ensure both side of the steak are well coated, cover the baking tray with plastic wrap and marinate for 1-4 hours. Alternatively, you could marinate in a Stasher Bag or Ziploc bag.

Heat a grill on medium-high heat. Add the carne asada and cook for approximately 5-7 minutes on each side. Remove the steak to a cutting board and let it rest for another 5 minutes.

Using a sharp knife, slice the carne asada at an angle against the grain. From there, you can further chop the carne asada into smaller pieces.

"Mexican food is one of the best culinary experiences that people can have." Karla Souza

"I prefer my Mexican food to have a little bit of an animal in it. That's some of the best food." George Lopez

CARNE ASADA

Source: Author

Ingredients

Flank steak, tenderized

1 Tbsp Comino Powder

1 Tbsp Tony Chachere's

2 Tbsp garlic powder

1 Tbsp oregano

1 Tbsp Lawrey's Seasoned Salt

½ cup lemon juice

½ cup soy sauce

Preparation

Mix together all ingredients except the meat. Marinade meat at least 12 hours, then cook on a charcoal grill. Serve with Arroz Central Café (page 260), refried beans and flour or corn tortillas.

SOPA DE ALBONDIGAS (MEATBALL SOUP)

"Albondigas simply means meatballs, but in Mexico, it's almost always meatball soup."

Source: Adventures in Mexican Cooking

Ingredients

Meatballs:

1 lb. lean ground beef	½ small onion, minced
2 Tbsp bread crumbs	1 Tbsp fresh mint, minced
1 egg, slightly beaten	½ tsp salt
¼ tsp ground cumin	1 clove garlic, minced
¼ tsp black pepper	2 Tbsp rice, uncooked
¼ cup tomato sauce	

Soup:

1 small onion, chopped	1 clove garlic, minced
1 Tbsp bell pepper, minced	1 stalk celery, diced
1 Tbsp oil	
6 cups beef or chicken broth	1 (16oz) can diced tomatoes
½ tsp ground cumin	1 tsp oregano
½ cup cilantro	Salt and pepper to taste

1 cup each of chopped vegetables; carrots, Italian or summer squash, potatoes etc.

Instructions

Meatballs: Combine all ingredients except tomato sauce which should be added last, using only enough to make the mixture moist, but firm enough to hold together as balls. Form small meatballs by rolling between your palms. Moisten your hands frequently with

SOPA DE ALBONDIGAS (MEATBALL SOUP)

cold water while forming the balls to prevent the meat from sticking. Set aside.

Soup: Sauté onion, garlic, bell pepper and celery in the oil until tender. Add the stock, diced tomatoes, cumin, oregano, cilantro salt and pepper and bring to a boil. Add meatballs slowly so that the boiling does not stop. Skim if necessary.

Add chopped vegetables, as desired. Lower heat to simmer, cover and cook for about 30 minutes.

"Let's get one thing straight: Mexican food takes a certain amount of time to cook. If you don't have the time, don't cook it. You can rush a Mexican meal, but you will pay in some way. You can buy so-called Mexican food at too many restaurants that say they cook Mexican food. But the real food, the most savory food, is prepared with time and love and at home. So, give up the illusion that you can throw Mexican food together. Just understand that you are going to have to make and take the time." Denise Chavez

CEVICHE DE JAIBA Y CAMARONES
(CRAB AND SHRIMP CEVICHE)

Source: Adventures in Mexican Cooking

Ingredients

½ lb. shrimp, peeled and deveined

½ lb. real crab meat (not that imitation crap!)

½ cup lime or lemon juice

½ red onion, cut into thin slivers

1 small tomato, seeded and chopped

2 Tbsp fresh cilantro, chopped

2 tsp fresh serrano or jalapeno, seeded and finely chopped

Salt and pepper, to taste

1 avocado, peeled and sliced

6 black olives, sliced

Instructions

Thaw shrimp, if frozen. Rinse shrimp and crab and pat dry with paper towels. In a glass bowl, marinate the shrimp overnight in the citrus juice. In the morning, add the crab meat and all the ingredients except the avocado and olives. Mix and chill for 2 hours.

Divide among 6 cocktail glasses or arrange on a lettuce leaf on small salad plates. Garnish with avocado and olive slices.

PROSCIUTTO-AND-FONTINA PANINI

Source: Café Nervosa; from the Sitcom, Frasier

Ingredients

1 (5.25-oz.) package focaccia or 1 (8-oz.) package Boboli

8 very thin slices prosciutto (about 2 oz.)

¼ cup (1 oz.) shredded fontina cheese

1 cup trimmed arugula

2 (1/8-inch-thick) red onion slices, separated into rings

2 tsp balsamic vinegar

1/8 tsp pepper

Instructions

Slice each bread round in half horizontally. Divide prosciutto slices between bottom halves of bread, and top each bread half with cheese, arugula, and onion slices. Drizzle vinegar over sandwiches, and sprinkle with pepper; cover with top halves of bread. Wrap sandwiches tightly in foil, and bake at 300°F for 15 minutes.

CALZONES

Source: Author

Ingredients

Filling:

1 lb. Italian sausage   8 oz. mozzarella cheese

16 oz. ricotta cheese   ¼ cup fresh parsley, chopped

1 bunch fresh spinach, steamed, drained and chopped

½ tsp salt   ¼ tsp white pepper

Pizza dough, shaped into four 8 inch rounds   1 egg

Parmesan cheese, grated*

Sauce:

1 Tbsp olive oil   1 medium onion, chopped

2 cloves garlic, minced   1 cup chicken stock

4 large tomatoes, peeled and chopped   1 (6 oz.) can tomato paste

1 Tbsp fresh basil, chopped   1 tsp fresh oregano, chopped

2 Tbsp fresh parsley, chopped   ½ tsp salt

¼ tsp white pepper

Preparation

Filling: Skin and cook sausage, crumbling it into small pieces. Mix together mozzarella and ricotta cheese, salt, white pepper, parsley and egg. Add spinach and sausage and mix.

Sauce: Saute onion and garlic in olive oil. Add remaining ingredients and simmer for I hour.

Preheat oven to 375°F.

Calzones: Mix 1 egg with ¼ cup water in a small bowl. Place equal

CALZONES

amounts of filling in the four 8 inch rounds of pizza dough. Using a finger, dip into the egg and water mixture and apply a thin coat along edge of dough. Fold over and seal edges. Bake in 375°F oven on a pizza pan until golden brown.

To serve, spoon sauce over individual servings and sprinkle with grated parmesan cheese.

*Note: Not the stuff in the cans.

"Calzones are just baked fold-over pizzas." Author

"There's nothing more romantic than Italian food." Elisha Cuthbert

"I instruct the prep cooks to roll out some lasagna noodles and to start preparing béchamel in large quantities. We will resort to a couple of baked pasta entrees, flavored with meat and sausage and, depending on what Eddie sends over, a cioppino." Meredith Mileti, Aftertaste: A Novel in Five Courses

GERARD NEBESKY'S PAELLA

"For your next party, forget that pot of chili and try cooking paella, the world's most sophisticated comfort food.

Paella may be the world's perfect one-pot party food. A medley of seafood, chorizo, chicken, saffron, peppers, and rice, it's impressive and sophisticated – and the kind of meal you can still manage well into your third glass of wine. "It's always a hit," says Gerard Nebesky, a California chef who, a decade ago, began cooking paella for large gatherings at wineries and festivals. "The social aspect is probably the best part."

Paella originated with rice farmers in Valencia, Spain, who used the rabbits and vegetables from their own land for the dish. Seafood was later introduced as the meal expanded along the coast. To make a great paella, all you really need, besides a bit of patience, is a large, flat-bottomed pan; some saffron; and the confidence to intentionally burn it to make the socarrat, or charred rice, at the bottom of the pan. 'Dirty rice will make you a hero'", says Nebesky.

Ingredients

• ½ cup olive oil

• 1 red bell pepper, cut into ½ inch-wide strips

• 1 cascabel chili (or another chili without heat)

• kosher salt

• 6 chicken thighs (bone in, skin on)

• 8 oz. chorizo

• 1 large yellow onion, diced

• 8 cloves garlic, minced

• 1 15-oz can diced tomatoes

• 4 cups chicken stock

GERARD NEBESKY'S PAELLA

- 30 threads saffron
- 1 Tbsp smoked paprika
- 8 littleneck clams
- 2 cups short-grain white rice
- 12 jumbo head-on Gulf shrimp
- 8 oz. cod, cut into 2-inch chunks
- 8 mussels
- 8 oz. green beans, cut into 2-inch pieces
- ½ cup canned chickpeas
- 2 lemons, cut into wedges
- ¼ cup parsley, chopped

Directions

Heat a 12-inch, flat-bottomed pan (it should be more than 2 inches deep) over medium-high heat. Add the olive oil, red bell pepper, and chili; sauté until browned. Season with salt, and remove bell peppers.

Place the chicken in the pan, skin side down, then brown on all sides, about 10 minutes. Add and brown the chorizo. Add the onion and garlic; cook until translucent. Add the tomatoes and cook until syrupy, about 10 minutes. Add the chicken stock; bring to a boil. Crush the saffron threads and smoked paprika using a mortar and pestle, and stir into the sauce. Add the clams. Remove them as they open, about 10 minutes.

Pour the rice into the pan in an even layer, moving the chicken so it settles to the bottom. Do not stir. (Use a short- to medium-grain white rice. Longer grains tend to burn, and brown rice will not work because it has to be covered to cook.)

WONTON NOODLES

Source: Sarah Kim

Ingredients

Wontons:

7 oz. shrimp, chopped (may substitute ground pork)

7 oz. ground beef   2 green onions, chopped

1 Tbsp light soy sauce   ½ tsp salt

Soup:

3 cups chicken broth   2 garlic cloves, smashed

1 ½ Tbsp light soy sauce   2 tsp sugar

Toppings:

Chopped green onions   Bok choy or Chinese broccoli

Egg noodles

Directions

Wonton Filling: Chop off the whites of 2 green onions, set aside the white part for the soup. Chop the green part of the green onions, set aside in a small dish.

In a large bowl add 7 oz. ground beef and 7 oz. chopped shrimp. Use a potato masher and mash until smooth 20 times and alternatively, if the masher doesn't work, place everything on a cutting board and chop. Return everything into a bowl. Add ½ tsp salt, 2 chopped green onions, 1 Tbsp light soy sauce, and stir.

Wontons: Lay out wonton wrappers, add 2 tsp of filling on each wrapper, brush the edges with water and fold over into a triangle. Cross each end back, pushing the meat side forward.

Soup: In a large pot add 3 Cups Chicken Broth, leftover whites of the green onions from earlier, 1 ½ Tbsp light soy sauce, 2 tsp sugar and 2 pieces of crushed garlic clove. Let it boil, then simmer for 5-

Wonton Noodles

10 minutes. Remove garlic, ginger and green onions.

Vegetables: Add any vegetables to cook now, Chinese broccoli or bok choy and cook until dark green. Remove from the pot once dark green, cool in cold running water and set aside

Dumplings: In boiling water cook dumplings in batches for 4 minutes or until they float. It's very important to not overcook the dumplings. Do not go over the time. Remove dumplings with a slotted spoon or strainer, but quickly.

Egg Noodles: Cook egg noodles according to package directions. I'm boiling mine until cooked, and testing for doneness by tasting.

Assembling Together Wonton Noodles: In a bowl add cooked wontons, noodles, vegetables, and pour in the soup. Top with chopped green onions.

"When it comes to Chinese food I have always operated under the policy that the less known about the preparation the better. A wise diner who is invited to visit the kitchen replies by saying, as politely as possible, that he has a pressing engagement elsewhere." Calvin Trillin

OSSO BUCO (VEAL SHANKS)

Source: Author

Ingredients

4 (1 lb.) veal shanks, trimmed	1 cup all-purpose flour
½ cup olive oil	4 cups beef stock or consommé
1 ½ cups dry white or red wine	1 cup plum tomatoes, chopped
1 small onion, diced	1 stalk celery, diced
4 garlic cloves, minced	1 small carrot, diced
1 bay leaf	1 sprig fresh rosemary
1 sprig fresh thyme	2 whole cloves
Salt and pepper, to taste	

Garnish:

3 Tbsp fresh Italian parsley, chopped	1 Tbsp lemon zest

Preparation

Preheat oven to 350°F. Season each shank with salt and pepper, dredge in flour, shaking off excess.

In a large Dutch oven, heat oil. Brown both sides of shanks, about 3 minutes per side. Pour stock or consommé and wine over meat so that it is immersed in liquid. Cover and bring to a simmer. Add vegetables and continue simmering 5 to 10 minutes. Add seasonings, cover Dutch oven and place it in the oven. After 1 hour, check the tenderness of the meat. Continue cooking until the meat is fork tender (the meat easily pulls apart when you insert a fork and twist).

Transfer to an ovenproof serving dish and keep warm. Boil remaining juices to reduce, about 15 minutes. Baste shanks with reduced juices and bake 10 to 15 minutes more, basting 3 to 4 times to glaze. Garnish with parsley and lemon zest to serve.

BERMUDA ONION PIE

"Bermuda has its own version of the classic Quiche Lorraine; a perfect supper dish with a tossed salad."

Source: What's Cooking in Bermuda by Betsy Ross

Ingredients

1 (8 inch) pie shell, baked

6 slices bacon

6 Bermuda onions

1 clove garlic, minced

½ cup Swiss cheese, grated

2 eggs, beaten

1 cup heavy cream

½ tsp salt

¼ tsp pepper

1/8 tsp nutmeg

1/8 tsp cayenne pepper

Directions

Preheat oven to 350°F.

Fry bacon until crisp. Crumble into the pie shell. Slice the onions thinly and fry them in the bacon fat. Add garlic and, salt and pepper. When onions are brown and limp, drain on paper towel to remove grease. Arrange over the bacon in the pie shell and sprinkle with cheese.

Beat remaining ingredients together and pour into pie shell. Bake at 350°F for 40 minutes. Serve immediately.

CONCH STEW

Pronounced "conk", the meat of conchs is eaten raw in salads or cooked; as in burgers, chowders, fritters, and gumbos. All parts of the conch meat are edible. It has a mild taste of the sea, in the sense that its flavors are not too strong, and if you put on lemon, or hot sauce, or whatever, it will easily be overpowered, if that's your desire. But, if you you're going to cover the flavor...why eat it? Its best attribute is its texture, firmer than you would have expected. It tastes a little bit like clams, escargot, scallops or maybe even octopus. Conch is most indigenous to the Bahamas, and is typically served in fritter, salad, and soup forms. In addition to the Bahamas, conch is also eaten in the West Indies (Jamaica in particular); locals in Jamaica eat conch in soups, stews and curries. Restaurants all over the islands serve this particular meat. In Puerto Rico, conch is served as a ceviche, often called ensalada de carrucho (conch salad), consisting of raw conch marinated in lime juice, olive oil, vinegar, garlic, green peppers, and onions. It is also used to fill empanadas. The Bermudians like it best in a stew.

Source: Betsy Ross; What's Cooking in Bermuda

Ingredients

2 medium sized conch shells (can be purchased frozen)

¼ lb. salt pork, cubed

1 large Bermuda onion, chopped

1 cup water

2 large Bermuda onions, quartered

2 large carrots, chopped

2 large potatoes, cubed

Small sprig of thyme

Sprig of parsley

Conch Stew

2 Tbsp flour

2 Tbsp ketchup

1 Tbsp Worcestershire sauce

1 tsp vinegar

¼ tsp pepper

¼ cup black rum or sherry

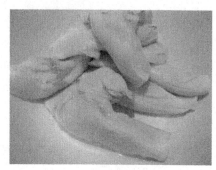

Directions

Stand conch shells in an inch of boiling water until the meat leaves the shells. Use only the white meat; cut into cubes (or use prepared, frozen or fresh, conch meat).

Cook salt pork. In uncovered pressure cooker, until golden. Add chopped onion and cook until golden (salt pork will continue to brown). Add conch meat, cover with 1 cup water and cook, under pressure in covered pressure cooker, for 30 minutes. Remove from heat and reduce pressure before removing cover.

Remove cover, add prepared vegetables, thyme and parsley. Cover with water and cook, under pressure, for another 5 minutes. Reduce pressure.

Remove cover, mix flour with ½ cup water and stir into the stew mixture. Remove the thyme and parsley. Stir in remaining ingredients. Serve with cooked rice.

CONCH CHOWDER

Source: Norman Van Aken; Norman's Restaurant, Orlando, Florida

Ingredients

¼ lb. bacon, diced   ¼ cup olive oil

6 cloves garlic, sliced   1 large onion, diced

2 jalapenos, minced (remove stems and seeds)

4 celery stalks, diced   1 large carrot, diced

1 bulb fennel, diced   1 yellow pepper, diced

2 Tbsp fresh thyme, chopped   2 Tbsp fresh oregano, chopped

2 Tbsp fresh marjoram, chopped   2 Tbsp fresh basil, chopped

3 bay leaves   1 Tbsp red pepper, crushed

4 cups plum tomatoes, peeled and crushed   2 cups tomato sauce

10 cups shellfish or chicken stock

2 ½ lbs. conch meat, cleaned and ground

10 small new potatoes, cleaned and diced

Hot red pepper sauce, to taste

Directions

Cook potatoes until tender; drain and reserve. In a very large soup pot or Dutch oven, cook the bacon with olive oil over medium heat. When bacon is almost cooked, add the onion, celery, carrots, fennel, garlic, jalapenos and yellow peppers and cook until carrots are tender, about 5 minutes. Add herbs, bay leaves and crushed red pepper. Stir in the crushed tomatoes and tomato sauce. Stir in the stock, ground conch and potatoes and bring to a simmer. Add hot red pepper sauce and simmer for 10 minutes. Serve with Bimini Bread. Recipe on page 51.

CONCH FRITTERS

Source: Author

Ingredients

¾ cup all-purpose flour

1 egg

½ cup milk

¼ tsp cayenne pepper

1 tsp Lawrey's Seasoned Salt

½ tsp salt

¼ tsp pepper

1 cup conch meat, chopped

1 small onion, diced

½ green bell pepper, diced

2 stalks celery, diced

2 cloves garlic, minced

Dipping Sauce:

2 Tbsp ketchup

2 Tbsp lime juice

1 Tbsp mayonnaise

1 tsp hot sauce

¼ tsp onion powder

¼ tsp garlic powder

Salt and pepper, to taste

Preparation

Heat 2 cups cooking oil, over medium heat, in a large skillet.

In a medium size bowl, combine the flour, egg, and milk. Add the cayenne pepper, seasoned salt, salt, and pepper. Mix in the conch meat, onion, bell pepper, celery, and garlic.

Drop batter with an ice cream scoop into the hot oil, and cook until golden brown, about 5 minutes. Turn to other side, if needed, and continue cooking until golden on both sides, about 3 minutes. Drain on paper towels.

Dipping Sauce:

In a bowl, mix the ketchup, lime juice, mayonnaise, hot sauce, onion powder, garlic powder, salt, and pepper. Serve dipping sauce on the side with the fritters.

CONCH STEW

Source: Capn' Ron

Ingredients

3 slices (thick-sliced) bacon

1 medium onion, chopped

2 Tbsp butter

2 medium jalapeno peppers, chopped

1 medium pablano pepper, chopped

2 celery stalks, chopped

2 Tbsp all-purpose flour

1 cup chicken broth

1 can diced tomatoes

2 cups conch, chopped

1 Tbsp Butt Kickin' Blacken Jamaican Jerk

Instructions

Chop bacon into ¼ inch pieces. Place in a 3 quart pot and cook over medium heat until the fat has been rendered from the bacon. Add the butter then add the onion and the peppers (if using). Cook over medium heat until soft. About 7 minutes. Add the flour, and stir it in well until the flour just starts to turn a little brown. Add the chicken broth, and stir well to blend the flour mixture (roux) into the liquid without any lumps. Add the tomatoes to the pot along with the Conch and Butt Kickin' Blacken. Bring to a boil, then turn the heat down and let simmer for about an hour. This gives time for the flavors to blend, and the Conch to cook. Taste a piece of the Conch. If it's rubbery, continue to cook until its soft textured.

Butt Kickin' Blacken contains neither salt nor sugar, and is available at www.capnrons.com. Adjust recipe if using a different seasoning.

ALSATIAN TART

Source: Steven Wheeler; Mushroom Magic

Ingredients

12 oz. pie pastry

4 Tbs. unsalted butter

3 medium onions, halved and sliced

3 ½ cups assorted wild mushrooms such as ceps, bay boletes, morels, chanterelles, saffron milk-caps, oyster, field and honey mushrooms, brushed clean and coarsely chopped

2 tsp. fresh thyme leaves, chopped

1 tsp. salt

¾ tsp. freshly ground pepper

Pinch of grated nutmeg

1/3 cup whole milk

1/3 cup crème fraiche

1 egg

2 egg yolks

Directions

Preheat an oven to 375°F and lightly grease a quiche dish with butter. Roll out the pastry on a lightly floured surface and line the dish. Rest the pastry in the fridge for 1 hour. Place 3 squares of wax paper in the tart crust, fill with rice and bake for 25 minutes. Lift out paper and rice and leave to cool.

Melt the butter in a frying pan, add the onions, cover and cook slowly for 20 minutes. Add mushrooms and thyme and continue cooking for another 10 minutes. Season with salt, pepper and nutmeg.

Pour milk and crème fraiche in a bowl and beat in the egg and egg yolks. Spread the mushroom mixture in the crust then pour in the milk and egg mixture. Bake for 15 to 20 minutes or until center is firm to the touch.

GYOZA (POT STICKERS)

Source: Shigeko Mia: My first Mother-in-Law; a truly wonderful cook and lady and the best mother-in-law a man could ask for.

Ingredients

1 lb. ground beef   1 lb. ground pork

1 pkg. Kombu Dashi (find in oriental markets)

Black pepper, to taste

1 tsp garlic powder

1 Tbsp soy sauce

1 Tbsp sesame oil

½ cup sake

4-5 cloves garlic, minced

1 cup green onions, chopped

2 cups Napa cabbage, finely chopped

4 (10 oz.) pkg. wonton wrappers

Directions

Heat oil in a large skillet over medium high heat. Add finely chopped cabbage, chives (green onions), and garlic and cook, stirring frequently, until cabbage is wilted. Mix in ground beef and the rest of the ingredients and cook until meat is evenly brown.

Place approximately 1 Tbsp of the meat mixture in center of each wonton wrapper. Fold wrappers in half over filling and seal by moistening the inside edge of the wrappers and pressing together.

In approximately 2 Tbsp preheated vegetable oil, cook gyoza, covered, 2-3 minutes on each side until meat is done and gyozas are lightly browned.

For dipping sauce: Mix together ¼ cup soy sauce and one Tbsp rice vinegar.

Lasagna

Source: Betty Lafredo; Fairbanks, Alaska (slightly modified by the author)

Ingredients

1 lb. ground beef or 1 pkg. mild Italian sausage, skins removed

2 cloves garlic, minced   1 Tbsp fresh parsley, chopped

1 Tbsp fresh basil, chopped   1 tsp salt

1 (14.5 oz.) can tomatoes, diced   1 (15 oz.) can tomato sauce

1 (6 oz.) can tomato paste   ½ cup white wine

¼ cup sugar   2 eggs

1 tsp salt

½ tsp white pepper

2 Tbsp fresh parsley, chopped

½ cup parmesan cheese, grated

48 oz. cottage cheese

32 oz. mozzarella cheese

9 lasagna noodles, uncooked

Preparation

Preheat oven to 350°F.

Brown meat and drain. Add next 9 ingredients and simmer for 30 minutes.

Mix together remaining ingredients except for mozzarella cheese and lasagna noodles and layer as follows: In a 9X13 inch pan, layer 3 lasagna noodles, cottage cheese mix, meat sauce and mozzarella cheese. Repeat for 3 sets of layers. Bake in 350°F oven for 45 minutes.

NOTES

FOR RESERVATIONS CALL: 1-318-371-1331

NOTES

_____

_____

_____

_____

_____

_____

_____

_____

_____

_____

_____

_____

_____

_____

_____

_____

MEATS & POULTRY

TEXAS STYLE SMOKED BEEF BRISKET

Source: Author

Ingredients

1 12-14 lb. whole brisket   2 Tbsp coarse kosher salt

2 Tbsp coarse ground black pepper   1 tsp cayenne pepper

2 Tbsp garlic powder

Preparation

Store your brisket in the refrigerator until you are ready to start trimming. Cold briskets are much easier to work with. Flip your brisket over so the point end is underneath. Remove any silver skin or excess fat from the flat muscle. Trim down the large crescent moon shaped fat section until it is a smooth transition between the point and the flat. Trim any excessive or loose meat and fat from the point. Flip the brisket over and trim the top fat cap to about ¼ of an inch thickness across the surface of the brisket.

In a mixing bowl or empty spice container, mix the salt, pepper, and garlic. Shake over the brisket to evenly distribute the spices on all sides.

Preheat your smoker to 225°F using indirect heat and hardwood smoke. Place the brisket on the smoker with the point end facing your main heat source. This is a thicker part of the brisket and it can handle the additional heat. Close the lid and smoke until and internal thermometer reads 165°F (usually takes around 8 hours).

On a large work surface, roll out a big piece of butcher paper (or foil) and center your brisket in the middle. Wrap the brisket by folding edge over edge, creating a leak proof seal all the way around. Return the wrapped brisket to the smoker, seam side down.

Close the lid on the smoker and, maintaining 225°F, continue cooking until the internal temperature of the brisket reaches 202°F in the thickest part of the meat (takes anywhere from 5-8 hours).

Remove the brisket to a large cutting board and allow to rest for 1 hour before slicing. Slice both the point and the flat against the grain with a sharp knife and serve immediately.

RACK OF LAMB WITH CABERNET SAUCE

Source: Author

Ingredients

Lamb Seasoning:

1 ½ tsp kosher salt	1 tsp black pepper
1 tsp paprika	½ tsp garlic powder
½ tsp onion powder	¼ tsp cayenne pepper
¼ tsp dried thyme	¼ tsp dried basil
¼ tsp dried marjoram	¼ tsp dried oregano

Cabernet Sauce:

1 tsp lamb seasoning	2 Tbsp butter
2 tsp all-purpose flour	½ cup cabernet sauvignon wine
2/3 cup beef broth	2 Tbsp water
3 tsp Dijon mustard	2 tsp parsley, minced

"Democracy is two wolves and a lamb voting on what to have for lunch. Liberty is a well-armed lamb contesting the vote." Benjamin Franklin (1706-1790)

RACK OF LAMB WITH CABERNET SAUCE

Lamb:

2 lamb racks

1 Tbsp olive oil

Preparation

Heat oven to 425°F.

Mix together seasoning ingredients in a bowl.

Heat olive oil in large skillet to medium.

If you like you can trim some fat from the racks. You also can slice them in half for smaller racks. Sprinkle seasoning on all sides of each rack.

Over medium heat, sear each rack on all sides until browned, about 2 to 4 minutes on each side. Put racks into roasting pan, meat side up, (curved side down) and bake for 15 minutes to 130°F (for medium), or 20 mins for medium-well. When lamb is done, take it out of the oven and cover pan with foil and let lamb sit for 10 minutes.

Cabernet Sauce:

While lamb is cooking, make cabernet sauce by melting butter in the searing skillet (Do NOT wash out skillet -- you want the cooked bits of lamb or "fond" in there for flavor). When melted, add flour and cook for 2 to 3 minutes. Stir in other ingredients starting with the wine and beef broth, then simmer for about 5 minutes to reduce the liquid. You can add a bit of cornstarch if you want it thicker.

When lamb is done, cut the racks into single bone chops or leave it whole depending on your presentation. Serve with Cabernet sauce on the side.

BEEF TIPS AND RICE

Source: Taste of Southern

Ingredients

1lb sirloin tip, stew meat or round steak, cut into bite size pieces

3 cups Beef Broth

1 Onion, medium sized, sliced

1 Tbsp Bacon grease, butter or vegetable oil

2 Tbsp Cornstarch

Salt and Pepper to taste

2-3 cups of prepared Rice

Instructions

Place a medium sized sauce pot on medium heat. Add bacon grease or cooking oil. Add beef and onions. Stir the meat and onions until the meat is lightly brown. Add beef broth and bring to a rolling boil. Cover, reduce heat to medium-low and simmer for 1 hour or until beef is tender.

In a small bowl, mix Cornstarch with cold water, stir well. Slowly add the cornstarch to the beef and broth, stirring constantly. Simmer another 10 minutes or until gravy has thickened.

Place rice in a medium size sauce pot. Run cool water in the pot, swirling the rice around and draining until the water drains fairly clear then add enough water back to the pot to cook the rice.

Place pot over medium-high heat and bring to a rolling boil. Cook for about 2 minutes then, reduce heat. Let rice continue to simmer on medium-low heat until most of the water has been absorbed. Watch for small pockets to appear in the rice. Do not stir but watch it carefully. Cover with a tight fitting lid and remove from heat. Let the rice rest, covered, for about 10 more minutes. Fluff the rice with a fork prior to serving. Serve beef tips over the rice.

BEEF TIPS AND RICE

This is a classic Southern comfort food.

Source: Author

Ingredients

3 lbs. sirloin tip steaks, cut into 1-inch cubes

1/3 cup all-purpose flour

5 Tbsp olive oil, divided

1 large onion, chopped

2 garlic cloves, minced

4 cups water

¼ cup soy sauce

¼ cup Worcestershire sauce

1 tsp seasoning salt

½ tsp black pepper

1/3 cup water

3 Tbsp all-purpose flour

Hot cooked rice

¼ cup red wine

1 Tbsp parsley, for garnish

Preparation

In a large Dutch oven, heat 2 Tbsp olive oil over medium heat. Add onion and garlic. Cook for about 5 minutes or until tender. Remove from pan and set aside.

In a bowl, toss together beef tips and flour. Add remaining 3 Tbsp of oil to the Dutch oven. Place beef tips in Dutch oven and brown on all sides. Cook for about 10 minutes, stirring regularly, then return onions and garlic back to the Dutch oven. Add 3 cups water, soy sauce, Worcestershire sauce, seasoned salt and pepper, stirring well. Bring to a boil. Reduce heat and cover. Let simmer for 1 hour, stirring occasionally. Add red wine and cook for another 5 minutes.

In a small bowl, combine 1/3 cup cold water and 3 Tbsp flour, mix well. Add flour mixture to the beef tips, cooking for 2-3 minutes or until mixture thickens.

Serve over hot cooked rice. Garnish with parsley.

CHICKEN JERUSALEM

Source: Author

Ingredients

4-6 chicken breast halves, skinned and boned

½ lb. small, fresh, baby mushrooms 1 (10 oz.) can artichoke hearts

2 cups chicken stock   2 cloves garlic, minced

½ small onion, finely chopped   1 cup white wine

1 Tbsp fresh Italian parsley   1 stick butter

1 cup heavy cream   Salt and white pepper to taste

Parmesan cheese, fresh grated

2 Tbsp fresh parsley, finely chopped

Preparation

Drain, rinse and drain artichoke hearts. Rinse and drain again. Clean and remove stems from baby mushrooms.

In a medium skillet, melt ¼ of the stick of butter and sauté the garlic and onion. Add the chicken stock. Bring to a boil, and cook until liquid is reduced by about half. Stir in wine, and continue to cook until reduced and slightly thickened. Add the mushrooms, artichoke hearts and parsley to the chicken stock mixture. Reduce heat, and simmer until mushrooms are tender. Stir in the heavy cream and cook, stirring occasionally, until thickened. Season with salt and white pepper.

Using a veal mallet, pound chicken breasts until approximately ¼ inch thick. Salt and pepper both sides of the flattened chicken breasts and coat with flour. In a large skillet, over medium heat, melt the remaining ¾ stick of butter and cook chicken until just done and golden on both sides. Do not over cook. Transfer to a large serving dish with sides. Pour sauce over the chicken, sprinkle with Parmesan cheese, parsley and serve.

Chicken with White Squash

Source: Author

I love white (scalloped) squash and usually slice them horizontally about ½ inch thick (making round squash steaks), season with salt and pepper, coat with cornmeal and fry until just tender and golden brown. I wanted to try different ways to prepare it and here is one of them.

Ingredients

4 boneless, skinless chicken breasts

2 Tbsp. olive oil

4 cups white squash, chopped in ½ inch cubes

Sea salt to taste

Mrs. Dash to taste

Preparation

Heat olive oil in a 10 inch pan with a lid. Add chicken and cook, covered over medium heat turning once, until golden brown on both sides. Add squash, arranging around chicken. Sprinkle with sea salt and Mrs. Dash, cover and continue cooking until squash is tender but not mushy. Serves four.

Chicken Jerusalem recipe on previous page

CHICKEN FLORENTINE CREPES

In the culinary arts, the word Florentine (pronounced "FLOR-en-teen"), or the term à la Florentine, refers to a recipe that is prepared in the style of the Italian region of Florence. The easiest way to remember what it means is that a Florentine-style recipe features spinach.

And while spinach is characteristic of a dish prepared à la Florentine, the traditional Florentine method is gently simmering the spinach in melted butter.

The technique is said to originate with Florence-born Catherine de Medici, or rather her chefs, who accompanied her to France upon her marriage to the Duke of Orleans and future king.

Source: Author

Make 2 dozen crepes and set aside

Ingredients

2 chicken breasts, skinned and boned

¾ cup spinach cooked, fresh or frozen

2 Tbsp heavy cream	½ lb. mushrooms, chopped
1 ½ cup asiago cheese, grated	1 stick butter
2 shallots, finely chopped	1 cup milk
5 Tbsp flour	1 cup cream
1 cup white wine	1 tsp. garlic powder
½ tsp salt	½ tsp white pepper
¼ tsp nutmeg	¼ cup sundried tomatoes

Preparation

Preheat the oven to 350°F.

Heat 2 Tbsp butter in a skillet over medium heat. Chop the chicken

CHICKEN FLORENTINE CREPES

into small pieces and cook in the butter for about 7 minutes until cooked. Add the chopped spinach and cook for another 2 minutes. Remove from the skillet and set aside.

In the same skillet, melt 2 more Tbsp butter and sauté shallots until tender. Add mushrooms and cook until all liquid is gone.

Over medium heat, melt remaining butter in a sauce pan, stir in flour and cook until golden. Add one cup of milk, rapidly stirring with a whisk, until smooth. Add wine and continue stirring until thickened and smooth. Stir in cream, salt, white pepper and nutmeg.

Combine chicken, spinach, mushrooms and ½ cup of the sauce. Add the cheese to the remaining sauce and spoon a layer in the bottom of a large baking dish. Fill the crepes with 2 Tbsp of the chicken mixture, roll and place them in the baking dish. Pour the remaining sauce over the crepes and sprinkle with parmesan cheese. Bake at 350°F for 30 to 40 minutes. Makes approximately 16.

FLANK AND GREENS

Source: Brad Herriage

Ingredients

1 ½ lbs. flank steak, fat removed and scalloped

2 cups onions, chopped

12 cups mixed greens, washed and chopped

6 cups beef stock

5 Tbsp flour, browned

6 cups long grain white rice, cooked

Seasoning mix:

1 Tbsp sweet paprika

2 tsp salt

2 tsp dry mustard

1 ½ tsp onion powder

1 tsp garlic powder

1 tsp dried thyme leaves

1 tsp ground ginger

¼ tsp white pepper

½ tsp black pepper

½ tsp ground cumin

¼ tsp cayenne pepper

Directions

Combine seasonings in a small bowl. Sprinkle all surfaces of the flank steak evenly with the seasoning mix and rub in well.

Preheat a heavy 5 quart pot over high heat to 350°F.

FLANK AND GREENS

Add the seasoned meat and brown it on all sides about 2-3 minutes each side. Add onions, the remaining seasoning mix and ½ cup of each type greens. Cover and cook, scraping bottom of pot to loosen the brown bits, for 8 minutes. Add one cup of the stock and cook, covered, for 15 minutes, checking occasionally for sticking. Add the browned flour and mix until completely absorbed, is no longer visible and the meat looks moist and pasty. Add the remaining stock and greens, bring to a boil, reduce heat to medium and cook until meat and greens are tender, checking occasionally for sticking, about 20 minutes. Serve with the rice.

"The best comfort food will always be greens, cornbread, and fried chicken." Maya Angelou

"Collard, turnip, mustard or tender greens served up with any southern meal tastes like home." Author

ROAST CORNISH HENS WITH WALNUT STUFFING AND WINE SAUCE

This is one of the tastiest dishes you will ever make! It is elegant, delicious, smells so good while its cooking and will impress whoever you invite over for dinner (supper if you were raised in the South).

Source: The New McCall's Cookbook, 1973

Ingredients

3 Tbsp Bacon drippings	1 cup onion, chopped
1 cup green pepper, diced	6 slices bacon, cooked and crumbled
3 cups small dry white bread cubes	1 cup walnuts, chopped
1 ½ tsp salt	½ tsp dried thyme leaves
½ tsp rubbed sage	Watercress sprigs
6 (1 lb. size) frozen Rock Cornish hens, thawed	

Directions

Make Stuffing: In hot bacon drippings in a medium skillet, sauté chopped onion and green pepper, stirring, until tender.

Add vegetables to rest of stuffing ingredients; toss lightly with fork, to mix. Use mixture to stuff hens. Close openings in hens with wooden picks; tie legs together.

Arrange hens, breast side up, in a shallow roasting pan without a rack.

Preheat oven to 400°F. Make Basting Sauce. Brush some over the hens. Roast hens 1 hour, brushing occasionally with rest of sauce, until golden.

Discard string, wooden picks. Arrange hens on round platter; keep warm. Make Wine Sauce.

Garnish hens with watercress. Makes 6 servings.

ROAST CORNISH HENS WITH WALNUT STUFFING AND WINE SAUCE

Basting sauce:

½ cup butter

1 clove garlic, crushed

½ cup white wine

½ tsp rubbed sage

1 ½ tsp salt

Directions

In a small sauce pan, combine all ingredients and bring to a boil. Reduce heat and simmer for 15 minutes. Use to baste Cornish hens and other poultry.

Wine Sauce:

3 Tbsp flour

1 cup white wine

1 cup currant jelly

1 tsp dry mustard

1 tsp salt

Directions

Gradually add the flour to the drippings in the roasting pan, stirring until smooth.

Add white wine, currant jelly, dry mustard and salt. Bring mixture back to boiling, stirring to loosen any brown bits in the roasting pan.

Reduce heat and simmer, stirring occasionally, until it thickens. Pass wine sauce along with the hens. Makes about 2 1/3 cups sauce.

CHICKEN AND DUMPLINGS

Source: Clara Wilson

Ingredients

3-4 chicken breasts	½ tsp salt
½ tsp pepper	2 carrots, chopped
1 stalk celery, finely diced	1 medium onion, diced
½ tsp dried thyme (¼ tsp ground)	½ tsp turmeric
½ tsp garlic powder	1 bay leaf
6 cups chicken broth	½ cup heavy cream

Dumplings:

1 cup all-purpose flour	1 cup butter, unsalted
1 cup milk	1 tsp salt

Directions

In a heavy stock pot, boil chicken and next 8 ingredients until chicken is done. Remove chicken and bay leaf. After chicken has cooled, shred the meat.

While chicken is simmering, make the dough for the dumplings. Cut in flour, butter and salt until crumbly. Add milk and stir with a fork until just blended. Form into a ball on a floured board. Roll to ¼ inch thick. Cut into 1 inch wide strips.

Bring chicken broth mixture to a slow boil. Add canned broth, if needed, to make 6 cups. Stir in heavy cream and chicken. Separate pastry strips into 1 to 1 ½ inch lengths, dropping gradually into the slow boiling broth, stirring carefully to keep separated. After all dumplings have been added, simmer for about 10 minutes. Adjust seasoning as necessary. Let sit for 10 minutes then add more broth, if needed, to bring to desired consistency. Should be slightly soupy. Serve immediately.

CHICKEN SPAGHETTI

Ingredients

1 large fryer, cooked, deboned and chopped (save broth)

1 stick butter

2 large onions, chopped

½ stalk celery, chopped

1 bell pepper, chopped

2 cans cream of chicken soup

2 cans cream of mushroom soup

Salt and pepper to taste

2 (12 oz. pkg) spaghetti, cooked

2 cups broth

1 cup cheddar cheese, grated

Directions

Preheat the oven to 350 degrees F. Bring a large pot of water to a boil. Add the chopped chicken to the boiling water and boil for a few minutes, then return the heat to medium-low and simmer, 30 to 45 minutes. Remove the chicken and 2 cups of the chicken cooking broth from the pot. When the chicken is cool, pick out the meat (a mix of dark and white) to make 2 generous cups.

Cook the spaghetti in the same chicken cooking broth until al dente. Do not overcook.

Sauté onions, celery and bell pepper in butter until tender. Add soups and chicken broth. Stir occasionally to prevent sticking. Add chopped chicken then mix with cooked spaghetti.

Place the mixture in a casserole pan and top with the remaining 1 cup cheese. Bake until bubbly, about 45 minutes. (If the cheese on top starts to get too cooked, cover with foil).

"MAID-RITES"

"The Name Says it All"

Source: My friend; Dick Dorrell, GBNF

Ingredients

1 lb. ground beef

1 onion, finely chopped

¾ cup Ketchup

3 Tbsp mustard

3 Tbsp vinegar

3 Tbsp sugar

Salt and pepper to taste

1 purple onion, thinly sliced

Directions

In a medium frying pan, brown hamburger meat. Add onion, ketchup, mustard, vinegar, salt pepper and sugar. Cook, over medium heat, until all liquid is gone and meat is caramelized (almost scorched).

Serve on sesame seed bun with sliced purple onion.

LOOSE MEAT SANDWICH

Inspired by Maid-Rite in Iowa, Loose Meat Sandwiches are simple yet so very delicious. Make a batch in 10 minutes or less! Also slow cooker friendly.

Ingredients

1 lb. ground beef (85/15 recommended)

¼ cup water

1 Tbsp yellow mustard

1 tsp sugar

Salt and freshly ground black pepper

½ cup onion, finely chopped

4 hamburger buns, split for serving

Ketchup, mustard, mayonnaise, pickles for serving

Instructions

In a large skillet, combine beef, water, mustard, sugar, 1 teaspoon salt, and 1 teaspoon pepper. Simmer over medium heat until the beef is cooked through, about 5 minutes, breaking up clumps of meat with a spoon. Stir in onion.

Serve meat on buns with toppings on the side such as ketchup, mustard, mayonnaise, and pickles.

BEST BBQ RIBS EVER

By Meathead Goldwyn

BBQ ribs are the Holy Grail; the tastiest part of the hog. Mastering them marks the difference between the tyro, pyro, and pit master.

You can make it happen. Here's the real barbecue ribs recipe, good enough to bring home a trophy in a cook-off. In fact, many readers have done exactly that with this ribs recipe. There may be a few more steps in this process than you like, but it's not hard and we're talking restaurant grade here. Better. You don't need a special smoker, although it helps. You can cook killer real smoked barbecue ribs on most charcoal and gas grills once you understand the concepts. Remember, if you boil ribs, the terrorists win.

These are the best BBQ pork ribs you will ever eat. There are so good you would ask for them as your "last meal". We're talking classic Southern barbecue ribs here, the barbecue ribs that win barbecue championships. They are a mélange of flavors: A complex spice rub, elegant hardwood smoke, tangy sweet sauce, all underpinned and held together by the distinct flavor of pork. They are juicy and tender and they tug cleanly off the bone but don't fall off the bone. Their smoked scent clings to your fingers for hours.

We will be cooking low and slow at about 225°F, so allow 5 to 6 hours for St. Louis Cut (SLC) Ribs or Spare Ribs, and 3 to 4 hours for Baby Back Ribs. Thicker, meatier slabs take longer, and if you use rib holders so they are crammed close to each other, add another hour.

Ingredients

1 slab Baby Back Ribs (optional St. Louis Cut Ribs or Spare Ribs)

4 Tbsp of Meathead's Memphis Dust

1 tsp Morton's kosher salt (¼ tsp per pound of meat)

1 cup of barbecue sauce (optional)

BEST BBQ RIBS EVER

About the ribs. The jargon butchers use to name different rib cuts can be confusing. Baby backs lie near the spine. Spareribs attach to them and run all the way down to the chest. St. Louis Cut Ribs are the meatiest and most flavorful ribs. They are spareribs with the tips removed so they form a nice rectangular rack. I sometimes call the "center cut ribs". You can use Baby Back Ribs for this recipe if you prefer. They are a bit leaner, smaller, and cook faster. Country ribs are really not ribs, they are chops and should be cooked very differently, so don't use them for this recipe. For more on the different cuts of ribs, click here.

About the salt. Remember, kosher salt is half the concentration of table salt so if you use table salt, use half as much. Click here to read more about salt and how it works.

Also. 8 ounces by weight of hardwood chunks, chips, or pellets. It doesn't matter how many slabs you are cooking, 8 ounces should be enough. You don't have to be precise, just measure it in some fashion so you have a baseline for your next cook. Then you can add or subtract if you wish. I prefer chunks of apple, oak, or hickory for pork. Never use any kind of pine unless you want meat that tastes like turpentine. Never use construction lumber because it is often treated with poisonous chemicals to discourage rot and termites. You do not need to soak the wood because wood does not absorb much water. That's why they make boats with it. Click the link to read more about wood and the myth of soaking wood.

Directions

Rinse the ribs in cool water to remove any bone bits from the butchering. If the butcher has not removed the membrane from the underside, do it yourself. It gets leathery and hard to chew, it keeps fat in, and it keeps sauce out. Insert a butter knife under the membrane, then your fingers, work a section loose, grip it with a paper towel, and peel it off. Finally, trim the excess fat from both sides. If you can't get the skin off, with a sharp knife, cut slashes through it

BEST BBQ RIBS EVER

every inch so some of the fat will render out during the cooking. Remove the membrane on ribs.

Salt is important. It penetrates deep and amplifies flavor. It helps proteins retain moisture. And it helps with bark, the desired crust on the top formation. Click here to read more about how salt works. It is truly the magic rock. If you can, give the salt 1 to 2 hours to be absorbed. The process of salting in advance is called dry brining. The rule of thumb is 1/2 teaspoon of kosher salt per pound of meat, but ribs are about 50% bone, so use about 1/4 teaspoon per pound. Beware of double salt jeopardy! Rubs and spice blends are a great way to add flavor to meat. Commercial rubs almost always contain salt because salt amps up flavor and helps form a crust. Brines are also a great way to add flavor as well as moisture. Meat that is labeled "enhanced" or "flavor enhanced" or "self-basting" or "basted" has been injected with a brine at the packing plant.

Some folks insist on putting the barbecue rub on the night before, but it isn't necessary. The molecules in spices are too large to penetrate more than a tiny fraction of an inch. Any time before cooking time, just coat the meat with a thin layer of water. The water helps dissolve the spices. Then sprinkle enough Meathead's Memphis Dust, an award winning barbecue rub spice blend, to coat all surfaces but not so much that the meat doesn't show through. That is about 2 tablespoons per side depending on the size of the slab. Spread the Memphis Dust on the meat and rub it in.

Fire up your barbecue smoker or set up your grill for 2-zone or indirect cooking. 2-zone cooking on a grill is the secret to keeping the temp down so you don't shrink the proteins and make the meat tough. Adjust the temp. Preheat your cooker to about 225°F and try to keep it there throughout the cook. This is crucial: You can absolutely positively no way no how rely on bi-metal dial thermometers. Use a good digital oven thermometer.

On a charcoal grill, adjust the air intake dampers at the bottom to

BEST BBQ RIBS EVER

control heat on charcoal grills. Intake dampers are more effective than exhaust dampers for controlling the temp because they reduce the supply of oxygen to the coals. Take your time getting the temp right. Cooking at 225°F will allow the meat to roast low and slow, liquefying the collagen in connective tissues and melting fats without getting the proteins knotted in a bunch. It's a magic temp that creates silky texture, adds moisture, and keeps the meat tender. If you can't hit 225°F, get as close as you can. Don't go under 200°F and try not to go over 250°F. Click here for more about how to calibrate your grill. To learn more about what happens inside the meat when it is cooking read my article on meat science. Read my article on the thermodynamics of cooking to learn how different grills cook differently. Add about 4 ounces of dry wood at this time. Do not soak the wood! This is a myth. Put the wood as close to the flame as possible. Put the slabs in the cooker in indirect heat, meaty side up, close the lid, go drink a beer, read a book or make love.

When the smoke dwindles after 20 to 30 minutes, add another 4 ounces of wood. That's it. Stop adding wood. On your first attempt, resist the temptation. Nothing will ruin a meal faster and waste money better than over smoked meat. You can always add more the next time you cook, but you cannot take it away if you over smoke. If you have more than one slab on, halfway through the cook you will need to move the ribs closest to the fire away from the heat, and the slabs farthest from the flame in closer. Leave the meat side up. There is no need to flip the slabs. You can peek if you must, but don't leave the lid open for long.

This optional trick involves wrapping the slab in foil with about an ounce of water for up to an hour to speed cooking and tenderize a bit. Almost all barbecue ribs competition cooks use the Texas Crutch to get an edge. But the improvement is really slight and I never bother for backyard cooking. If you crutch too long you can turn the meat to mush and time in foil can soften the bark and remove a lot of rub. I recommend it only for barbecue competitions

BEST BBQ RIBS EVER

when the tiniest improvement can mean thousands of dollars. Skip it and you'll still have killer ribs. But if you've seen it on TV and must try it, click here to learn more about The Texas Crutch. The Texas Crutch is it is baked into a popular technique called the 3-2-1 method which I do not recommend. Two hours in foil or butcher paper is far too long and can make the meat mushy. Try the Texas Crutch after you master the basics.

Although I insist that you buy a good digital meat thermometer for grilling, this is one of the few meats on which you cannot use a meat thermometer because the bones have an impact on the meat temp and because the meat is so thin. Allow 5 to 6 hours for Barbecue St. Louis Cut Ribs and Barbecue Spare Ribs, or 3 to 4 hours for Barbecue Baby Back Ribs. The exact time will depend on how thick the slabs are and how steady you have kept the temp. If you use rib holders so they are crammed close to each other, add another hour. Then check to see if they are ready. I use the bend test (a.k.a. the bounce test). Pick up the slab with tongs and bounce it gently. If the surface cracks as in the picture above, it is ready. Here are some other tricks to tell when ribs are ready.

Some folks serve ribs without barbecue sauce, but most folks love their sauce. Just go easy. Let the meat shine through. When the meat is done, paint both sides with your favorite homemade barbecue sauce or store-bought barbecue sauce and cook for another 15 minutes or so. Don't put the sauce on earlier than then. It has sugar and there is a risk it can burn. Now here's a trick I like: Sizzle on the sauce. Put the ribs with sauce directly over the hottest part of a grill in order to caramelize and crisp the sauce. On a charcoal grill, just move the slab over the coals. On a gas grill, crank up all the burners. On a water smoker, remove the water pan and move the meat close to the coals. On an offset smoker, put a grate over the coals in the firebox and put the meat there. With the lid open so you don't roast the meat from above, sizzle the sauce on one side and then the other. The sauce will actually sizzle and bubble. Stand by your grill

BEST BBQ RIBS EVER

and watch because sweet sauce can go from caramelized to carbonize in less than a minute! One coat of a thick sauce should be enough, but if you need two, go ahead, but don't hide all the fabulous flavors under too much sauce. If you think you'll want more sauce, put some in a bowl on the table.

If you've done all this right, you will notice that there is a thin pink layer beneath the surface of the meat. This does not mean it is undercooked! It is the highly prized smoke ring caused by the combustion gases and the smoke. It is a sign of Amazing Ribs. Now be ready to take a bow when the applause swells from the audience.

Meathead's Simple Dust

Makes about 3 cups. At about 2 Tbsp per slab of ribs, this is enough for 24 slabs. Store the extra in a zipper bag or a glass jar with a tight lid. Use enough to cover the meat surface but still let some meat show through.

Ingredients

¾ cup dark brown sugar, firmly packed

¾ cup white sugar

½ cup American paprika

¼ cup garlic powder

2 Tbsp ground black pepper

2 Tbsp ground ginger powder

2 Tbsp onion powder

2 tsp rosemary powder

POULET BASQUAISE

Source: Anthony Bourdain

Ingredients

1 whole chicken, about 4 lb., cut into 8 pieces

Salt   Pepper

Pinch of cayenne pepper   2 Tbsp olive oil

1 Tbsp butter   1 red bell pepper, cut into fine julienne

1 green bell pepper, cut into fine julienne   1 onion, thinly sliced

16 oz. can Italian plum tomatoes   ½ cup white wine

½ cup water   ½ cup chicken stock

3 sprigs of flat parsley, finely chopped   Rice pilaf

Directions

Season the chicken all over with salt, pepper, and cayenne. Heat the large pot over medium-high heat and add the oil. When the oil is hot, add the butter. When the butter has foamed and subsided, add the chicken, skin side down, and brown on that side only. Remove the chicken and set aside on the plate. Add the peppers and onion to the pot and reduce the heat to medium low. Cook for about 10 minutes, then add the tomatoes and cook until the liquid is reduced by half. Stir in the wine, scraping, as always, to get the good stuff up. Cook until the wine is reduced by half, then add the water and the stock. Return the chicken to the pot, making sure to add all the juice on the plate. Cover the pot and cook on low heat for about 25 minutes. Remove the chicken to the platter. Turn the heat to high and reduce the sauce for 5 minutes. Season with salt and pepper and add the parsley. Pour the sauce over the chicken and serve with rice pilaf.

Oven Roasted Squab

Source: Author

Ingredients

4 squabs, ¾ lb. each, cleaned and trussed	1 small onion, diced
½ lb. button mushrooms, sliced	1 clove garlic, crushed
¾ cup chicken stock	3 Tbsp butter
1 Tbsp olive oil	1 sprig of rosemary
3 leaves basil, chopped	Salt, pepper

Preparation

Place oven rack in lower third of oven. Preheat oven to 450°F.

Place butter and olive oil in a large, heavy Dutch oven over moderately high heat. Dry the squabs well with a towel, then place them in hot oil. Brown the squabs on all sides, about 5 minutes total. Remove.

Add the onion and garlic to the oil and sauté until tender. Sprinkle the squabs evenly with the salt and pepper. Put them on their sides in the Dutch oven with all legs facing in the same direction. Cook for 4 minutes on one side, then 4 minutes on the other side. Finally, turn the squabs breast side up, and cook for 4 minutes more. The squabs should be rare to medium-rare at this point. Add mushrooms, rosemary, basil and chicken stock. Cover and bake another 5 minutes. Squabs should now be medium to medium-rare.

Serve on a bed of oven roasted vegetables. Sprinkle with fresh blueberries.

ROAST DUCK

Source: Julia's Album

Ingredients

6 lb. whole Pekin duck	Salt
5 garlic cloves, chopped	1 lemon, chopped

Glaze:

½ cup balsamic vinegar	1 lemon, freshly squeezed
¼ cup honey	

Instructions

Defrost duck in the refrigerator for a couple of days if frozen. Once the duck is completely defrosted, take the duck out of the refrigerator 30 minutes prior to cooking to bring it more or less to room temperature.

Preheat oven to 350°F. You will be roasting the duck for a total of 3 hours (3 hours will be divided into 4 time chunks where you will be flipping the duck, brushing it with glaze, etc. - see the instructions below).

Prepare the duck:

Remove the giblets from inside the duck. Rinse the duck, inside and outside, with cold water. Pat dry with paper towels.

Set the duck on the working surface. Score the duck's skin on the breast in a diamond pattern, making sure you only cut the skin, without reaching the meat. Poke the other fatty parts of the duck with the tip of the knife all over, to ensure fat release, especially in very fatty parts. You don't need to poke the duck legs as the skin is pretty thin there (except for where the duck legs connect to the duck body). Season the duck very generously with salt both inside the cavity of the duck and outside on the skin, legs, all over. Place the duck breast side up.

Put 5 chopped garlic cloves and lemon slices inside the duck cavity (these are just for flavor, not for eating - you will discard them after cooking). The duck will have flapping skin on both ends - fold that skin inwards, to hold the garlic and lemon inside. Tie up the duck legs with butcher's twine.

ROAST DUCK

Roast the duck for 3 hours in 4 distinctive steps:

Place the bird breast side up on a large roasting pan with a rack (roasting pan should have a roasting rack to lift the duck from the bottom of the pan and allow the fat to drip below the duck). Roast the duck, breast side up, for 1 hour at 350 F.

After 1 hour of roasting, flip the duck on its breast and roast it breast side down (roast the other side) for 40 minutes, at 350°F.

Remove the roasting pan with the duck from the oven (you now have roasted the duck for 1 hour + 40 minutes), carefully remove the duck to a platter (making sure the lemons and garlic from the cavity do not fall out - keep the skin on both ends of the duck folded), and carefully pour off all the duck fat juices from the roasting pan into a large heat-proof bowl or container.

Flip the duck breast side up again on a rack in a roasting pan (the pan will have no fat juices now). In a small bowl, combine ½ cup balsamic vinegar with the freshly squeezed juice of 1 lemon. Brush all of the duck with the balsamic mixture (especially the scored duck breast) and cook the duck breast side up for another 40 minutes at 350°F, brushing every 10 minutes with the mixture.

Now, in a separate small bowl, combine ¼ cup honey and 3 Tbsp of balsamic vinegar lemon mixture that you will have left over from the previous step. Brush the breast side of the duck with this honey-balsamic mixture, and roast for another 40 minutes, brushing the duck breast side every 10 minutes with honey balsamic mixture. You can even carefully broil the duck for the last 10 to 15 minutes if you like (do it carefully, checking the duck regularly to make sure it doesn't char too much).

After the duck is cooked, remove it from the oven, let duck stand for 15 minutes. Then, carefully remove and discard the lemon from the cavity (being careful not to get burned). Carve the duck and serve!

BEEF BOURGUIGNON

Recipe Courtesy of Julia Child

Ingredients

One 6 oz. piece of chunk bacon   3 ½ Tbsp olive oil

3 lbs. lean stewing beef, cut into 2-inch cubes   1 carrot, sliced

1 onion, sliced   Salt and pepper

2 Tbsp flour   1 Tbsp tomato paste

3 cups red wine, young and full-bodied (like Beaujolais, Cotes du Rhone or Burgundy)

2 ½ cups to 3 ½ cups brown beef stock   2 cloves garlic, mashed

½ tsp thyme   A crumbled bay leaf

18 to 24 white onions, small   3 ½ Tbsp butter

Herb bouquet (4 parsley sprigs, one-half bay leaf, one-quarter teaspoon thyme, tied in cheesecloth)

1 lb. mushrooms, fresh and quartered

Cooking Directions

Remove bacon rind and cut into lardons (sticks ¼ inch thick and 1 ½ inches long). Simmer rind and lardons for 10 minutes in 1 ½ quarts water. Drain and dry.

Preheat oven to 450°F.

Saute lardons in 1 tablespoon of the olive oil in a flameproof casserole over moderate heat for 2 to 3 minutes to brown lightly. Remove to a side dish with a slotted spoon.

Dry beef in paper towels; it will not brown if it is damp. Heat fat in casserole until almost smoking. Add beef, a few pieces at a time, and sauté until nicely browned on all sides. Add it to the lardons.

In the same fat, brown the sliced vegetables. Pour out the excess

BEEF BOURGUIGNON (CONTINUED)

fat. Return the beef and bacon to the casserole and toss with ½ tsp salt and ¼ tsp pepper. Then sprinkle on the flour and toss again to coat the beef lightly. Set casserole uncovered in middle position of preheated oven for 4 minutes. Toss the meat again and return to oven for 4 minutes (this browns the flour and coves the meat with a light crust).

Remove casserole and turn oven down to 325°F. Stir in wine and 2 to 3 cups stock, just enough so that the meat is barely covered. Add the tomato paste, garlic, herbs and bacon rind. Bring to a simmer on top of the stove. Cover casserole and set in lower third of oven. Regulate heat so that liquid simmers very slowly for 3 to 4 hours. The meat is done when a fork pierces it easily.

While the beef is cooking, prepare the onions and mushrooms. Heat 1 ½ Tbsp butter with one and one-half tablespoons of the oil until bubbling in a skillet. Add onions and sauté over moderate heat for about 10 minutes, rolling them so they will brown as evenly as possible. Be careful not to break their skins. You cannot expect them to brown uniformly. Add ½ cup of the stock, salt and pepper to taste and the herb bouquet. Cover and simmer slowly for 40 to 50 minutes until the onions are perfectly tender but hold their shape, and the liquid has evaporated. Remove herb bouquet and set onions aside.

Wipe out skillet and heat remaining oil and butter over high heat. As soon as you see butter has begun to subside, indicating it is hot enough, add mushrooms. Toss and shake pan for 4 to 5 minutes. As soon as they have begun to brown lightly, remove from heat.

When the meat is tender, pour the contents of the casserole into a sieve set over a saucepan. Wash out the casserole and return the beef and lardons to it. Distribute the cooked onions and mushrooms on top.

Skim fat off sauce in saucepan. Simmer sauce for a minute or 2,

BEEF BOURGUIGNON (CONTINUED)

skimming off additional fat as it rises. You should have about 2 ½ cups of sauce thick enough to coat a spoon lightly. If too thin, boil it down rapidly. If too thick, mix in a few tablespoons stock. Taste carefully for seasoning.

Pour sauce over meat and vegetables. Cover and simmer 2 to 3 minutes, basting the meat and vegetables with the sauce several times.

Serve in casserole, or arrange stew on a platter surrounded with potatoes, noodles or rice, and decorated with parsley.

Julia Child's Beef Bourguignon

"This is my invariable advice to people: Learn how to cook- try new recipes, learn from your mistakes, be fearless, and above all have fun!" Julia Child, My Life in France

"You never forget a beautiful thing that you have made,' [Chef Bugnard] said. 'Even after you eat it, it stays with you - always." Julia Child, My Life in France

SAUTÉED VEAL SCALLOPS IN WILD MUSHROOM CREAM SAUCE

Source: Food Network

Ingredients

8 veal cutlets, pounded into scaloppini

Flour for dredging

Salt and pepper to taste

2 Tbsp olive oil

2 Tbsp unsalted butter

Fresh lemon juice to taste

Fresh chervil, minced, to taste

For the sauce:

2 Tbsp olive oil

2 Tbsp unsalted butter

½ cup shallots, minced

1 tsp fresh thyme, minced

½ lb. wild mushrooms, such as chanterelles, shiitake, oyster or a combination

Salt and pepper to taste

1 clove garlic, minced

½ cup dry white wine

1 cup veal demi-glace

1 cup heavy cream

Directions

Dredge scallops in flour, shaking off excess, and season with salt and pepper. In large skillet set over moderate flame, heat olive oil and butter until hot. Add scallops and sauté for 1 minute on each side. Transfer to sauce for just a minute and season mixture with fresh lemon juice and chervil.

For the sauce:

Make the sauce: In a sauté pan set over moderately high flame, heat the oil and butter until hot. Add the shallots and cook, stirring, 1 minute. Add the mushrooms, thyme and salt and pepper and cook, stirring occasionally, for 3 to 5 minutes, or until mushrooms are soft. Add the garlic and cook, stirring, 1 minute. Add the wine and reduce by half. Add the demi-glace and simmer 5 minutes. Add the cream and reduce until lightly thickened. Correct seasoning. Cover with a round of buttered waxed paper and keep hot.

BEEF WELLINGTON

Source: Author

Ingredients

1 (3 lb.) beef tenderloin

1 small onion, minced

½ cup cremini mushrooms, finely chopped

½ cup portabella mushrooms, finely chopped

½ cup shitake mushrooms, finely chopped

½ tsp pepper, coarse ground

All-purpose flour, as needed

2 Tbsp warm water

1 pkg. (12-oz.) prepared beef demi-glace

3 Tbsp butter

½ cup red wine

1 tsp kosher salt

Olive oil

1 pkg. frozen puff pastry, thawed

1 egg yolk, lightly beaten

Salt and pepper to taste

Preparation

In medium skillet, melt butter. Add onion and mushrooms. Saute mixture over medium heat. As moisture begins to cook out, turn heat to low, stirring occasionally, until mixture is dry looking (about 10 to 15 minutes). Add red wine and cook until dry again. Stir in salt and pepper.

Brush beef with olive oil. In large skillet, sear beef until it turns brown on all sides. Cover tenderloin and keep at room temperature.

Roll puff pastry to length that extends 2 inches past each end of the tenderloin, and twice as wide as the diameter; lightly flour as needed to prevent sticking. Spread thin layer of mushroom mixture on puff pastry, keeping 1-inch border all around. Lay tenderloin on top of mushroom mixture; fold puff pastry around, creating seam on bottom and tucking ends under. Place on baking sheet lined with parchment paper, seam side down, and refrigerate 15 minutes.

BEEF WELLINGTON

Preheat oven to 425°F. Combine egg yolk and water to form an egg wash. Brush over puff pastry and roast 20 minutes. Turn temperature down to 400°F and bake an additional 15 minutes. If the crust begins to get dark, tent with foil. For medium-rare, remove beef from oven when meat thermometer registers 125°F and rest 10 minutes before slicing. Heat demi-glace in small saucepan.

To serve, cut into 1 inch slices and serve with demi-glace.

"The nutritional composition of beef provides much-needed protein, vitamins and iron.... Let us also not gloss over what is beef's most obvious benefit: Livestock take inedible and untasty grains and convert them into a protein-packed food most humans love to eat." Jayson Lusk, The Food Police: A Well-Fed Manifesto About the Politics of Your Plate

"No matter what it is you are cooking, buy the best ingredients you can afford. I don't care if it's a simple salad or Beef Wellington. A quality product stands alone and won't need any dressing up." Joe Bastianich

COQ AU VIN

Julia Child's Coq Au Vin is undeniably the best. While Coq au vin might sound fancy, it is really just a simple chicken dish that anyone can master. Don't be intimidated, this recipe is very easy to follow.

Ingredients

4 slices thick cut bacon

3 lbs. chicken breasts and legs, skin on   1 yellow onion, chopped

2 tsp minced garlic   2 bay leaves

1 sprig fresh rosemary, minced   2 cups red wine

2 cups chicken broth   2 Tbsp butter

3 Tbsp flour   10 oz. mushrooms, sliced

¼ tsp pepper   ½ tsp salt (or, to taste)

Directions

Preheat oven to 250°F.

Fry the bacon over medium heat in a Dutch oven or large heavy-bottomed pot. After it's fried, remove the bacon and place on paper towels to drain. Once cool, chop bacon and set aside. Keep the bacon grease in the pot.

Turn heat to high and place chicken, skin-side down in the pot. Sear chicken until golden brown on both sides, about eight minutes. Then, add the onions, garlic, bay leaves and rosemary. Continue sautéing until the onions begin to soften, about six minutes.

Add the chicken broth and red wine. Bring to a boil, then reduce heat to a simmer. Cover and let simmer for 30 minutes.

After 30 minutes, carefully remove the chicken from the pot and place in an oven-safe dish. Keep chicken warm in the oven while you work on the sauce.

Stir the flour and butter (butter should melt instantly in the pot)

JULIA CHILD'S COQ AU VIN

into the red wine sauce. Bring back up to a boil and stir constantly----sauce should be begin to thicken. Add mushrooms, chopped bacon, salt and pepper and continue cooking for 10-12 minutes. Keep in mind that the sauce will also thicken up a bit when it cools.

Place chicken back in sauce and serve with roasted potatoes, noodles or a big green salad.

Yield: 4 servings

"Coq au vin, only with white wine," Delphine announced. "It is too warm for red, and we are too busy to be made drowsy with heavy food." Ellen Herrick, The Forbidden Garden

"I still feel that French cooking is the most important in the world, one of the few that has rules. If you follow the rules, you can do pretty well." Julia Child

"You learn to cook so that you don't have to be a slave to recipes. You get what's in season and you know what to do with it."
Julia Child

ORIENTAL STUFFED CHICKEN ROLLS

Source: Cheryl Berrios

Ingredients

5 chicken breast halves, boneless

2 cups buttermilk baking mix

1/3 cup green onions, chopped

2 Tbsp cooking oil

1 cup shrimp, minced (optional)

1 (8 oz.) can water chestnuts, diced

¾ cup bean sprouts, rinsed and drained

3 Tbsp soy sauce

1 Tbsp instant chicken bouillon

2 Tbsp cornstarch

¼ cup water

2 eggs

2 Tbsp water

Directions

Pound chicken with a veal mallet until flattened. Coat with dry buttermilk mix and set aside. Combine cornstarch with ¼ cup water and set aside. Lightly beat eggs with 2 Tbsp water and set aside.

Sauté onions until wilted. Add water chestnuts, bean sprouts, soy sauce, shrimp (optional) and bouillon. Stir and add cornstarch and cook until thick. Place 2 Tbsp filling at one end of each chicken breast, roll up and secure with a toothpick. Dip in beaten eggs then roll in remaining baking mix. Fry at 400°F in cooking oil until golden brown. Keep warm in 300°F oven if not serving immediately.

STUFFED CHICKEN ROLLS

Source: Taste of Home

Ingredients

6 (8 oz.) chicken breast halves, boneless, skinless

6 slices fully cooked ham

6 slices Swiss cheese

¼ cup all-purpose flour

¼ cup grated Parmesan cheese

½ tsp rubbed sage

¼ tsp paprika

¼ tsp pepper

¼ cup canola oil

1 (10 ¾ oz.) can condensed cream of chicken soup, undiluted

½ cup chicken broth

Fresh parsley, chopped (optional)

Directions

Flatten chicken to ¼ inch thickness. Top with ham and cheese. Roll up and tuck in ends. Secure with toothpicks.

In a shallow bowl, combine the flour, cheese, sage, paprika and pepper. Coat chicken on all sides. In a large skillet, brown chicken in oil over medium-high heat.

Transfer to a 5 quart slow cooker. Combine soup and broth and pour over chicken. Cover and cook on low for 4-5 hours or until chicken is tender. Remove toothpicks. Garnish with parsley if desired.

ROY'S BROILED BURGERS

Source: Marilyn Thomas

Ingredients

1 lb. hamburger (93/7)

1 egg

1 tsp Worcestershire sauce

2 tsp mustard

2 tsp ketchup

Cheese (optional)

Directions

Set oven on "Broiler".

Combine all ingredients, except cheese, and mix well. Separate 8 hamburger buns and place open side up on a baking sheet. On each open face bun spread mixture on very thin, creating 16 open face burgers. Broil until meat is brown. Add cheese and cook 1 more minute, if desired.

Serve open-faced with your choice of lettuce, tomato, pickles, onions, ketchup, etc.

BROILED SPAM® BURGERS

"This unique recipe was probably created during World War II as a new way to prepare SPAM® which was widely used in that time of shortages and rationing. These open-faced sandwiches are delicious and economical."

Source: Author

Ingredients

1 (12 oz.) can SPAM®, finely chopped

4 hardboiled eggs, peeled and chopped

1 (8 oz.) pkg. cheddar cheese, shredded

½ cup onion, finely chopped

½ cup mayonnaise

1 tsp chili powder

½ tsp salt

¼ tsp hot sauce (optional)

12 hamburger buns, split

Directions

Preheat oven on broil and set an oven rack about 6 inches from the heat source. Combine all ingredients, mixing well. Place hamburger bun halves on a baking sheet, open side up, and spread meat mixture evenly over each bun half.

Broil in the preheated oven until brown and bubbly, about 5 to 10 minutes.

Serve open-faced with your choice of lettuce, tomato, pickles, onions, ketchup, etc.

NOTES

NOTES

RUBS & SEASONINGS

CAJUN SEASONING

Source: Author

Ingredients

1 Tbsp onion powder

1 Tbsp garlic powder

2 Tbsp paprika

2 Tbsp salt

1 Tbsp black pepper

1 tsp cayenne pepper

1 tsp dried oregano

1 tsp dried thyme

1 tsp dried basil

½ tsp. coriander

½ tsp. cardamom

Preparation

In a small bowl, mix together all ingredients. Store in a covered jar or spice container.

"Cooking is a part of our way of life in New Orleans, and when it comes to good Cajun Cooking, you will need the Holy Trinity. The Holy Trinity consists of onion, bell peppers, and celery. This is the base for just about every famous dish from gumbo to jambalaya. After these three ingredients, every chef will add his/her own unique touch. But remember, it must start with the Holy Trinity." **Mulate's; The original Cajun restaurant**

"When the taste changes with every bite and the last bite is as good as the first, that's Cajun." **Paul Prudhomme**

CAJUN TURKEY INJECTOR MARINADE

Source: Author

Ingredients

1 cup beer

½ cup crab boil

1/2cup olive oil

½ cup butter

2 Tbsp garlic powder

2 Tbsp onion powder

2 Tbsp Cajun seasoning

1 tsp Tabasco

½ tsp cayenne

1 Tbsp smoked paprika

Preparation

Combine all ingredients in a saucepan. Heat until butter is melted. Stir and continue heating until sauce is very liquefied. Strain to remove solids. Inject while still warm enough to stay liquid.

"Somewhere lives a bad Cajun cook, just as somewhere must live one last ivory-billed woodpecker. For me, I don't expect ever to encounter either one."

William Least Heat Moon (William Trogdon)
'Blue Highways' (1982)

ACADIANA TABLE CAJUN SEASONING BLEND

:Source: George Graham - AcadianaTable.com

Ingredients

¼ cup salt

¼ cup black pepper

2 Tbsp onion powder

1 Tbsp celery salt

¼ cup granulated garlic

2 Tbsp sweet paprika

2 Tbsp white pepper

1 Tbsp cayenne pepper

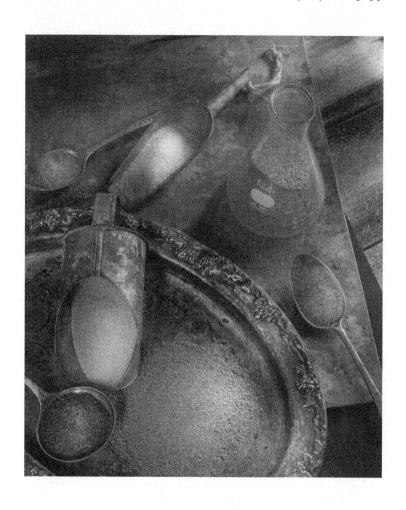

JAMAICAN JERK SEASONING MIX

Source: Author

Ingredients

4 Tbsp onion powder

2 Tbsp garlic powder

4 tsp thyme

4 tsp allspice

2 tsp black pepper

½ tsp cayenne pepper

1 tsp cinnamon

1 tsp cloves

½ tsp cardamom

½ tsp coriander

2 tsp salt

1 Tbsp brown sugar

2 Tbsp chili powder

1 Tbsp dried, ground orange peal

Preparation

Combine all ingredients. Store in a covered jar or spice container.

"You can't just eat good food. You've got to talk about it too. And you've got to talk about it to somebody who understands that kind of food."

Kurt Vonnegut

POULTRY SEASONING

Source: Clara Wilson

Ingredients

1 Tbsp marjoram

1 Tbsp sage

1 Tbsp thyme

2 tsp ground rosemary

2 tsp parsley

½ tsp celery salt

Directions

Combine all ingredients. Store in a covered jar or spice container.

TEXAS BRISKET RUB

Source: Author

Ingredients

1 Tbsp black pepper

1 tsp ground oregano

5 Tbsp chili powder

3 Tbsp salt

5 Tbsp paprika

5 Tbsp brown sugar

2 Tbsp onion powder

2 Tbsp garlic powder

1 tsp cayenne pepper

2 tsp cumin

2 Tbsp dried, ground orange peal

Preparation

Combine all ingredients. Store in a covered jar or spice container.

LAMB SEASONING

Source: Author

Ingredients

2 Tbsp kosher salt

4 tsp black pepper

4 tsp paprika

2 tsp garlic powder

2 tsp onion powder

1 tsp cayenne pepper

1 tsp dried thyme

1 tsp dried basil

1 tsp dried marjoram

1 tsp dried oregano

Preparation

Combine all ingredients, mixing well. Store in a covered jar or spice container.

MEATHEAD'S SIMPLE DUST

Source: Meathead

Ingredients

¾ cup dark brown sugar, firmly packed

¾ cup white sugar

½ cup American paprika

¼ cup garlic powder

2 Tbsp ground black pepper

2 Tbsp ground ginger powder

2 Tbsp onion powder

2 tsp rosemary powder

Directions

Makes about 3 cups. At about 2 Tbsp per slab of ribs, this is enough for 24 slabs. Store the extra in a zipper bag or a glass jar with a tight lid. Use enough to cover the meat surface but still let some meat show through.

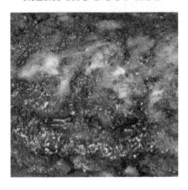

SWEET MEMPHIS BBQ RUB

Melissa Cookston has cemented her place as, not only a great Southern Delta chef, but also as one of the preeminent Pitmasters in the World. Five time Whole Hog World Champion, Two time World Grand Champion, the winner of the Inaugural Kingsford Invitational, and literally thousands of other trophies have proven her to be the Winningest Woman in Barbecue.

Source: Melissa Cookston

Makes about 3 ½ cups

Ingredients

1 cup turbinado sugar

½ cup white sugar

½ cup kosher salt

1 Tbsp onion powder

2 Tbsp granulated garlic

1 ½ tsp cayenne pepper

1 tsp black pepper, finely ground

2 tsp dry mustard

¼ cup chili powder

1 tsp ground cumin

1/3 cup paprika

Instructions

In a mixing bowl, add all ingredients and stir until well incorporated. Store in an airtight container for up to 3 months.

CC SPICE

Source: Author

Ingredients

4 Tbsp black pepper

1 tsp salt

¼ tsp cayenne pepper

1 tsp smoked paprika

1 tsp thyme

1 tsp oregano

1 tsp basil

½ tsp. coriander

½ tsp. cardamom

Preparation

Combine all ingredients thoroughly and store in a dry, airtight container. Use for New Orleans Style BBQ Shrimp, page 80.

Author on his 2013 Harley-Davidson Road Glide Ultra

"Black Pearl"

EMERIL'S ESSENCE CREOLE SEASONING (ALSO REFERRED TO AS BAYOU BLAST)

Source: Chef Emeril Lagasse; A Travel for Taste

Ingredients

2 ½ Tbsp paprika

2 Tbsp salt

2 Tbsp garlic powder

1 Tbsp black pepper

1 Tbsp onion powder

1 Tbsp cayenne pepper

1 Tbsp dried leaf oregano

1 Tbsp dried thyme

Directions

Combine all ingredients thoroughly and store in an airtight jar or container.

"The secret of happiness is variety, but the secret of variety, like the secret of all spices, is knowing when to use it."

Daniel Gilbert

"Spice is life. It depends upon what you like... have fun with it. Yes, food is serious, but you should have fun with it."

Emeril Lagasse

"Once you get a spice in your home, you have it forever. Women never throw out spices. The Egyptians were buried with their spices. I know which one I'm taking with me when I go."

Erma Bombeck

NOTES

NOTES

SAUCES & GRAVIES

"If a man does not have sauce, then he is lost. But the same man can get lost in the sauce." Gucci Mane

SHRIMP SAUCE

Source: Jo Baker

Ingredients

2 Tbsp butter

1 medium onion, chopped

1 clove garlic, minced

1 3oz. can mushrooms (or fresh if desired)

1 can mushroom soup

1 cup sour cream

1/3 cup catsup

2 cups shrimp, boiled and peeled

Directions

Sauté onions and garlic in butter until onion is tender. Add mushrooms and cook 5 minutes. Add soup, sour cream and catsup. Simmer for 5 minutes. Add cooked shrimp and serve.

ORANGE SRIRACHA SAUCE

Source: Author

Ingredients

½ cup hoisin sauce

2/3 cup orange juice

½cup honey

1 ½ Tbsp Sriracha sauce

2 Tbsp sesame oil

1 tsp garlic powder

½ tsp cardamom

1 Tbsp sesame seeds, toasted

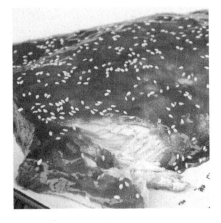

Preparation

Make the marinade by mixing together the hoisin sauce, orange juice, honey, Sriracha sauce, sesame oil, garlic powder and cardamom together in a small bowl.

If smoking salmon, place the salmon in a flat dish and pour ½ of the marinade over the salmon. Flip the salmon a couple times to ensure that all the salmon is coated in the marinade. Cover with plastic wrap and place in the fridge for 3-4 hours. Flip the salmon every hour. Pour the remaining ½ cup of marinade in a small saucepan. Let it come to a low boil and let it reduce until it thickens and turns into a nice glaze. This takes about 10-15 minutes or so. Remove from heat.

Once the salmon has finished smoking, place it on a serving platter. Brush with the glaze. Sprinkle with toasted sesame seeds. Serve.

SWEET & SOUR APRICOT SAUCE

Source: Cheryl Berrios

Ingredients

¼ cup apricot preserves

½ cup light brown sugar, packed

2 Tbsp cider vinegar

2 Tbsp soy sauce

½ tsp dry mustard

Directions

Combine all ingredients in a small saucepan. Cook over medium heat, stirring frequently, until sugar is dissolved. Cool then store in refrigerator until ready to use.

BROWN SAUSAGE GRAVY

I lived on a farm in West Texas until I was 10. Although I didn't know it at the time, we were poor. The picture is of my sister and me. The windmill provided our water. This is a brown "water" gravy that I grew up eating on my mother's homemade biscuits (minus the sausage and extra pepper). There are some recipes that you just do not need to dress up with other "stuff". Sometimes less really is more. Although, in this case, more black pepper is a good thing! This is the only recipe that's ever been asked for at our B&B.

Source: Author

Ingredients

¼ lb. ground pork sausage (I use Jimmy Dean)

3 Tbsp bacon grease

¼ cup all-purpose flour

Water

½ tsp salt

1 tsp black pepper (or to taste)

Preparation

Brown sausage in a large skillet over medium heat. Remove sausage, leaving the drippings in the skillet.

Add bacon grease to the sausage drippings. Stir in the flour, stirring frequently until mixture is a medium to dark brown roux.

Gradually whisk in water, a little at a time, stirring constantly until the mixture is smooth, adding more water to obtain the desired consistency (not runny but not pasty). Remember that the gravy will continue to thicken as it cooks. Return sausage to the skillet, stirring to incorporate. Season with salt and pepper (add additional pepper if desired). Reduce heat, and simmer for about 5 minutes, stirring occasionally. Serve with homemade biscuits.

SAVORY SAUSAGE GRAVY

Source: Gary

Ingredients

1 lb. breakfast sausage

½ cup onion, finely chopped

1 tsp garlic, minced

¼ cup flour

3 Tbsp bacon drippings

2 ½ cups milk

1 tsp black pepper

¼ tsp ground rosemary

¼ tsp dried sage

1 tsp dried basil

Preparation

In a large skillet over medium heat, cook sausage, onion, and garlic until sausage is beginning to brown. Add bacon drippings and stir in flour until sausage mixture is well coated. Gradually add milk, stirring constantly. Mixture will continue to thicken as it cooks. The amount of milk can be adjusted for desired thickness.

Stir in black pepper, rosemary, sage and basil. Continue to cook over medium heat, stirring constantly until gravy thickens, about 5 minutes. Remove from heat.

Serve hot over your favorite biscuits or toast.

"I come from a family where gravy is considered a beverage."

Erma Bombeck

SEAFOOD ALFREDO SAUCE

Source: Author

Ingredients

2 sticks butter

1 onion, minced

1 bundle green onions, finely chopped

1 clove garlic, minced

½ bell pepper, cored and finely chopped

2-3 sticks celery, finely chopped

½ tsp salt

¼ tsp white pepper

¼ tsp garlic powder

1 Tbsp fresh parsley, chopped

2 cups heavy cream

1 can cream of mushroom soup

1 can cream of celery soup

½ cup sour cream

Preparation

In a large skillet over medium heat, melt the butter and sauté the next 5 ingredients until tender. Add the salt, pepper, garlic powder and parsley. Stir in the heavy cream, mushroom soup, celery soup and the sour cream. Cook over medium heat 10 to 15 minutes or until thickened.

Add shrimp, crawfish, mussels, scallops or combinations of each. Cook until just done. Serve over pasta or French bread.

BARBECUE SAUCE

Source: Author

Ingredients

1 stick butter

1 clove garlic, minced

1 onion, finely chopped

½ cup catsup

2 Tbsp lemon juice

2 cups vinegar

1 Tbsp mustard

½ cup brown sugar

½ tsp black pepper

2 tsp salt

½ tsp cayenne pepper

2 Tbsp Worcestershire Sauce

Preparation

In a sauce pan, melt the butter. Add onion and garlic and sauté until tender. Add remaining ingredients, bring to a boil then reduce to simmer and cook for 15 minutes, uncovered. Using a submersible blender, puree sauce until smooth or slightly chunky.

"Barbecue sauce is like a beautiful woman. If it's too sweet, it's bound to be hiding something." **Lyle Lovett**

SPAGHETTI SAUCE

Source: Author

Ingredients

2 tablespoons olive oil

1 large onion, minced

5 cloves garlic, crushed

½ cup chicken broth

¼ cup sherry

1 (28 oz.) can crushed tomatoes

1 (15 oz.) can tomato sauce

1 (6 oz.) can tomato paste

1 Tbsp brown sugar

1 tsp dried oregano

½ tsp salt

¼ tsp pepper

¼ cup fresh basil, chopped

¼ cup fresh parsley, chopped

Preparation

Heat olive oil in a large pot over medium heat. Add onion and sauté in the olive oil until tender, about 5 minutes. Add garlic and sauté another 2 minutes.

Pour in chicken broth, sherry, crushed tomatoes, tomato sauce, tomato paste, brown sugar, oregano, salt, pepper, basil, and parsley. Reduce the heat to low and simmer for 1 hour. Use an immersion blender to puree the mixture until the desired consistency is achieved, leaving it slightly chunky, or completely smooth.

SALSA DI FUNGI E' CARCIOFI
(SALSA WITH MUSHROOMS AND ARTICHOKE HEARTS)

Source: An Italian Kitchen

Ingredients

3 Tbsp olive oil

½ onion, chopped (Cipollini)

3 cloves garlic, minced (Aglio)

8 (oz.) whole fresh mushrooms, sliced (Fungi)

1 (6 oz.) jar marinated artichoke hearts (Carciofi)

1 Tbsp pine nuts

¼ cup white wine

1 Tbsp balsamic vinegar

¼ tsp white pepper

Salt to taste

French bread

Directions

Blend all ingredients in a blender or food processer until desired smoothness. Serve on sliced French bread.

"They eat the dainty food of famous chefs with the same pleasure with which they devour gross peasant dishes, mostly composed of garlic and tomatoes, or fisherman's octopus and shrimps, fried in heavily scented olive oil on a little deserted beach."

-Luigi Barzini, Author of The Italians (1964)

CABERNET SAUCE

Source: Author

Ingredients

2 Tbsp butter

2 tsp all-purpose flour

½ cup cabernet sauvignon wine

2/3 cup beef broth

1 tsp lamb seasoning (recipe in Rubs & Seasonings)

2 Tbsp water

3 tsp Dijon mustard

2 tsp fresh parsley, minced

Preparation

If you are cooking lamb, make cabernet sauce by melting butter in the searing skillet (Do NOT wash out skillet -- you want the cooked bits of lamb or "fond" in there for flavor). When melted, add flour and cook for a minute or so. Stir in other ingredients starting with the wine and beef broth, then simmer for a bit to reduce the liquid. You can add a bit of cornstarch if you want it thicker.

CARAMEL SAUCE

How to make Caramel Sauce that you'll want to put on everything

Source: Claire Saffitz; Bon Appétit Test Kitchen

We can all agree that sauce makes just about every savory food better, and the same most definitely goes for dessert. Enter homemade caramel sauce, an irresistibly delicious substance able to improve everything from store-bought pound cake to ice cream with a single generous drizzle. Here's how to make caramel sauce the "Basically" way.

Stir 1 cup sugar, ⅛ tsp cream of tartar, and 3 Tbsp water in a medium heavy saucepan (this is a must) to combine. A flimsy pan will have hot spots, causing the caramel to burn in places.

Bring sugar mixture to a boil over medium heat, stirring occasionally and scraping around sides to dissolve sugar. Normally, stirring can lead to a grainy caramel, but the cream of tartar prevents crystallization.

Once the sugar mixture is at a rapid boil, reduce heat to medium-low and cook, swirling the pan occasionally. After about 4 minutes, the syrup around the edges will start to turn golden.

Keep cooking, swirling as the edges darken to equalize the color and distribute the heat throughout the pan, until caramel is amber, another 2–3 minutes. Pay close attention, as the caramel darkens quickly.

Continue to cook, swirling, until caramel is dark amber and a wisp of smoke appears, 1–2 minutes. Remove from heat and stir in 4 Tbsp. unsalted butter a tablespoonful at a time until smooth (mixture will sputter).

Stirring constantly, gradually add ½ cup room-temperature heavy cream. Stir until caramel is silky smooth and thick. If caramel hardens in spots, set back over medium heat and stir until solids dissolve.

Stir 1 tsp. kosher salt into caramel sauce and let cool (it will continue to thicken as it cools). Transfer to an airtight container. It will keep in the refrigerator 1 month. Reheat gently to liquefy before using.

Serve caramel sauce on an ice cream sundae, with apple pie, whipped into frosting, or spooned over Monkey Bread. Recipe makes about 1 cup.

"GRAND" OR "MOTHER" SAUCES OF FRENCH CUISINE

One of the first lessons in culinary school is about the importance of the five mother sauces. They're not only the building blocks of classic French cuisine, but they'll give you the foundations to becoming an incredible cook, too. They may seem intimidating at first, but they're all based on simple ingredients and easy techniques.

We've all had a taste of each of them at some point, be it ladled over pasta, stirred into soup or slathered on that succulent hunk of steak. But how many of us actually know where our sauces come from? This introduction will help you unearth the secrets behind the 5 'mother' sauces of classical French cuisine, from the delicate hollandaise to the indulgent Espagnole, from which the myriad sauces we know of today were derived.

Originally, there were four basic French mother sauces developed by Antonin Careme in the 19th century. Careme created a myriad of signature sauces, but the base came down to four main recipes, hence the name mother sauce. These four sauces are Sauce Tomat (Tomato), Béchamel, Veloute and Espagnole (Brown). Careme is considered one of the godfathers of haute cuisine. In the early 20th century, renowned chef Auguste Escoffier added Hollandaise, the fifth mother sauce.

Most derivative sauces of Brown sauce require that a demi-glace be made first. Brown sauce, made from beef or veal stock, is one of the "Grand" or "Mother" sauces of French cuisine. It is intensely flavored and rich and obviously pairs well with all forms of red meat although it can be used on vegetables as well. A Grand sauce is a base sauce from which a panoply of derivative sauces are then made. The primary derivative made from Brown sauce is demi-glace. Demi-glace is then in turn used to make a host of additional sauces such as Bordelaise, Robert sauce, Chasseur sauce or Madeira sauce. Or, demi-glace can certainly stand on its own.

DEMI-GLACE SAUCE

Source: Author

Ingredients

Sachet:

1 bay leaf

6 to 8 sprigs fresh parsley

1 tsp thyme, dried

8 to 10 whole peppercorns

Sauce:

2 Tbsp butter

¼ cup celery, chopped

¼ cup all-purpose flour

½ cup onions, chopped

¼ cup carrots, chopped

5 cups beef stock

Preparation

Place the bay leaf, thyme, parsley sprigs, and peppercorns onto a square of cheesecloth. Tie it up into a bundle with cooking twine.

Heat the butter in a saucepan over medium heat and add the onions, celery and carrots. Sauté about 3 to 5 minutes or until carrots are tender. Stir in flour and cook for about 5 minutes, stirring frequently until the flour is lightly browned. Whisk in 3 cups of the beef stock. Bring to a boil over medium-high heat then lower heat to a simmer. Add the sachet and cook until reduced by about one-third.

Remove pan from heat and remove sachet. Set it aside. Pour the sauce through a wire mesh strainer lined with a piece of cheesecloth. Return the sauce to the pan, stir in the remaining 2 cups of stock and return the sachet to the pan.

Bring back to a boil and then lower heat and simmer for about 50 minutes or until the sauce has reduced by half. Discard the sachet. Strain the sauce through a fresh piece of cheesecloth.

Demi-glace will keep in the refrigerator for a couple of weeks, and in the freezer for months.

MADEIRA SAUCE

Source: Author

Ingredients

¼ stick butter

1 small onion, finely chopped

½ lb. white or cremini mushrooms, sliced

½ tsp pepper, freshly ground

1 bay leaf

¼ tsp dried thyme

1 cup Madeira wine

1 cup demi-glace (recipe on previous page)

¼ cup heavy cream (optional)

Salt, to taste

Preparation

In a medium sized sauce pan over medium heat, melt the butter then the shallots. Sauté the shallots until translucent, about 2 minutes. Add the mushrooms and cook until tender, about 3 minutes. Remove the mushrooms and reserve.

Add the pepper, thyme and bay leave to the sauce pan and cook for 1 minute. Add ¼ cup Madeira wine and reduce by half, about 3 to 5 minutes.

Add the remaining Madeira wine and bring the sauce to a boil. As soon as the wine comes to a boil, reduce heat to a simmer. Add the demi-glace to the sauce and whisk until well blended. Return the reserved mushrooms to the sauce pan, stir, then add the optional heavy cream if you are using it.

Reduce this sauce until it is thick enough to coat the back of a spoon. Taste and adjust seasoning with salt and pepper.

ESPAGNOLE SAUCE

Espagnole is a classic brown sauce, typically made from brown stock, mirepoix, and tomatoes, and thickened with roux. Given that the sauce is French in origin, where did the name come from? According to Alan Davidson, in The Oxford Companion to Food, "The name has nothing to do with Spain, any more than the counterpart term allemande has anything to do with Germany. It is generally believed that the terms were chosen because in French eyes Germans are blond and Spaniards are brown.

Source: Epicurious

Ingredients

1 medium carrot, chopped	1 medium onion, chopped
½ stick butter	¼ cup all-purpose flour
4 cups hot beef demi-glace	¼ cup canned tomato purée
2 cloves garlic, chopped	1 celery rib, chopped
½ tsp whole peppercorns	1 bay leaf

Preparation

Melt butter in a heavy saucepan over moderate heat and cook carrot and onion, stirring occasionally, until golden, about 7 to 8 minutes. Add flour and cook roux over moderately low heat, stirring constantly, until medium brown, about 6 to 10 minutes. Add hot stock, whisking constantly to prevent lumps. Add tomato purée, garlic, celery, peppercorns, and bay leaf and bring to a boil, stirring constantly. Reduce heat and simmer about 45 minutes, uncovered, stirring occasionally, until reduced to about 3 cups.

Pour sauce through a fine-mesh sieve into a bowl, discarding solids.

"Sauces in cookery are like the first rudiments of grammar - the foundation of all languages." Alexis Soyer

BÉCHAMEL SAUCE OR WHITE SAUCE

This used to be one of the first lessons in home economics classes; invariably white and pasty, it coated many a bland dish. When well made, however, it has a proper place in homey, creamed dishes, often making leftovers stretch or giving cooked foods new life. And it is important as a base for soufflés. The French term for this medium-thick white sauce is béchamel. The foolproof way to attain a perfectly smooth sauce is to have the milk hot when added to the butter and flour. It uses an extra pot, but as you become more proficient, this cautionary measure may not be necessary.

Source: September 1996, The Fannie Farmer Cookbook

Ingredients

2 Tbsp butter

2 Tbsp flour

1 ¼ cups milk, warmed

Salt

Freshly ground pepper

Instructions

Melt the butter in a heavy-bottomed saucepan. Stir in the flour and cook, stirring constantly, until the paste cooks and bubbles a bit, but don't let it brown — about 2 minutes. Add the hot milk, continuing to stir as the sauce thickens. Bring it to a boil. Add salt and pepper to taste, lower the heat, and cook, stirring for 2 to 3 minutes more. Remove from the heat. To cool this sauce for later use, cover it with wax paper or pour a film of milk over it to prevent a skin from forming.

Stir in ½ cup grated Cheddar cheese during the last 2 minutes of cooking, along with a pinch of cayenne pepper to make a cheese sauce.

VELOUTE SAUCE

Don't get nervous about the names of some of these classic sauces like Veloute (veh-loo-TAY). It's a fancy French name for a white sauce that is stock based and thickened with a white roux.

The stock used is usually chicken, veal, or fish. Veloute is considered one of the five "mother sauces" that almost all of the classic French sauces are derived from.

Source: Emeril Lagasse

Ingredients

3 Tbsp butter

3 Tbsp flour

2 cups chicken stock

Salt

Freshly ground white pepper

Directions

In a saucepan, over medium heat, melt the butter. Stir in the flour and cook for 2 minutes. Whisk in the stock, ½ cup at a time. Whisk until smooth. Season with salt and pepper. Bring the liquid to a boil and reduce the heat to low and cook for 15 minutes. Remove from the heat and serve.

HOLLANDAISE SAUCE

Hollandaise is a tangy, buttery sauce made by slowly whisking clarified butter into warm egg yolks. So the liquid here is the clarified butter and the thickening agent is the egg yolks. Hollandaise is an emulsified sauce, and we use clarified butter when making a Hollandaise because whole butter, which contains water and milk solids, can break the emulsion. Clarified butter is just pure butterfat, so it helps the emulsion remain stable.

Hollandaise sauce can be used on its own, and it's particularly delicious on seafood, vegetables, and eggs.

This is a delicious and creamy hollandaise sauce. If you love a good hollandaise sauce, you will love how easy this is!

Source: Author

Ingredients

4 large egg yolks

¼ tsp salt

Pinch of white pepper

2 Tbsp fresh lemon juice

1 stick butter, melted or clarified butter

Preparation

Combine eggs yolks, salt, pepper and lemon juice in a blender. Cover the blender with a lid and blend the yolk mixture at high speed for 3 seconds. With the blender still running, uncover and slowly pour in the hot melted butter. The sauce will begin to thicken with half of the butter blended in. Season with a little extra salt and pepper, if needed.

HOLLANDAISE SAUCE

Ingredients

4 Tbsp butter

4 egg yolks

2 Tbsp fresh lemon juice

Salt and white pepper

Directions

In a small saucepan, melt four tablespoons of butter. Do not let it brown.

In a medium-sized bowl, beat together four egg yolks, two tablespoons fresh lemon juice, white pepper and salt.

To combine the eggs with the melted butter requires a little technique we like to call tempering. If you simply add the eggs directly to the warm butter, the eggs will curdle, which is not good. Unless you enjoy unattractively lumpy and congealed sauces. Which you shouldn't.

To temper the eggs, add a teaspoon of the melted butter to the egg mixture and beat with a whisk. Gradually introducing the hot liquid to the cold keeps the mixture from curdling.

Keep adding the melted butter to the egg mixture slowly until you've added about five tablespoons. Be sure to keep whisking the entire time. Really the entire time. Do not stop.

Add the egg mixture to the saucepan.

Turn the heat to low and very quickly cook the mixture — no more than 15 seconds, still whisking constantly.

If your hollandaise sauce doesn't seem thick enough, you can return to the heat and continue cooking it in five second increments — if the heat gets too high you run the risk of the eggs ending up scrambled. Keep whisking the Hollandaise sauce the entire time, until it reaches the consistency you desire.

If the sauce gets too thick, you can thin with a few drops of warm water before serving.

SAUCE TOMAT

You guessed it, sauce Tomat is simply tomato sauce – one of the five French mother sauces. This sauce can be made with various types of tomatoes, making it one of the most diverse staple sauces that uses French cooking techniques. Though this sauce is prepared in many different ways across the world, Auguste Escoffier's recipe is consistently considered the standard in many culinary circles. This is Auguste Escoffier's version of the classic.

Basic sauce Tomat recipe

Ingredients

2-3 oz. salt pork	3 oz. carrots, peeled and diced
3 oz. white or yellow onion, diced	2 oz. whole butter
2-3 oz. flour, all-purpose	5 lbs. tomatoes, quartered
1 qt. white veal stock	1 clove crushed garlic
Salt and pepper to taste	Pinch of salt

Directions

Render the salt pork by placing the pork in a heavy-bottomed pan with a Tbsp of water over medium heat and cover for five minutes.

Add butter and sauté the carrots and onion to fork tender.

Sprinkle flour in and continue to cook toward a blonde roux.

Add tomatoes and cook until they soften.

Add veal stock and garlic cooking over medium heat for one to two hours to reduce the water content, thicken the sauce and concentrate the flavors.

Puree in a blender and pass through a fine mesh strainer or chinois.

Season and add a pinch of sugar to offset the acid in the tomatoes.

Learning how to make a basic sauce Tomat is among the essential cooking basics.

ROASTED GARLIC TOMATO SAUCE

Source: Author

Ingredients

2 Tbsp olive oil	1 onion, diced
1 red pepper, diced	5 oz. button mushrooms, sliced
6 oz. tomato paste	¼ cup dry sherry
1 tsp salt	1tsp brown sugar
¼ tsp chili pepper flakes	½ tsp garlic powder
½ tsp smoked paprika	½ tsp thyme
1 tsp oregano	1 tsp parsley
½ tsp dried basil leaves	2 (28 oz.) cans crushed tomatoes

3 heads roasted garlic, cloves removed from skins

3 fresh basil leaves, chopped

Preparation

In a large saucepan sauté the onion, peppers, and mushrooms in the olive oil over medium-high heat until soft and lightly golden, 7 minutes. Stir in the tomato paste and cook for 3 minutes. Pour in the sherry, add the salt, brown sugar, pepper flakes, garlic powder, paprika, thyme, oregano, parsley, basil, and the tomatoes, stir to combine and bring to a boil. Reduce the heat to a slow simmer and cook for 30 minutes, stirring occasionally. Mash the roasted garlic cloves. Add the roasted garlic and stir to combine. Continue to simmer for 30 minutes. Add fresh basil. Puree with an immersion blender.

Serve with any dish calling for tomato sauce.

NOTES

NOTES

SEAFOOD

"Most seafood should be simply threatened with heat and then celebrated with joy." Jeff Smith; Joy, Cooking, Heat

Fisherman's Wharf Cioppino

Ingredients

1/4 cup olive oil	1 onion, chopped
1 green bell pepper, chopped	1 tablespoon minced garlic
2 (16 ounce) cans diced tomatoes	1 (16 ounce) can chicken broth
1 cup white wine	1 (6 ounce) can tomato paste
1/4 cup dried parsley	2 teaspoons crushed dried basil
1 teaspoon oregano	1/2 teaspoon red pepper flakes

1/4 teaspoon ground black pepper

1 pound shrimp, peeled and deveined

1 pound cod fillets, cut into 2-inch chunks

8 clams in shell, scrubbed, or more to taste

8 mussels, cleaned and de-bearded, or more to taste

Directions

Heat oil in a large saucepan over medium-high heat. Saute onion and bell pepper in hot oil until tender, about 5 minutes; add garlic and continue to sauté until garlic is fragrant, about 1 minute. Transfer mixture to a large stockpot.

Stir tomatoes, chicken broth, white wine, tomato paste, parsley, basil, oregano, red pepper flakes, and black pepper with the onion mixture in the stockpot; bring to a boil, cover the pot, reduce heat to medium-low, and simmer until the tomatoes are softened, about 15 minutes.

Stir shrimp and cod chunks into the tomato mixture. Arrange clams and mussels in the liquid so they are partially submerged. Cover pot again and continue cooking until the clams and mussels open, 7 to 10 minutes.

FISHERMAN'S CIOPPINO

This recipe is based on the one used at the original Rafello's Fish Market.

Ingredients

Seafood:

2 cups crab meat with a hearty portion of "crab fat" if available

1 lb. large raw prawns　　　2 lbs. raw clams (preferably Manila)

1 lb. calamari rings

Optional: 2 lbs. firm fish filets, cut into chunks (use halibut, sea bass, salmon—or a combination)

Sauce:

2 to 3 cloves garlic, finely chopped　　　2 medium onions, chopped

1 cup thinly sliced celery　　1 large green bell pepper finely chopped

3 14 oz. cans diced tomatoes　　　½ cup Italian parsley, chopped

1 can tomato paste　　　　　　　1 cup clam juice

1 to 2 cups water　　　　　　　　¼ cup olive oil

½ tsp crushed red pepper

Instructions

Preparing the sauce:

In a large stockpot over medium-high heat, sauté garlic, onions, celery, green pepper and parsley in olive oil until tender.

Add stewed tomatoes, tomato paste, clam juice and crushed red pepper.

Bring to a low boil, then lower heat and simmer for at least an hour, adding water if needed to keep the volume of liquid the same.

FISHERMAN'S CIOPPINO

Making the cioppino:

Add crab, crab fat, raw clams and fish (if using) to sauce. Simmer for about 15 to 20 minutes. Add calamari rings during the last five minutes.

While the cioppino is simmering, bring a pot of water to a boil and season with a pinch of salt.

Cook prawns for one minute, then add to cioppino during the last two or three minutes of cooking. Cioppino is done when all clams have opened.

Serving the cioppino:

Serve the cioppino over freshly cooked rigatoni (to soak up the broth). Accompany the stew with a crusty sourdough bread and a bottle of red.

MARYLAND CRAB CAKES

Ingredients

1 large egg	2½ Tbsp mayonnaise
1½ tsp Dijon mustard	1 tsp Worcestershire sauce
1 tsp Old Bay seasoning	¼ tsp salt
¼ cup celery, finely diced	2 Tbsp fresh parsley, finely chopped
1 lb. lump crab meat	½ cup panko
Olive oil	

Directions

Line a baking sheet with aluminum foil. Combine the egg, mayonnaise, Dijon mustard, Worcestershire, Old Bay, salt, celery, and parsley in a large bowl and mix well. Add the crab meat (be sure to check the meat for any hard and sharp cartilage) and panko; gently fold mixture together until just combined, being careful not to shred the crab meat. Shape into 6 crab cakes (about ½ cup each) and place on prepared baking sheet. Cover and refrigerate for at least 1 hour.

Preheat a large nonstick pan to medium heat and coat with olive oil. When oil is hot, place crab cakes in pan and cook until golden brown, about 3-5 minutes per side. Be careful as oil may splatter. Serve immediately with tartar sauce or a squeeze of lemon.

Quick Tartar Sauce:

Ingredients

1 cup mayonnaise	1½ Tbsp sweet pickle relish
1 tsp Dijon mustard	1 Tbsp red onion, minced
1 Tbsp lemon juice	Salt and black pepper, to taste

Directions

Mix all ingredients together in a small bowl. Cover and chill.

CIOPPINO

Source: Author

Ingredients

1/3 cup olive oil   1 large onion, chopped

½ green pepper, chopped   3 cloves garlic, minced

1 bunch green onions, chopped   2 cans (14.5 oz.) diced tomatoes

1 can (15 oz.) tomato sauce   1 ½ cup dry red wine

¼ cup fresh parsley, chopped   1 Tbsp fresh basil, chopped

1 tsp fresh oregano, chopped   2 bay leaves

1 can whole clams, with juice   1 stick butter

½ lb. each of cod or halibut, red snapper or striped bass, small fresh shrimp and small scallops

½ lb. frozen small rock lobster tails or Dungeness crabs

1 dozen small, fresh, hard-shell clams and or mussels, scrubbed and rinsed, removing beards from mussels. Discard any open clams or mussels. Let stand in cold salted water for 5 minutes. Pour off salted water.

Preparation

In a heavy stock pot, sauté onion, green pepper and garlic until tender. Add next 9 ingredients, bring to boil, cover and simmer for 45 mins. Add butter, stir in seafood and simmer until clams pop open, about 5-7 min. Remove the bay leaves and season with salt and pepper to taste.

NOTE: Do not overcook the seafood.

SHRIMP SAUCE PIQUANT

Source: ©From the Kitchen of Deep South Dish

Ingredients

2 pounds of medium shrimp, peeled and deveined

2 teaspoons plus 1 tablespoon of Cajun seasoning (like Slap Ya Mama), divided

2 tablespoons of canola oil

2 tablespoons of all-purpose flour

2 cups of chopped onion

1 cup of chopped green bell pepper

1/2 cup of chopped celery

5 cloves of garlic, chopped

2 cups of slow roasted tomatoes, pureed,* or canned tomato sauce

4 cups of shrimp stock*

Juice of half a lemon

Instructions

Pat the shrimp dry with paper towels and sprinkle with 2 teaspoons of the Cajun seasoning. Refrigerate until needed.

Heat the oil in a heavy bottomed stockpot over medium high heat, stirring in the flour. Cook, stirring constantly, until the roux becomes a medium brown, caramel colored. Add the onion, bell pepper and celery and cook over medium heat, stirring often until vegetables are soft, about 5 minutes. Add the garlic and cook another minute. Stir in the remaining 1 tablespoon of Cajun seasoning and 1 cup of the shrimp stock, bring to a boil and continue at a medium boil, stirring often for about 5 minutes. Add the tomato sauce, return to a boil, reduce heat to medium low and let simmer for 1 hour, stirring occasionally.

SHRIMP SAUCE PIQUANT

After the first hour, stir in another cup of shrimp stock, bring to a boil, reduce heat and simmer 30 minutes longer. Repeat, adding a cup of the stock and cooking another 30 minutes.

Add the lemon juice and cook for another 10 minutes, then add the last cup of stock, bring to a boil, add the shrimp, and simmer for another 15 to 20 minutes.

Spoon over rice in bowls and serve with buttered French bread to sop up the juices.

*Cook's Notes: May substitute canned tomato sauce and commercial seafood, chicken or vegetable broth/stock.

"If you love heat, you're gonna love Shrimp Sauce Piquant. Shrimp is cooked in a slow simmered, spicy tomato sauce. Piquant translated from French means literally "pricking" and that is what this spicy sauce piquant is meant to do, prick the tongue."

BLACKENED REDFISH

Source: Paul Prudhomme

Ingredients

1 Tbsp paprika

1 tsp onion powder

1 tsp cayenne pepper

½ tsp dried oregano leaves

2 ½ tsp salt

1 tsp garlic powder

½ tsp thyme leaves

1 ½ cups unsalted butter, melted

6 skinless redfish, pompano or tilefish fillets, or other firm-fleshed fish, each 8 to 10 ounces and about ½ inch thick

Instructions

In a small bowl, combine the paprika, salt, onion powder, garlic powder, cayenne, thyme and oregano. Mix well. Set aside.

Place a large cast-iron skillet over high heat until very hot, about 10 minutes. It will get smoky, so turn on the exhaust fan and turn off the smoke detector.

Meanwhile, pour 2 tablespoons of melted butter in each of 6 small ramekins; set aside and keep warm. Pour the remaining butter into a shallow bowl. Dip each fillet in the butter so that both sides are well coated. Sprinkle the spice mix generously and evenly on both sides of the fish, patting it on by hand.

When the skillet is heated, place the fillets inside without crowding and top each with 1 teaspoon of melted butter. Cook, uncovered, until the underside looks charred, about 2 minutes. Turn the fillets over and again pour 1 teaspoon of butter on top; cook until done, about 2 minutes more. Transfer to warmed plates and repeat with the remaining fish. Serve immediately, with a ramekin of butter on each plate.

SEAFOOD FETTUCINE ALFREDO

Source: Karrie; Tasty Ever After

Ingredients

1 lb. uncooked fettuccine noodles

3 Tbsp unsalted butter, divided

2 Tbsp olive oil, divided

1 lb. large shrimp, peeled, deveined, rinsed, salted and peppered

8 large scallops, rinsed well, salted and peppered

3 green onions, finely chopped

1 medium shallot, finely chopped

4 garlic cloves, minced

8 oz. button mushrooms, sliced

½ cup white wine

2 cups heavy cream

½ cup fresh Parmesan cheese, grated

Salt and white pepper to taste

Instructions

Cook fettuccine noodles al dente, according to package directions, drain, and set aside.

In a large skillet over medium-high heat, add 1 tablespoon butter and 1 tablespoon olive oil. Add shrimp to skillet in single layer. Cook until shrimp turns pink on each side and just cooked through, about 3 minutes. Place on plate. Set aside. Add another 1 table-spoon butter and 1 tablespoon olive oil to pan. Add scallops in a single layer and cook for 90 seconds on each side. Remove and place on plate with shrimp. Set aside.

Add remaining 1 tablespoon butter to pan with green onions, shallots, and garlic, and sauté for 1 minute. Add sliced mushrooms and sauté for 3 minutes. Add white wine, and reduce to half.

Add cream and stir constantly until slightly thickened, about 2-3 minutes. Stir in Parmesan cheese, taste sauce and add salt and pepper, if needed. Add scallops, shrimp and cooked fettuccine noodles, stir together until everything is well coated and heated through, about 2 minutes. Serve immediately with parmesan cheese.

LOBSTER SOUFFLÉ, PLAZA ATHENÉE

Ingredients

3 Live lobsters or 10 to 12 frozen 1 lb. rock lobster tails (thawed)

¼ cup carrot, finely chopped	¼ cup onion, finely chopped
1 Tbsp parsley, chopped	1 Tbsp chives, chopped
1 tsp paprika	1 cup heavy cream
½ cup sauterne	2 Tbsp cognac
3 Tbsp butter	3 Tbsp flour
1 cup milk	¼ cup heavy cream
¼ cup dry sherry	5 Tbsp butter
6 Tbsp flour	2 tsp salt
1 tsp cayenne	¼ cup milk
6 egg yolks	½ cup parmesan cheese, grated
6 egg whites, room temperature	½ tsp cream of tartar

Directions

On a wooden board lay lobster on back. Sever spinal cord by inserting point of knife through to back shell where body and tail of lobster come together. With sharp knife, split body down middle, cutting through the under- shell. Discard dark vein and small sac 2 inches below head. Crack large claws with nutcracker.

With sharp knife, cut lobster and shell into large pieces (if using tails, cut into thirds). In hot oil in large skillet, sauté lobster pieces (shell and all), turning occasionally, 5 minutes until red and remove to bowl. In drippings in same skillet, sauté carrot, onion, parsley, and chives until carrot and onion are tender for about 2 minutes and return lobster to skillet. Add paprika, 1 cup cream, the sauterne

LOBSTER SOUFFLÉ, PLAZA ATHENÉE

and cognac. Cook gently, covered for 10 minutes.

Remove lobster, cut away shell and discard. Slice lobster meat ¼ inch thick and set aside. Over medium heat, simmer the cream mixture, stirring, to reduce to 1 cup. Force through coarse strainer and reserve for Lobster Sauce.

Lobster Sauce:

In small saucepan melt 3 Tbsp butter. Remove from heat and stir in 3 Tbsp flour until smooth. Gradually stir in 1 cup milk and bring to boiling, stirring. Remove from heat stir in cream, sherry and reserved mixture. In a bowl combine 1 cup sauce with cut-up lobster turn into 1½ quart shallow baking dish and reserve rest of sauce.

Preheat oven to 375°F.

Soufflé:

In medium sauce- pan melt butter. Remove from heat stir in flour, 1 teaspoon salt and dash cayenne until smooth. Gradually stir in milk and bring to boiling, stirring. Reduce heat simmer until mixture becomes very thick and leaves bottom and side of pan and remove from heat. With wire whisk, beat mixture into egg yolks in large bowl mix well and beat in cheese.

In large bowl, with electric mixer at high speed, beat egg whites with cream of tartar and 1 tea- spoon salt just until stiff peaks form when beater is slowly raised. With wire whisk or rubber scraper, fold egg whites, one half at a time, into egg-yolk mixture just until well combined. Pour over lobster in baking dish and bake 35 to 40 minutes until puffed and nicely browned.

Just before serving, gently reheat reserved lobster sauce. Serve soufflé at once with sauce.

OYSTERS MARIE LAVEAUX

Marie Laveaux was the voodoo queen of Bourbon Street. Legend has it that the pirate Jean Lafitte often met Marie at the Old Absinthe House late in the evening where they enjoyed oysters on the half shell while trading secrets of Barataria Bay.

Source: Chef John Folse

Ingredients

Oysters:

3 dozen select oysters, reserve liquid   3 Tbsp butter

1 tsp garlic   1 tsp parsley, chopped

½ ounce Pernod or Herbsaint

Directions

In a heavy-bottomed sauté pan, melt butter over medium-high heat. Stir in garlic and parsley and sauté 2 minutes. Add oysters and cook until edges begin to curl, but do not overcook. Deglaze with Pernod and cook 1 minute. Remove oysters, reduce liquid to half volume and reserve for sauce.

Sauce:

¼ pound butter   ½ cup onions, diced

¼ cup celery, diced   2 Tbsp garlic, minced

¼ cup green onions, sliced

½ cup white crabmeat (or ½ cup chopped cooked shrimp)

2½ Tbsp flour   3 cups heavy whipping cream

1 ounce dry white wine

Reserved cooked liquid from oysters   Reserved oyster liquid

1/8 tsp nutmeg   ¼ cup red bell peppers, diced

¼ cup yellow bell peppers, diced   Salt and pepper to taste

OYSTERS MARIE LAVEAUX

Parmesan cheese for topping

Directions

Preheat oven to 375°F. In a 1-quart heavy-bottomed saucepan, melt butter over medium-high heat. Add onions, celery, garlic and green onions and sauté 3 minutes. Stirring constantly, add crabmeat or shrimp and sauté 1 minute. Whisk in flour until a white roux is achieved then whisk in cream and wine. Bring to a low boil, stirring constantly as mixture thickens. Pour in cooked liquid from oysters and reserved oyster liquid. Reduce heat to simmer and cook 10–15 minutes, adding hot water if sauce becomes too thick. Add nutmeg and bell peppers then season with salt and pepper. Place 6 oysters in each au gratin dish, top with a generous serving of sauce and bake until bubbly. If desired, sprinkle Parmesan cheese on top prior to baking. Serve with garlic croutons.

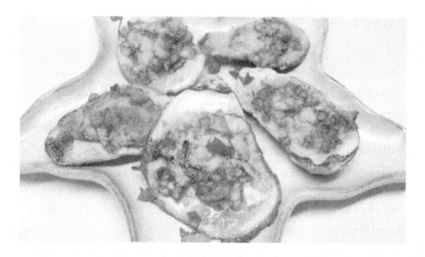

"If you don't love life you can't enjoy an oyster; there is a shock of freshness to it and intimations of the ages of man, some piercing intuition of the sea and all its weeds and breezes..... shiver you for a split second." Eleanor Clark

SMOKED SALMON

Source: Author

Ingredients

5 pounds salmon, trout or char

Maple syrup for basting

Brine:

1 quart cool water

1/3 cup kosher salt

1 cup brown sugar

¼ tsp white pepper

¼ tsp crushed bay leaves

¼ tsp allspice

¼ tsp cardamom

Preparation

Mix together the brine ingredients and place your fish in a non-reactive container (plastic or glass), cover and put in the refrigerator. This curing process eliminates some of the moisture from the inside of the fish while at the same time infusing it with salt, which will help preserve the salmon.

You will need to cure your salmon at least 4 to 8 hours, even for thin fillets from trout or pink salmon. A really thick piece of king salmon might need as much as 36 hours in the brine. Double the brine if it's not enough to cover the fish.

Take your fish out of the brine and pat it dry. Set the fillets on your cooling rack, skin side down. Let the fish dry under a cool fan for 2 to 4 hours (or up to overnight in the fridge). You want the surface of the fish to develop a shiny skin called a pellicle. The pellicle, which is a thin, lacquer-like layer on top of the fish, seals it and

SMOKED SALMON

offers a sticky surface for the smoke to adhere to. The salt in the brine will protect your fish from spoilage.

Even though this is hot smoking, you still do not want high temperatures. Start with a small fire and work your way up as you go. It is important to bring the temperature up gradually or you will get that white albumin "bleed" on the meat. Start the process between 120° F and 150°F for up to an hour, then finish at 175°F for a final hour or two. What the smoker is set at is not necessarily what the actual temperature is. Smoking is an art, not a science. To keep temperatures mild, always put water in your drip pan to keep the temperature down.

After an hour in the smoker, baste the fish with the maple syrup; do this every hour. This is a good way to brush away any albumin that might form. In most cases, you will get a little. You just don't want a lot of it. You goal should be an internal temperature of about 130°F to 140°F. (I keep the smoke on the whole time, but if you want a lighter smoke, finish the salmon without smoke or in a 200° F oven.)

Cool and Store the Fish. Once your fish is smoked, let it rest on the cooling rack for an hour before you put it in the fridge. Once refrigerated and wrapped in plastic, smoked fish will keep for 10 days. If you vacuum-seal it, the fish will keep for up to 3 weeks, or freeze your fish for up to a year.

See also: ***Orange Sriracha Sauce in Rubs & Sauces.***

LOBSTER THERMIDOR

Source: Gourmet chef Louis P. De Gouy

Ingredients

2 (1 to 1 ½ lb.) live lobsters	½ stick unsalted butter
½ tsp paprika	1/8 tsp salt
¼ tsp black pepper	2 Tbsp medium-dry Sherry
1 cup heavy cream, scalded	2 large egg yolks

Instructions

Plunge lobsters headfirst into an 8-quart pot of boiling salted water*. Loosely cover pot and cook lobsters over moderately high heat 9 minutes from time they enter water, then transfer with tongs to sink to cool.

When lobsters are cool enough to handle, twist off claws and crack them, then remove meat. Halve lobsters lengthwise with kitchen shears, beginning from tail end, then remove tail meat, reserving shells. Cut all lobster meat into ¼ inch pieces. Discard any remaining lobster innards, then rinse and dry shells.

Heat butter in a 2-quart heavy saucepan over moderate heat until foam subsides, then cook mushrooms, stirring, until liquid that mushrooms give off is evaporated and they begin to brown, about 5 minutes. Add lobster meat, paprika, salt, and pepper and reduce heat to low. Cook, shaking pan gently, 1 minute. Add 1 tablespoon Sherry and ½ cup hot cream and simmer 5 minutes.

Whisk together yolks and remaining tablespoon Sherry in a small bowl. Slowly pour remaining ½ cup hot cream into yolks, whisking constantly, and transfer to a small heavy saucepan. Cook custard over very low heat, whisking constantly, until it is slightly thickened and registers 160°F on an instant-read thermometer. Add custard to lobster mixture, stirring gently.

Preheat broiler. Arrange lobster shells, cut sides up, in a shallow baking pan and spoon lobster with some of sauce into shells. Broil lobsters 6 inches from heat until golden brown, 4 to 5 minutes. Serve remaining sauce on the side.   *Use 1 Tbsp salt for every 4 quarts of water.

PAN SEARED SCALLOPS WITH BACON CREAM SAUCE

Source: Meghan; Cake 'n Knife

Ingredients

6 slices bacon, chopped

½ Tbsp butter

1 cup heavy cream

½ cup Parmesan, freshly grated

½ tsp olive oil

6 large scallops

Salt & pepper

Chopped chives for garnish

Instructions

In a medium skillet, cook chopped bacon over medium-high heat until crisp. Remove the bacon with a slotted spoon to a paper towel -lined plate to drain.

Add butter, cream, and Parmesan to the skillet with the bacon grease. Reduce the sauce over medium heat by half. Stir in the cooked bacon. Season with salt and pepper to taste. Keep warm over low heat.

In a separate skillet, heat ½ tsp olive oil over medium-high heat. Season scallops with salt and pepper. Once the pan is hot (make sure it's really hot!), add the scallops to the pan. Sear until golden brown on one side, approximately 1 minute, and turn over. Sear on the other side for 1 minute until golden brown. Remove to a paper towel-lined plate to drain.

Serve the scallops over a layer of bacon cream sauce. Garnish with chives.

NOTES

_____

_____

_____

_____

_____

_____

_____

_____

_____

_____

_____

_____

_____

_____

NOTES

SOUPS, STEWS & CHILI

"Let food be thy medicine and medicine be thy food." Hippoc-
rates

CREAMY COLCANNON SOUP

Source: Author

Ingredients

1 small head of cabbage, cored and chopped

Equal amount of diced potatoes

1 medium onion, diced

3 slices Wrights thick sliced bacon, cut in ¼ inch pieces

½ stick butter

Salt and pepper to taste

1 cup heavy cream

Preparation

In a large pot cook bacon until brown. Add onions and sauté until tender. Add cabbage and potatoes and add enough water to come about halfway up the vegetables. Bring to boil, reduce to simmer and cook until cabbage and potatoes are tender. Remove from heat. Using an immersible blender purée until smooth. Stir in butter, heavy cream, salt and pepper. Continue stirring until butter is melted.

CHASEN'S FAMOUS CHILI

Chasen's Restaurant in Hollywood, California probably made the most famous chili. The owner of the restaurant, Dave Chasen (1899-1973), ex-vaudeville performer, kept the recipe a secret, entrusting it to no one. Chauffeurs, studio people, actors and actresses would come to Chasen's to buy the chili. Liz Tayler had it shipped to every movie set for lunch; so the story goes.

Ingredients

½ lb. pinto beans	2 (14 oz. cans) tomatoes
1 lb. green bell peppers, seeded and chopped	
1 ½ lbs. onions, chopped	1 ½ Tbsp vegetable oil
2 cloves garlic, minced	½ cup parsley, finely chopped
1 stick butter	2 ½ lbs. ground beef
1 lb. ground pork	2 tsp salt or to taste
1/3 cup chili powder (add more to make it hotter)	
1 ½ tsp black pepper	½ tsp ground cumin

Directions

Rinse beans, put in a bowl and cover with two inches of water. Allow to soak overnight. Transfer beans AND water to a large stock pot. Bring to a boil and simmer, covered, in the same water until tender, about 2 to 2 ½ hours. Add tomatoes and simmer 5 minutes. Heat butter in a large skillet and sauté green peppers over medium heat for 5 minutes. Add onions and cook until tender, stirring frequently. Add garlic and parsley. In a second large skillet, add oil and cook beef and pork for 15 minutes. Add onion mixture to the meat, stir in chili powder and cook 10 minutes. Add meat mixture to beans in a large pot. Season with salt, pepper and cumin. Simmer, covered, 1 hour. Remove cover and cook 30 minutes longer. Skim fat off top. NOTE: This chili freezes very well and Dave Chasen believed it was best when reheated.

Chicken Corn Chowder

Source: Author

Ingredients

4 slices bacon, sliced in ¼ inch pieces

1 medium onion, quartered and thinly sliced

4 medium potatoes, cubed

1 cup water

2 Tbsp olive oil

2 large chicken breasts, cubed

1 pkg (16 oz.) frozen, whole kernel corn

1 cup heavy cream

1 tsp sugar

½ stick butter

¼ tsp white pepper

Salt to taste

2 cups milk

½ tsp tarragon

½ cup white wine

Preparation

In a large stock pot over medium heat, sauté bacon until lightly browned. Add onion, potatoes and 1 cup water. Bring to a boil and simmer, covered, until potatoes are tender, about 10 minutes. Brown chicken in 2 Tbsp olive oil then cut into ½ inch cubes. Add chicken, corn, cream, sugar, butter and remaining ingredients. Simmer over low heat, covered, for 10 minutes.

TACO SOUP

Source: Clara Wilson

Ingredients

2 lbs. ground beef

1 large onion, chopped

2 cans Ranch Style Beans

2 cans yellow hominy, drained

1 can whole kernel corn, drained

2 cans diced, stewed tomatoes

2 cans Rotel tomatoes

1 pkg. dry taco seasoning

1 pkg. dry Ranch style seasoning

Directions

In a large sauce pan, brown meat and onion together. Add all other ingredients, bring to a boil and simmer for 30 minutes. Serve with grated cheddar cheese and Fritos.

JAILHOUSE CHILI

Source: Betty Parks

Ingredients

3 Tbsp oil	3 lbs. ground round
1 medium onion, chopped	2-3 cans tomato sauce (16 oz.)
1 qt. water	6 Tbsp chili powder
5 cloves garlic, minced	Salt and black pepper to taste
1 tsp cumin	1 tsp marjoram

½ to 1 tsp cayenne pepper (how hot do you like it?)

1 tsp oregano	1 tsp turmeric
1 Tbsp sugar	1 Tbsp paprika

For thickening:

3 Tbsp flour

6 Tbsp corn meal

1 cup water

Directions

Heat oil in a heavy stock pot. Add meat and onions and cook over medium heat until meat starts to brown then drain. Add tomato sauce and water. Bring to a boil then cook over low heat, covered, for 1 ½ to 2 hours. Add remaining ingredients, except thickening ingredients, and cook another 30 minutes. Add thickening ingredients and cook another 5 minutes.

"I like chili, but not enough to discuss it with someone from Texas." Calvin Trillin

GREEK LEMON SOUP

Source: Chef Jim Scritchfield, Clock Restaurant; Monterey, CA

Ingredients

2 cans chicken and rice soup

¼ tsp white pepper

¼ cup lemon juice

6 egg yolks

1 cup cream

Salt to taste

1 fresh lemon

Directions

Beat together egg yolks and lemon juice. Pour cans of soup into a sauce pan, add pepper and salt, bring to a boil and reduce heat to a high simmer. Add cream and egg yolk mixture. Simmer until slightly thickened.

Place a very thin slice of lemon in each serving bowl. Serve with Russian Dark Rye bread and butter.

CUMBER SOUP

Source: Fanny Farmer Cookbook; Courtesy of my friend, Bill Bennett

Ingredients

3 cucumbers, peeled and sliced

2 Tbsp butter

3 Tbsp flour

2 cups chicken stock

1 onion, quartered and thinly sliced

1 cup milk

Pinch of nutmeg or mace

½ cup cream

2 egg yolks, lightly beaten

Salt to taste

White pepper to taste

Angostura Bitters

Directions

Peel, slice and seed cucumbers. Cook 10 minutes in butter. Stir in flour then gradually add chicken stock, stirring constantly. Scald together milk, onion and nutmeg or mace. Combine the mixtures and puree. Bring to a boil and stir in cream and two egg yolks. Season with salt and white pepper.

For Chilled Cucumber Soup:

Omit the egg yolks, chill before adding the cream and season with a few drops of Angostura Bitters.

GREEK CHICKEN SOUP WITH LEMON

Avgolemono soup is the classic Greek chicken penicillin. It is a heavenly, velvety soup with a savory chicken broth, tart lemons and egg yolks. The combination creates a smooth and comforting soup perfect for a new twist on the classic chicken soup.

Source: Mila Furman; Girl and the Kitchen

Ingredients

2 quarts chicken broth	1 cup cooked chicken, shredded
1 medium onion finely diced	½ cup long grain white rice
1 bay leaf	12 lemon zest strips, about 2 lemons zested
2 large eggs	2 large egg yolks
¼ cup lemon juice from zested lemons	Salt and pepper to taste
Dill sprigs for garnish	

Instructions

To a large pot, add 1 Tbsp olive oil, onion and lemon strips.

Saute for 7 minutes over medium-low heat until onions are tender. Add chicken broth to the pot along with the rice and bay leaf and bring to a boil over medium heat. Reduce heat to and simmer until rice is tender, about 20 minutes.

Remove and discard bay leaf and lemon zest strips. Increase heat to high and return stock to boil, then reduce heat to low. Place immersion blender into the pot and blend for a few seconds.

In a separate bowl, whisk eggs, yolks, and lemon juice lightly until combined. Add extra salt, pepper and lemon juice if desired. While whisking constantly, slowly ladle about 2 cups of hot broth into egg mixture, whisking until combined. Add chicken. Pour egg-stock mixture back into pot; cook over low heat, stirring constantly, until soup is slightly thickened, about 4 to 5 minutes. Remove from heat and serve immediately. Garnish with lemon zest and fresh dill.

BLACK BEAN SOUP

Source: Cheryl Berrios

Ingredients

1 lb. dried black beans

¼ cup butter

1 small onion, diced

2 stalks celery, diced

2 cloves garlic, minced

2 quarts water

1 ham bone/hock

1 bay leaf

Pinch of thyme

Salt and pepper, to taste

¼ cup sherry

Lemon slices for garnish

Hard boiled eggs, chopped for garnish

Directions

Soak beans 1 hour using quick soak method. Drain. Melt butter in a heavy pot. Sauté onions, celery and garlic until tender. Add water, beans, ham bone/hock, salt and pepper. Bring to a boil, cover, reduce heat, cover and simmer 3 hours.

Transfer to a blender and puree. Return to pot, adding more water for desired consistency. Bring to a boil, add sherry and adjust seasoning, if needed.

RIO GRANDE STEW

Source: Better Homes and Gardens, March 1977

Ingredients

2 lbs. stew meat	2 Tbsp olive oil
3 cups water	10 ½ oz. beef broth
½ cup celery, chopped	1 medium onion, chopped
2 cloves garlic, minced	1 (15 oz.) can garbanzo beans
1 Tbsp dried oregano, crushed	1 Tbsp dried coriander
2 tsp ground cumin	2 bay leaves
1 ½ tsp salt	3 medium carrots, sliced

2 ears fresh corn on the cob, cut into 1 inch pieces

1 head of cabbage, cut into 8 wedges

Directions

In a large Dutch oven, brown the meat in oil. Add water, beef broth, celery, onion, garlic, oregano, coriander, cumin, bay leaves and salt. Bring to a boil, reduce heat, cover and simmer until meat is tender, about 2 hours. Skim off fat. Stir in carrots, corn on the cob, and undrained garbanzo bean. Arrange cabbage on top. Simmer, covered, 20 to 30 minutes or until vegetables are done. Season to taste with additional salt and pepper.

Salsa:

Combine 1 (16 oz.) can diced, stewed tomatoes, 1 medium onion, finely chopped, 1 (4 oz.) chopped green chilies, 1 clove garlic, minced, ¼ cup chopped fresh parsley and ½ tsp salt. Pass salsa to spoon over each serving.

BEEF STEW

Source: Author

Ingredients

2 lb. beef chuck stew meat, cubed into 1" pieces

2 Tbsp. olive oil   1 onion, chopped

2 carrots, peeled and sliced into rounds (quarter thickest sections)

2 stalks celery, chopped

Salt to taste   Black pepper to taste

3 cloves garlic, minced   1 (14.5 oz. can) tomato sauce

6 cups beef broth   1 cup red wine

1 Tbsp. Worcestershire sauce   1 tsp. dried thyme

½ tsp oregano   2 bay leaves

1 lb. baby potatoes, quartered   1 cup frozen peas

¼ cup parsley, freshly chopped   1 Tbsp sugar

Preparation

In a large Dutch oven (or pot), over medium heat, heat oil. Add beef and cook on all sides until seared, 10 minutes, working in batches if necessary. Transfer beef to a plate.

In the same pot, cook onion, carrots, and celery until soft, 5 minutes. Season with salt and pepper. Add garlic and tomato sauce and cook until garlic is fragrant, 2 minutes. Add beef back to Dutch oven then add broth, wine, Worcestershire sauce, thyme, oregano and bay leaves. Bring to a boil then reduce heat to a simmer. Season with salt and pepper. Cover and let simmer until beef is tender, 30 minutes. Add potatoes, peas, parsley and sugar and simmer, covered, until potatoes are tender, 15 minutes. Remove bay leaves.

CROCK POT BEEF STEW

Source: RIVAL

Ingredients

2 lbs. beef, chuck or stew meat, cut in 1 inch cubes

¼ cup flour

1 ½ tsp salt

½ tsp black pepper

1 ½ cups beef broth

1 tsp Worcestershire

sauce

1 clove garlic, chopped

1 bay leaf

1 tsp paprika

4 carrots, sliced

3 potatoes, diced

2 onions, chopped

1 stalk celery, chopped

2 tsp Kitchen Bouquet (optional)

Directions

Place meat in crock pot. Mix flour, salt and pepper and pour over meat; stir to coat meat with flour. Add remaining ingredients and stir to mix well. Cover and cook on low 10 to 12 hours (high: 4 to 6 hours). Stir stew thoroughly before serving.

BAKED POTATO SOUP

A quick and delicious soup.

Source: Deena Coyle

Ingredients

4 large potatoes

2/3 cup butter

2/3 cup all-purpose flour

6 cups milk

¾ tsp salt

1/2 tsp pepper

1 ½ cup cheddar cheese, shredded

12 slices bacon, cooked and crumbled

4 green onions, chopped

8 oz. sour cream

Instructions

Bake then scrape potatoes out of peel. Set aside.

Melt butter in a large pan, stir in flour then add milk, salt and pepper. Stir in potatoes, cheese, bacon, onions and sour cream. Heat until bubbly.

"Not everyone can be a truffle. Most of us are potatoes. And a potato is a very good thing to be." Massimo Bottura, Massimo Bottura: Never Trust A Skinny Italian Chef

"There is all the pleasure that one can have in golddigging in finding one's hopes satisfied in the riches of a good hill of potatoes." Sarah Orne Jewett, The Country of the Pointed Firs

"What I say is that, if a man really likes potatoes, he must be a pretty decent sort of fellow." A.A. Milne

HEARTY BAKED POTATO SOUP

Source: Author

Ingredients

4 large potatoes, scrubbed	12 bacon slices
4 Tbsp butter	2 garlic cloves, minced
1 large onion, chopped	1 / 3 cup all-purpose flour
2 cups milk	1 cup heavy cream
2 cups chicken stock	1 tsp salt
½ tsp black pepper	1 tsp paprika
1 tsp dried parsley	½ tsp tarragon
1 ½ cup cheddar cheese, shredded	1 cup sour cream
Minced fresh chives, for garnish	

Preparation

Bake potatoes, cool and remove skin. Cut into chunks. Set aside.

Cook bacon in a skillet over medium heat until crisp. Remove bacon, reserving up to 1 tablespoon of the bacon fat. Once the bacon has cooled, crumble it into small pieces.

In a large pot, melt the butter over medium-low heat. Add the reserved bacon fat, garlic and onion and cook for 4 to 5 minutes, or until the onion is tender. Whisk the flour into the pan and stir for 1 to 2 minutes. Slowly whisk in the milk and half-and-half. Keep whisking until smooth. Stir in the chicken stock. Bring to a light simmer and stir in the salt, pepper, paprika and tarragon. Keep at a light simmer until the mixture has thickened slightly, 8 to 10 minutes.

Stir in the cheese, bacon, and sour cream. Remove the pot from the heat. Stir in the potatoes. Serve hot and garnish with chives, shredded cheese and bacon.

POTATO SOUP

Source: Valeria (Val) Corley

Ingredients

½ stick butter, cubed

1 onion, diced

¾ cup celery, chopped

5 cups potatoes, peeled and chopped

3 cups milk

3 cups water*

4 tsp chicken bouillon granules*

½ tsp salt

½ tsp pepper

¼ cup all-purpose flour

4 cups cheese, shredded

½ cup bacon, cooked and crumbled

Directions

In a large pot over medium heat, melt the butter. Add onion and celery and sauté until tender, about 8 to 10 minutes. Add potatoes and water, bring to a boil, reduce heat and simmer for 15 minutes. Stir in 2 cups of milk, chicken bouillon, salt and pepper. Whisk together flour in remaining cup of milk and stir into the soup mixture. Bring to a boil and cook 2 minutes, stirring constantly. Reduce heat to low and stir in the cheese and bacon. Continue stirring until cheese is melted and well incorporated.

*Use 3 cups of chicken broth instead of water and bouillon if desired.

KIMCHI SOUP (KIMCHI-GUK)

I'd like to introduce you to my family's special kimchi soup recipe today. It's called kimchiguk in Korean, is very easy to make and it's a well-balanced "one pot meal" when served with rice. You get the vitamins and minerals from well-fermented kimchi, and protein from pork and tofu. It's great for the winter: nutritious, warm, and satisfying.

Before there were modern methods of preservation and farming in Korea, we had to prepare food for the long, cold winter when vegetables were hard to come by. Neighbors would get together right before winter starts and prepare huge batches of Napa cabbage kimchi together, enough to last all of the families involved for the whole winter. This kind of event was called a kimjang. To make sure the kimchi didn't freeze over the winter, we stored it in onggi crocks and buried in the ground so the temperature was always above freezing and our families could eat nutritious kimchi all winter.

Source: Maangchi

Ingredients

2 cups of chopped kimchi	1 teaspoon of sugar
½ pound of pork shoulder (or pork belly), cut into bite sized pieces	
2 Tablespoons of hot pepper paste	5 cups of water
2 stalks of green onions, chopped	
1 package of tofu (14 ounces: 396 grams), cut into bite sized cubes	

Directions

Combine the kimchi, hot pepper paste, kimchi juice, pork, and sugar in a heavy bottomed pot. Add water and bring to a boil over high heat and cook for 30 minutes. Add tofu and lower the heat to medium low. Cook for another 10 minutes. Add green onion and remove from the heat.

KIMCHI SOUP

Ok. So, you may be wondering why I'm getting carried away with my interest in Kimchi Soup. Because...it is good! And most people, like me, probably had never heard of it before. If you can live with the smell until it is cooked, this soup is delicious (you may want to cook it outside)! Kimchi has never been high on my food list, but my daughter loves it. And I like this recipe she developed for Kimchi Soup. Don't plan on going on a first date after eating it, unless it is with some lovely Korean maiden who has eaten some before the date as well!

Source: My Daughter; Lenore Wilson McLaughlin

Ingredients

2 jars of kimchi

1 can Rotel tomatoes

1 clove garlic, crushed

1 onion, chopped

1 cup white wine or sake

1 cup soy sauce

¼ cup Sriracha sauce

1 Tbsp sesame oil

Chicken broth to cover

2 containers of tofu, cut into bite sized cubes

Frozen scallops, shrimp, squid rings

Directions

Combine the first 8 ingredients in a heavy pot. Add chicken broth, bring to a boil and cook for 30 minutes. Add tofu and lower the heat to medium low. Add seafood and simmer until seafood is cooked (5 to 10 minutes).

KIMCHI SOUP

Super easy and delicious Kimchi Soup! Tastes just like the ones from the Korean restaurants. I was so confused to see that this soup was so easy to recreate. The key ingredient is the chili pepper paste that makes the broth super yummy! I literally have no reason to ever go to a Korean restaurant ever again.

Source: Sarah Kim

Ingredients

1 lb. Napa cabbage kimchi, cut to bite sized pieces

1 lb. pork, cubed

1.5 lb. tofu, cut into rectangles

4 cups water

2 Tbsp Gochujang, chili pepper paste

2 tsp sugar

2 Tbsp oil

Button mushrooms, sliced

Enoki mushrooms

Directions

Heat oil in a Dutch oven. Add the meat and sear on all sides. Stir in kimchi, water, pepper paste and sugar.

Bring to a boil, and then simmer 45 minutes. Towards the end add mushrooms and Enoki mushrooms.

BEST CHICKEN SOUP EVER

Source: Clara Wilson

Ingredients

2 Tbsp olive oil	6 cloves garlic, minced
1 large onion, chopped	2 carrots, chopped
2 stalks celery, chopped	1 Tbsp fresh ginger, grated
1 tsp ground turmeric	8 cups chicken broth
3 boneless, skinless chicken breasts	1 Tbsp fresh parsley, chopped
½ tsp dried thyme	½ teaspoon salt
½ tsp white pepper	1 (10 oz. box) pearl couscous
1 cup frozen peas	

Instructions

In a large Dutch oven over medium heat add oil. When oil is hot, add onion, garlic, carrots and celery. Cook until onions are tender. Add grated ginger and turmeric. Saute for 30 seconds to incorporate, then add chicken broth, chicken breast, parsley, thyme, salt and pepper.

Bring soup to a boil and stir in couscous. Make sure the chicken is covered by the broth. Reduce heat to simmer and cook, uncovered, for 20-30 minutes or until chicken is fully cooked.

When chicken is cooked, remove to a cutting board and shred with two forks. Add chicken back to pot then stir in frozen peas. Adjust seasonings if needed.

"I am forbidden sugar, fat, and alcohol. So hooray, I guess, for oatmeal, lemon juice, and chicken soup." **Mason Cooley**

"A Jewish woman had two chickens. One got sick, so the woman made chicken soup out of the other one to help the sick one get well." **Henny Youngman**

NEW YEAR'S BLACK EYED PEA SOUP

"There are some among you who think that Mack Brown, Vince Young and some other Longhorns are the reason Texas won the 2005 national college football championship. But I can tell you that the real reason is this lucky black- eyed pea soup. The orange-colored soup recipe is one Dottie Wilkinson, an Austin resident and Longhorns fan, gave me in 1979 when I wrote an article about the New Year's custom of serving black- eyed peas.

The soup still fits Texas so well. Legumes are popular in this state and these are flavored with chili powder and smoked sausage, ingredients many Texans already have in their pantries and freezers. The soup is a great use of the Easter holiday ham bone. Toss it in the pot and it seasons those bland peas as the little pieces of meat fall off the bone and into the soup."
Kitty Crider

Source: Dottie and Joe Wilkinson

Ingredients

3 cups dried black-eyed peas	Ham bone with meat or ham hocks
3 cups celery, minced	3 cups onion, minced
3 cups carrots, minced	2 lb. smoked sausage, diced
2 Tbsp chili powder	

Directions

In a large pot, sauté celery, onion and carrots until just tender. Add 3 quarts water, peas and ham and bring to a boil. Reduce heat to simmer and cook until peas are soft, about two hours. (No need to soak peas.) Discard bone, leaving bits of ham in soup. Add smoked sausage and simmer 30 minutes. Add chili powder. If needed, add more water, salt or black pepper. Serve with cornbread. Makes about a gallon.

DUTCH PEA SOUP

Source: Stuff Dutch People Like

Ingredients

1 ½ cups dried green split peas   3 ½ oz. thick-cut bacon

1 (5-6 oz.) pork chop   1 stock cube (vegetable, pork or chicken)

2 celery sticks, diced   2-3 carrots, sliced

1 large potato, peeled and cubed   1 small onion, chopped

1 small leek, sliced   ½ cup celeriac (celery bulb), cubed

Salt and pepper, to taste   ½ cup chopped celery leaves

½ cup sliced smoked sausage (Dutch sausage, if you can find it)

Instructions

Boil 3¾ pints of water in a large soup pot, along with the split peas, stock cube, pork chop and bacon. Skim off any froth forming on top as the pot starts to boil. Put the lid on the pot and leave to boil softly for 45 minutes, stirring occasionally (it may catch if you don't).

Carefully take the pork chop out, debone and thinly slice the meat. Set aside. Add the vegetables to the boiling broth and leave to cook for another 30 minutes, adding a little extra water every time the soup starts to catch. Add the smoked sausage for the last 15 minutes. When the vegetables are tender, remove the bacon and smoked sausage with the tongs, slice thinly and set aside.

If you prefer a smooth consistency, puree the soup with a stick blender until it is as chunky or smooth as you like. Season to taste. Add the meat back to the soup, setting some slices of smoked sausage aside. Serve split pea soup in bowls or soup plates, garnished with slices of smoked sausage and chopped celery leaf.

CREOLE COURT-BOUILLON

Source: Author

Ingredients

5 to 6 redfish, cut in pieces	1 ½ lbs. shrimp, peeled & deveined
1 cup cooking oil	1 cup all-purpose flour
1 cup onions, finely minced	½ cup bell pepper, finely minced
1 cup celery, finely minced	2 cloves garlic, finely minced
2 (14.5 oz.) tomatoes, diced	1 (8 oz.) can tomato paste
1 Tbsp sugar	3 bay leaves
½ cup dry white wine	2 ½ tsp salt
2 tsp black pepper	2 tsp creole seasoning
½ cup green onion tops, minced	¼ cup fresh parsley, minced
Tabasco, to taste	4 Tbsp butter

Water to make about 3 quarts with the fish stock

Preparation

Boil bones and head of fish. Strain and reserve stock. Make a roux of oil and flour, stirring constantly until golden brown. Add onions, bell pepper, celery and garlic. Cook over low heat until tender. Place the tomato paste in a small bowl and whisk in the wine to blend. Add tomatoes, tomato paste mixture and bay leaves, cooking for 25 to 30 minutes. Add stock, water, salt pepper, creole seasonings and Tabasco (if desired). Bring to a boil and cook about 15 minutes. Reduce the heat to low then whisk in the butter until melted. Remove from the heat, taste, and adjust seasoning, if necessary. Add red fish, shrimp, onion tops and parsley and continue cooking until fish is just done, about 5 to 10 minutes. Serve over rice in bowls.

OYSTER BISQUE

Source: Author

Ingredients

6 Tbsp butter

3 Tbsp flour

2 cups whole milk

1 cup heavy cream

½ cup onion, finely minced

2 cloves garlic, finely minced

1 celery stalk, finely minced

1 Tbsp fresh parsley, minced

1/2 tsp dried tarragon

1 bay leaf

2 dozen oysters, shucked, drained and liquid reserved

Kosher salt

Freshly ground black pepper

Preparation

Melt 4 Tbsp butter over medium heat in a large saucepan. Add the flour and cook, stirring constantly, for 3 to 4 minutes. Stir in milk, cream, oyster liquid, onion, garlic, celery, parsley, tarragon and bay leaf. Bring the mixture to a simmer and cook for 3 to 4 minutes. Add the oysters. Bring back up to a simmer and cook for 3 to 4 minutes, or until the oysters curl. Remove the bay leaf and season to taste. Stir in the remaining 2 Tbsp butter and remove from the heat.

"Give me oysters and beer, for dinner every day of the year, and I'll be fine." Jimmy Buffett

NOTES

NOTES

VEGETABLES & SIDE DISHES

MICROWAVE BROCCOLI

Source: Carla Hubbard

Ingredients

1 head broccoli, rinsed well

3 Tbsp butter

Salt to taste

White pepper to taste

Directions

Placed rinsed broccoli in a microwaveable dish with a microwaveable cover. Arrange 3 Tbsp butter on broccoli. Add salt and white pepper to taste. Cover and microwave on high for 2 minutes. Other fresh vegetables such as; squash, cauliflower, carrots, etc. can be cooked this way. Some, like carrots, may require a one or two minute longer cooking time.

TEXAS ROADHOUSE GREEN BEANS

There are several copycat recipes of these delicious green beans.
This is my version.

Source: Author

Ingredients

2 (14.5 oz.) cans Del Monte Whole Green Beans, drained

2 cups chicken broth

¼ cup butter

1 Tbsp brown sugar

½ tsp salt

½ tsp white pepper

½ tsp black pepper

1 tsp chopped or minced garlic

4 slices bacon, diced (raw) or 4 ounces ham (cooked)

½ medium onion, diced

Preparation

Drain Del Monte Whole Green Beans and set aside.

Cook together broth, butter, brown sugar, peppers and salt for 5
minutes. Set aside.

Preheat a deep pan over medium heat. Cook bacon pieces until
browned. Add onions and garlic and cook until tender. Add the
broth mixture, let simmer for 20 minutes then stir in the green
beans. Bring mixture to a boil just long enough to heat through and
not overcook.

GREEN BEANS

This is a quick and tasty recipe for green beans. I use Del Monte Whole Green Beans as I have found that they taste better. Same with the Kikkoman soy sauce. It just tastes better.

Source: Author

Ingredients

2 (14.5 oz. cans) Del Monte Whole Green Beans, undrained

1 Tbsp bacon drippings or olive oil

2 Tbsp Kikkoman soy sauce

½ tsp onion powder

½ tsp salt

Preparation

Empty undrained Del Monte Whole Green Beans in a sauce pan. Add bacon drippings or olive oil, Kikkoman soy sauce and seasonings. Bring to a boil then simmer for 5 minutes.

MUSHROOM ASPARAGUS QUICHE

Source: Taste of Home

Ingredients

1 tube (8 ounces) refrigerated crescent rolls

2 tsp prepared mustard

1 ½ lbs. fresh asparagus, trimmed and cut into ½ inch pieces

1 medium onion, chopped

½ cup fresh mushrooms, sliced

¼ cup butter, cubed

2 large eggs, lightly beaten

2 cups mozzarella cheese, shredded

¼ cup fresh parsley, minced

½ tsp salt

½ tsp pepper

¼ tsp garlic powder

¼ tsp each dried basil, oregano and rubbed sage

Directions

Separate crescent dough into eight triangles; place in an ungreased 9 inch pie plate with points toward the center. Press onto the bottom and up the sides to form a crust; seal perforations. Spread with mustard; set aside.

In a large skillet, sauté the asparagus, onion and mushrooms in butter until asparagus is crisp-tender. In a large bowl, combine the remaining ingredients; stir in asparagus mixture. Pour into crust.

Bake at 375°F for 25-30 minutes or until a knife inserted in the center comes out clean. Let stand for 10 minutes before cutting.

GRANNY'S GREEN BEANS

Source: Granny Cox

Ingredients

6 (14.5 oz. cans) Del Monte Whole Green Beans, drained

10 slices bacon, cut into pieces

1 cup brown sugar

1 stick butter, melted

Directions

Combine all ingredients. Pour into a large cast iron skillet or a 9 X 13 inch casserole dish and bake at 350°F for 30 minutes. Simple but delicious.

"My most memorable meal is every Thanksgiving. I love the food: The turkey and stuffing; the sweet potatoes and rice, which come from my mother's Southern heritage; the mashed potatoes, which come from my wife's Midwestern roots; the Campbell's green bean casserole; and of course, pumpkin pie."

Douglas Conant

COLLARD GREENS WITH CAJUN FRIED TURKEY

Source: Author

Ingredients

2-3 Tbsp bacon drippings (use olive oil if preferred)

2 medium onions, chopped

6-8 cloves garlic, finely chopped

32 oz. chicken stock or water

1 Cajun fried turkey leg, thigh or wing (frozen from Thanksgiving or Christmas)

1 cup red wine

1 lb. fresh collard greens, washed, rinsed, trimmed and cut into pieces

Salt and pepper to taste

Preparation

Wash and rinse collard greens well. Remove stem from collard leaves. In large pot, add bacon drippings, onions and garlic. Sauté until tender. Add broth, water and turkey. Bring to a boil, reduce heat and simmer for 20-30 minutes. Remove turkey to a cutting board, let it cool enough to handle, remove from bone and cut across the grain into 1 inch pieces. Return to pot and add collard greens and wine. Cook on medium heat for 45 to 60 minutes or until collards are tender. The leaves will wilt down as they cook. Add salt and pepper to taste. The collard greens will be mildly spicy from the Cajun fried turkey.

STUFFED BELL PEPPERS

Source: Ruth Mire Hanson

I copied the directions, as it was written by my friend, Ruth Hanson of Gonzales, Louisiana. It may be a little difficult to follow, but the end result was delicious.

Ingredients

½ cup cooked rice

½ onion, chopped

1 clove garlic, diced

1 eggplant, diced

Stuffing of choice

Directions

For peppers cook rice (½ cups) ahead. Slice tops off peppers (save slices for seasoning) deseed. In a deep skillet insert peppers and steam about 10 min to partially cook peppers. Remove peppers w/ tongs and turn on bottoms. For stuffing I generally use things I have on hand often from last one or two cooked meals. I sauté onions, garlic and pepper slices cut up in small amount of oil. If adding diced tomatoes, diced eggplant add to sauté mix and continue cooking till soft. If you don't have tomatoes a couple of spoons jarred spaghetti sauce works well. Add in any meat, i.e. raw chicken cubed or cubed rotisserie chicken, ground beef; shrimp cut in small chunks or use canned shrimp. When pink is gone from meat take off heat. Stir into rice keeping it moist like dressing. Add in parmesan cheese and stir well. Stuff peppers generously. Top with bread crumbs, Italian or plain. In preheated 350°F oven bake approximately 30 min.

"To grow a tomato or a pepper and prepare a meal from your labor and care is primordially satisfying." Nell Newman

EGGPLANT-STUFFED BELL PEPPERS

Source: Author

Ingredients

2 eggplants, diced	8 whole bell peppers (color of choice)
1 pound ground pork	½ onion, chopped
2 stalks celery, diced	½ cup bell pepper, diced (from the tops)
2 Tbsp garlic, diced	2 cups chicken stock
1 cup crab meat	1 cup (90-110 pkg.) shrimp
4 cups cooked rice	Salt and black pepper, to taste
½ cup sliced green onions	Bread crumbs

Preparation

Preheat oven to 350°F. Cut the tops from the bell peppers and clean the pulp from inside. In a large pot, place bell peppers and cover by 2 inches with lightly salted water. Bring to a low boil and cook 5-8 minutes. Remove peppers from pot and place in cold water to cool. In the same pot, boil diced eggplant until tender, approximately 10-15 minutes. Strain and reserve stock for later use. In a 5-quart cast iron Dutch oven, cook ground pork over medium heat. Continue to stir and chop until meat begins to brown and render juices. Once meat is browned, add onions, celery, ½ cup bell pepper and garlic. Sauté 3-5 minutes or until vegetables are tender. Add stock as needed to retain moisture. Add boiled eggplant, blend well into the meat mixture and cook 15-20 additional minutes. Add shrimp and cook until they just turn pink. Gently fold in crab meat and green onions. Season to taste using salt and pepper. Stuff the mixture into the bell peppers, place on a large baking sheet. Top with bread crumbs. Bake 30 minutes or until peppers are tender.

RIZ PILAF À LA VALENCIENNE

Source: Restaurant de la Pyramide, Fernand Point, Vienne; Courtesy of Vincent Price

Ingredients

½ cup butter	1 cup eggplant, diced and peeled
1 small zucchini or summer squash, diced	
2 large mushrooms, sliced	1 clove garlic, minced
1 ripe tomato, peeled, seeded, and chopped	
3 pimientos (or 7 oz. can), minced	1 tsp salt
¼ tsp pepper	1 cup rice
1 ¾ cups chicken broth	12 mussels
½ cup water	

Directions

In a saucepan, melt the butter.

Add the eggplant, zucchini, mushrooms, garlic, pimientos, salt, and pepper. Cook over moderate heat for 10 minutes, stirring occasionally.

Stir 1 cup rice.

Add chicken broth and bring to a boil. Cover tightly and cook over low heat for 30 minutes. While rice is cooking, scrub thoroughly 12 mussels. Put them in a saucepan with ½ cup water, cover, and cook over high heat for 5 minutes, or until shells pop open. Keep warm.

Turn rice onto a warm serving dish and top with the mussels in their shells. When this pilaf is served with the Brochette des Corsaires, it is placed in a little mound alongside the brochette, with a little mound of Scupions à la Nicoise on either side.

PROSCIUTTO WRAPPED ASPARAGUS

Source: Author

Ingredients

1 bunch thin asparagus spears, trimmed

3 tablespoons olive oil

1 ½ Tbsp Parmesan cheese, grated

1 clove garlic, minced (optional)

1 tsp sea salt

½ tsp black pepper

Prosciutto

Preparation

Preheat oven to 425°F.

Parboil asparagus for 5 minutes. Place the asparagus into a mixing bowl, and drizzle with the olive oil. Toss to coat the spears then sprinkle with Parmesan cheese, garlic, salt, and pepper. Wrap asparagus, in bundles of 3 each, with prosciutto. Arrange the wrapped asparagus onto a baking sheet in a single layer.

Bake in the preheated oven until just tender, 12 to 15 minutes depending on thickness.

STUFFED YELLOW SQUASH

Source: Author

Ingredients

5-6 yellow squash

2 slices bacon, cooked and crumbled

1 onion, finely chopped

¾ cup Panko bread crumbs

½ stick butter, melted

2 Tbsp butter (to sauté onion)

Salt & pepper to taste

Paprika

2 cups cheddar cheese, grated

Preparation

Squash:

Cut squash in half lengthwise. Fill a bowl with ice water. Set aside. Bring a pot of salted water to a boil. Place squash in boiling water. Bring water back to a boil; cook squash until slightly tender, about 5 minutes. Place squash in ice water for 2 minutes. Remove, pat dry and lay on paper towel to drain. Scrape out seeds and stringy pulp from each squash half, leaving a large cavity for stuffing. Sprinkle insides of squash with salt & pepper.

Stuffing:

Sauté onion in 2 Tbsp melted butter until tender. Mix together scraped squash, bacon, onion, panko, melted butter, cheese, salt & pepper. Fill squash shells with mixture; sprinkle tops with paprika. Arrange stuffed shells in a lightly greased baking dish, sides touching.

Bake 20 to 30 minutes, until top is golden and bubbly.

RATATOUILLE

Source: Author

Ingredients

2 Japanese eggplants	6 roma tomatoes
2 yellow squash	2 zucchinis
3 Tbsp olive oil	1 onion, diced
4 cloves garlic, minced	½ red bell pepper, diced
½ yellow bell pepper, diced	2 carrots, diced
2 stalks celery, diced	Salt, to taste
Pepper, to taste	2 (14.5 oz.) cans diced tomatoes

2 Tbsp fresh basil, chopped (8-10 leaves)

Herb seasoning:

4 Tbsp olive oil	2 Tbsp fresh basil, chopped (8-10 leaves)
1 Tbsp garlic chives, minced	2 Tbsp fresh parsley, chopped
2 tsp fresh thyme	1 tsp fresh oregano, minced
Salt, to taste	Pepper, to taste

Preparation

Preheat the oven to 375°F.

Slice the eggplant, tomatoes, squash, and zucchini into approximately 3/16 inch rounds, then set aside.

Heat the olive oil in a 12-inch oven-safe pan over medium heat. Sauté the onion, garlic, bell peppers, carrots and celery until tender, about 10 minutes. Season with salt and pepper, then add the canned tomatoes and basil. Stir until the ingredients are fully incorporated. Remove from heat, then smooth the surface of the sauce.

RATATOUILLE

Arrange the sliced veggies in alternating patterns, (for example, yellow squash, eggplant, tomato, zucchini) on top of the sauce from the center to the outer edge of the pan. Season with salt and pepper. Cover the pan and bake for 40 minutes. Uncover, drizzle with 4 Tbsp olive oil and scatter the herb seasoning ingredients over the cooked ratatouille. Bake for another 20 minutes.

Serve while hot as a main or side dish.

SOUTHERN CABBAGE

Source: Author

Ingredients

1 head of cabbage

4 Tbsp butter or bacon drippings

Salt to taste

Black pepper to taste

1½ to 2 cups water (use chicken broth for additional flavor)

Preparation

Cut Cabbage into quarters, removing the hard stem. Slice each quarter, across the wedge, into 1-inch wide pieces.

In a large pot, add the cabbage and water. Bring to a boil over medium-high heat. Cover and reduce heat to medium low. Simmer for 12-15 minutes, stirring occasionally until cabbage is tender. Do not overcook. Stir in butter, salt and pepper and remove from heat.

MUSHROOMS & WILD RICE

Creamy Mushroom & Wild Rice is very good and easy to make in one pan. This wild rice and mushroom recipe is a perfect meatless main or side dish for any occasion.

Source: Author

Ingredients

2 Tbsp olive oil

1 small onion, diced

2 cloves garlic, minced

8 oz. fresh mushrooms, sliced

1 tsp salt

½ tsp pepper

½ tsp Herbs de Province seasoning

2 cups chicken broth

1 cup wild rice*

¼ cup heavy cream

½ cup parmesan cheese, shredded

Instructions

Heat the olive oil in a large skillet over medium-high heat. Add the onions and sliced mushrooms. Cook, stirring, until onions are tender. Add the minced garlic and cook for 3 minutes. Season with salt, pepper, and Herbs de Province seasoning. Add the broth and rice. Let the mixture come to a boil then reduce heat to low, cover the skillet and simmer for 15 to 20 minutes.

Remove the pan from the heat and allow the rice to stand for 5 minutes. Remove the lid and stir in the heavy cream and parmesan cheese.

*Cooking times for wild rice can vary.

"Nature alone is antique, and the oldest art a mushroom."

Thomas Carlyle

"I am... a mushroom; On whom the dew of heaven drops now and then."

John Ford

GARLIC MUSHROOMS

Pan seared Garlic Mushrooms are a staple side in any restaurant, bistro, pub or steakhouse, and a huge favorite in homes all over the world. You will love this easy and delicious 10-minute side dish that pairs with anything! Low carb and Keto approved!

Karina; Café Delights

Ingredients

4 Tbsp unsalted butter

1 Tbsp olive oil

½ onion, chopped

1 lb. cremini or button mushrooms

2 Tbsp dry white wine*

1 tsp fresh thyme leaves, chopped

2 Tbsp fresh parsley, chopped

4 cloves garlic, minced

Salt and pepper to taste

Instructions

Heat the butter and oil in a large pan or skillet over medium-high heat.

Sauté the onion until softened (about 3 minutes). Add the mushrooms and cook for about 4-5 minutes until golden and crispy on the edges. Pour in the wine and cook for 2 minutes, to reduce slightly. Stir through thyme, 1 tablespoon of parsley and garlic. Cook for a further 30 seconds, until fragrant. Season generously with salt and pepper (to your taste). Sprinkle with remaining parsley and serve warm.

*Use a good quality dry white wine, such as Pinot Gris, Chardonnay, or a Sauvignon Blanc

WILD RICE PILAF WITH SULTANAS AND PINE NUTS

Source: Author

Ingredients

1 box Uncle Ben's Wild and Long Grain Rice, reserve the seasoning

2 Tbsp olive oil

¼ cup pine nuts

1 onion, finely diced

1 ¾ cup boiling water

4 Tbsp sultanas (golden raisins)

¾ tsp salt

½ tsp saffron threads

Preparation

In a medium saucepan, over medium heat, add the oil. Add the pine nuts and cook until golden brown, about 1 to 2 minutes, stirring constantly. Transfer the pine nuts to a small bowl and set aside.

Add the onion to the saucepan you cooked the pine nuts in, and cook until softened and just starting to brown, about 5 to 7 minutes, stirring occasionally. Add the rice and cook 2 minutes, stirring frequently. Stir in the boiling water, sultanas, salt, and saffron and Uncle Ben's seasoning, turn the heat up to high, and bring it to a rolling boil.

Stir the rice then cover the saucepan, turn the heat down to low, and cook until tender, about 10 minutes (do not open the lid during this time). Turn the heat off and let the rice sit (covered) 15 minutes, then fluff with a fork. Transfer to a serving dish, sprinkle the toasted pine nuts on top and serve.

Option: Add ½ tsp cardamom, ¼ tsp cloves, and ½ cinnamon at the same time that you add the rice.

Stuffed Crook Neck Squash

Source: Valeria (Val) Corley; a recipe from Lebanon

Ingredients

6 to 7 small to medium yellow crook neck squash, stem removed

Stuffing:

1 lb. ground round	¼ cup Uncle Ben's original white rice
½ tsp salt	¼ tsp black pepper
¼ tsp ground oregano	¼ tsp cinnamon

1 (14.5 oz.) can diced tomatoes (¼ cup drained for stuffing, reserving the juice)

Sauce:

1 (28 oz.) can crushed tomatoes	1 cup water
Remaining diced tomatoes and reserved juice	¼ tsp cinnamon
Salt and pepper, to taste	¼ tsp ground oregano

Instructions

Slice the small necks in ½ inch sections until you reach an area of the main squash body that a large enough hole can be made to scoop out the insides (a narrow tool with a scooped end may be used). Discard the insides. Reserve the neck pieces.

Mix together ground round, rice, salt, pepper, oregano, cinnamon and ¼ cup drained tomatoes. Carefully stuff mixture into the hollowed out squash. Make small meatballs out of any remaining mixture.

In a large pot, pour the 28 oz. can of crushed tomatoes, the remainder of the 14.5 oz. can of diced tomatoes, the reserved liquid from the ¼ cup drained tomatoes, water, salt, pepper, oregano and cinnamon. Bring to a boil. Add stuffed squash, reserved neck pieces and meatballs. Cook on high heat 5 to 10 minutes, stirring carefully. Lower heat and simmer for about 1 hour. Serve over cooked rice.

PARMESAN VEGETABLE TIAN

Source: Georgia; The Comfort of Cooking

Ingredients

1 Tbsp olive oil

1 large onion, diced

2 garlic cloves, minced

1 medium zucchini, thinly sliced

1 medium yellow squash, thinly sliced

1 medium baking potato, thinly sliced

2 medium Roma tomatoes, thinly sliced

½ tsp Italian seasoning

Salt and freshly cracked pepper, to taste

¼ cup mozzarella cheese, shredded

2 Tbsp freshly grated Parmesan

Directions

Preheat oven to 400°F. Lightly coat a round pie pan with nonstick cooking spray. Set aside.

In a medium pan, heat olive oil. Add chopped onion and garlic, cooking until tender. Spread the onion and garlic mixture on the bottom of round pan. Evenly arrange the sliced vegetables on top, alternating as you go. Once you get all the way around, continue layering to fill the middle until no open space remains.

Drizzle all over with 1 Tbsp olive oil and sprinkle with Italian seasoning, salt and pepper. Cover with aluminum foil and bake covered for 30 minutes. Remove aluminum foil and sprinkle with mozzarella and Parmesan. Return to oven and bake uncovered for an additional 15 minutes, or until cheese is golden brown.

STUFFED BAKED ZUCCHINI

Source: Author

Ingredients

3 medium zucchini, ends trimmed	3 cups marinara sauce, divided
1 Tbsp olive oil	1 lb. lean ground beef
½ cup onion, chopped	1 tsp garlic, minced
½ cup mushrooms, chopped	¼ cup fresh Italian parsley, chopped
¼ cup fresh lemon balm, chopped	2 Tbsp fresh basil, chopped
1 tsp Italian seasoning	½ tsp salt
Black pepper to taste	¼ tsp crushed red pepper
1 ½ cups mozzarella, shredded	¼ cup Parmesan, shredded
2 Tbsp Italian style panko bread crumbs	

Preparation

Preheat oven to 375°F. Measure out 1 cup of the marinara sauce and set aside.

Slice zucchini in half, lengthwise. Scrape out the zucchini, chop and set aside. Place the scooped out zucchini halves in a 9" x 13" baking dish and add about 1" of water. Cover with foil and bake in preheated oven for 15 minutes. Remove from oven and set aside to cool.

Heat olive oil over medium heat in a medium size skillet. Add beef, onion and garlic and cook, stirring to break up the ground meat as it cooks. Cook until meat is done and veggies have softened. Add the chopped zucchini, mushrooms, marinara (except for reserved cup), parsley, lemon balm, basil, Italian seasoning, salt, black pepper, and crushed red pepper. Stir well to combine. Bring to a boil then reduce heat and allow to simmer over low heat for about 15 minutes.

Remove partially cooked zucchini from baking dish and pour off water. Pour the 1 cup of reserved marinara sauce into the empty

STUFFED BAKED ZUCCHINI

baking dish and place zucchini halves on top of the sauce, open sides up. Divide the filling between the zucchini halves. If you have extra filling, spoon it into the dish around the zucchini.

Cover the dish with foil, and bake for 15 to 20 minutes. Remove from oven. Remove foil and sprinkle zucchini stuffing with mozzarella, Parmesan and the panko bread crumbs. Return to oven, watching closely, and cook until cheese has melted and bread crumbs are golden brown.

BAKED ASPARAGUS CUSTARD

Source: Author

Ingredients

Custard:

2 lbs. asparagus, tough parts removed	2 eggs
1 egg yolk	1 tsp salt
¼ tsp ground nutmeg	Dash white pepper

1 medium leek (white and pale green parts only), minced

Sauce:

1 (10.5 oz.) can white asparagus spears, drained	½ tsp tarragon
¼ cup chicken broth	¼ cup heavy cream
¼ tsp salt	Dash white pepper
Cherry tomatoes, halved	Fresh parsley, chopped

Preparation

Cook asparagus in boiling salted water for 10 to 15 minutes or until tender. Drain well. Cut off tips and save for garnish (about 3 per serving). Chop remaining asparagus and puree in a blender (should have 2 cups).

In a mixing bowl, beat eggs, egg yolk, the 1 tsp salt, nutmeg, and pepper. Stir in the asparagus puree. Turn into 4 lightly greased 6 oz. custard cups. Place in a large baking pan and add boiling water to a depth of 1 inch. Bake in 400°F oven for 30 minutes or until set.

Meanwhile, place canned asparagus, chicken broth, cream, ¼ tsp salt and dash of white pepper in a blender and puree until smooth. Pour into a small saucepan, re-heat and season to taste.

Unmold custards onto serving plates and spoon sauce around them. Garnish with cherry tomatoes, parsley and asparagus tips.

GARLIC MASHED POTATOES

Source: Author

Ingredients

5 medium potatoes, cubed

½ stick butter, cut in Tbsp size pieces

½ cup heavy cream

3 cloves garlic, minced

1 tsp salt

½ tsp white pepper

Preparation

Place potatoes in a large pot, add water to cover by about one inch, bring to a boil and cook for about 15 minutes or until tender.

Strain the potatoes and place in a large mixing bowl. Add the butter, heavy cream, garlic, salt and white pepper. Mix on medium slow speed until butter is melted, all ingredients are well combined and potatoes are mashed.

Baked Asparagus Custard from Previous Page

NOTES

_____

_____

_____

_____

_____

_____

_____

_____

_____

_____

_____

_____

_____

_____

NOTES

_____

_____

_____

_____

_____

_____

_____

_____

_____

_____

_____

_____

_____

_____

WILD GAME

"I have always tempered my killing with respect for the game pursued ."

History

"And they say back roads lead you no where" is the beginning of the chorus to a song written by my friend, Sidney Cox and recorded by the Cox Family of Cotton Valley, Louisiana on their album "Just When We're Thinking it's Over". It's a beautiful song that speaks of a country boy stuck in a big city where all he wants is to get back to back roads. So get out of the city and break away from the highways and take a road trip down some of Louisiana's scenic byways and back roads where you'll find country kitchens, piney woods, cypress trees draped with Spanish moss and coastal wetlands teeming with wildlife. It's down back roads that you'll truly experience the taste of Louisiana's food, music, culture and natural beauty.

American beavers, nutria, muskrats, black bear, deer, and swamp rabbits are some of Louisiana's mammals. The state's best-known reptile might be the American alligator. But the area is also home to alligator snapping turtles, possums, raccoons, armadillos, turkeys, wild hogs, (red) fox squirrels, (gray) cat squirrels, a variety of wild ducks and migrating geese, crawfish, frogs and a large variety of other edible aquatic life. Then, of course, there are the snakes.

Cajuns living in rural areas made and continue to make hearty dishes like gumbo and jambalaya that usually contain seafood, vegetables, rice, spices and often; wild game. These are prepared in one cooking pot. Cajun cooking uses whatever foods are nearby like; crawfish, duck, alligator, okra, corn or tomatoes. Miz Bienvenu says: "When a Cajun cook is planning a meal, he or she simply opens the kitchen door and whatever is flying, swimming, walking by or growing in their gardens may well end up in the pot."

Louisiana Cajuns have been heard to say, "If it walks, crawls, flies or swims, I'll eat it!" That may be stretching it a little..... but not much!

Louisianans *will* eat almost anything! That's because Louisiana has some of the best food in the world..... if you don't ask too many questions about what's in it.

BEST BAKED RABBIT

Source: Ken Nipper

Ingredients

1-2 rabbits, cut into pieces

2 cups flour

2 cups crushed corn flakes

1 Tbsp salt

1 Tbsp garlic powder

1 ½ Tbsp onion powder

1 Tbsp sugar

1 Tbsp dry powdered yeast

4 Tbsp paprika

¼ cup olive oil

¼ cup cooking oil

Directions

Place flour, corn flakes, salt, garlic powder, onion powder, sugar, yeast and paprika in a food processor and process on high for one minute. Make sure the corn flakes are crushed so you will add enough. After one minute and the mixture is thoroughly mixed slowly add the olive oil while processing for another one minute.

Preheat oven to 350°F and grease a baking pan with the cooking oil.

Rinse rabbit pieces and drain. Dredge rabbit pieces in prepared coating mix and coat them thoroughly. Make sure rabbit is wet so coating sticks well, but not too wet or the coating will get lumpy and sticky. Place coated rabbit pieces on baking pan with oil. Cook in oven for 50 minutes. Use a spatula to remove stuck pieces after cooking.

HUNTER'S RABBIT

Recipe courtesy of Frank Vargas, chef at Louis' Basque Corner in Reno, NV.

Ingredients

½ cup olive oil   1 rabbit, cut into 6 to 8 portions

Salt and freshly ground black pepper   1 bay leaf

15 medium-size mushrooms, quartered or sliced

2 shallots, minced   1/3 cup all-purpose flour

Pinch dried thyme   Pinch dried parsley

1 cup white wine   1 to 2 cups chicken broth

Directions

Preheat the oven to 350°F.

In a large warmed Dutch oven over medium heat, add ¼ cup of olive oil. Sprinkle the rabbit with salt and pepper, to taste. Add the rabbit to the hot oil and brown on both sides. Remove the rabbit to a medium-size casserole dish.

In that same Dutch oven, over medium heat, add more olive oil. Add the mushrooms and shallots and sauté for about 2 minutes. Transfer the mushroom mixture to the casserole. Sprinkle the flour, thyme, parsley and the bay leaf over the rabbit and stir in the tomato sauce, wine, and the beef broth. You may add a pinch more of salt and pepper if you wish. Cover with foil and put in the oven to bake until the rabbit is tender, stirring every hour, about 2 to 3 hours. Rabbit meat should pull off easily from the bone with a fork. Remove from the oven and serve.

"I did not eat of cold beef, but of Welsh rabbit and stewed cheese."
John Byron, 'Literary Remains' (1725)

STEWED RABBIT

Recipe courtesy of Cora Faye's Café; Aurora, Colorado

Ingredients

2 rabbits	2 Tbsp cooking oil
2 Tbsp all-purpose flour	1 clove garlic, chopped
1 herb bouquet, chopped	1 large onion, finely chopped
½ cup mushrooms, chopped	1 cup white wine
1 cup boiling water	Kosher salt and freshly ground black pepper

Directions

Wash the rabbits in cold water and debone them by cutting at the joints like you would a chicken. Sprinkle generously with salt and pepper.

Place the cooking oil in a stewing pot (deep iron pot with a lid, if possible). When the oil is hot, place the rabbit pieces in the pot and let brown, about 5 minutes on each side. Once both sides are nicely seared, remove the pieces and set aside.

Reduce the heat and add the flour to the pot and stir frequently until the mixture is brown, about 3 minutes. Be careful not to burn. Once the flour is brown, throw in the garlic, herb bouquet and the onion. Stir frequently and cook for about 5 minutes. Place the seared rabbit back into the pot, along with the mushrooms. Cook for another 5 minutes. Add the wine and water to the pot and bring it back to a boil. Once it has boiled, reduce the heat and bring the liquid to a simmer. Place a tightly fitting lid on the pot, and let simmer for about 30 minutes. Season with salt and pepper again and continue to simmer until the rabbit is tender, about another hour. Serve hot over something like rice or mashed potatoes.

CRISPY CAJUN FRIED ALLIGATOR

Ingredients

1 lb. boneless alligator, fresh or frozen	1 cup buttermilk
2 Tbsp Cajun seasoning	1 tsp garlic powder
1 large egg	1 Tbsp spicy mustard
5 dashes Louisiana hot sauce	3 cups lard, or vegetable oil
2 cups flour	

Preparation

Pat the alligator meat dry. Place the alligator in a medium bowl and season with the Cajun seasoning, garlic powder, and hot sauce, and toss to coat evenly. Cover and allow marinating for at least 10 minutes at room temperature. Remove the alligator from the dry spices. Heat shortening in a large cast-iron skillet until it registers 350°F (176°C) or use a recommended electric deep fryer.

In a separate bowl whisk together the buttermilk, mustard, and eggs. Whisk well. In another bowl add the flour and season with some Cajun seasoning as well.

Dip the alligator in the flour and shake off. Then add into the buttermilk mixture and shake off. Then back into the flour and shake off. Repeat the process until all is done.

When the oil is ready, add the alligator pieces to the skillet in batches, shaking off any excess flour before adding them to the oil and being careful not to overcrowd the skillet. Start with the larger pieces.

Cook the alligator, using tongs to turn occasionally, until golden brown and cooked through, about 8 to 10 minutes. Keep an eye on the temperature of the oil, making sure the oil does not get too hot. Transfer the alligator to a plate lined with paper towels. Repeat the process until all the Alligator is cooked.

ALLIGATOR FINGERS

Recipe by: Jerry FLA "Quick and easy way to fix up gator bites for your friends - exotic, but taste like chicken! You can get frozen alligator meat online."

Ingredients

2 pounds alligator meat, cut into bite-size pieces

2 Tbsp vinegar	Salt and pepper to taste
Oil for frying	¼ cup all-purpose flour
1 cup cornmeal	2 Tbsp garlic powder
½ tsp cayenne pepper	2 tsp black pepper

Optional dipping sauce:

3 Tbsp mayonnaise	2 tsp prepared horseradish
1 Tbsp brown mustard	1 Tbsp red wine vinegar

Directions

Place alligator meat in a medium bowl, and mix with vinegar, salt, and pepper. Cover, and refrigerate about 10 minutes.

Pour oil into a large skillet to a depth of 1 inch, and heat over a medium-high flame.

Add to a large re-sealable bag the flour, cornmeal, garlic powder, cayenne pepper, and black pepper. Squeeze off excess liquid from meat, and add one handful of meat to the re-sealable bag. Shake to coat. Remove meat, shake off excess flour, and set on a plate. Repeat with remaining meat.

When oil is hot, place meat pieces into oil, being careful not to overcrowd. Fry until golden brown, about 3 minutes. Remove to paper towels, and serve hot.

To prepare dipping sauce, mix together in a small bowl the mayonnaise, horseradish, brown mustard, and red wine vinegar.

ROASTED DUCK IN PORT CHERRY WINE

Source: Le Gourmet TV

This deep golden glazed duck recipe is perfect for any holiday table.

Ingredients

5 Pound (1 whole duck) or 5-6 wild ducks

1 Tbsp Canola oil

1 Large shallots, finely chopped (+ 2 shallots, halved)

2 medium garlic cloves, minced

2 cups Port (ruby red port wine)

Salt to taste   12 large sage leaves

½ cup dried cherries

Directions

Trim excess skin and fat from duck and reserve for another use. Using fork, pierce skin all over. Place duck on rack in roasting pan; set aside.

Preheat the oven to 325°F.

In small saucepan, heat oil over medium heat and cook shallot and garlic for about 6 minutes or until softened. Add port and bring to the boil. Reduce heat and simmer for about 15 minutes or until reduced by half.

Sprinkle duck with salt, inside cavity and on skin. Place sage leaves and shallots into duck cavity. Remove about ½ cup of the port mixture and brush all over duck. Add dried cherries into remaining port and set aside.

Place duck in center of the preheated oven and roast for about 3 hours or until skin is crisp and golden brown. Allow to stand for 10 minutes before cutting.

Reheat port and cherries and serve with duck.

RAGONDIN (NUTRIA)

Nutria, the infamous 'river rat', were introduced to the U.S. west coast as an alternative to mink in the mid-1900's. Although 1.5 million nutria were trapped yearly for the fur trade in it's heyday, nutria fur is no longer in fashion and wild populations have rocketed. Despite looking like a giant rat, wild nutria are clean animals. They consume plants only and are among the healthiest of meats to consume...

Nutria meat is very high in protein, low in fat and actually healthy to eat. With the help of Mr. Noel Kinler and Edmont Mouton of the Louisiana Department of Wildlife and Fisheries, we cooked nutria stews, nutria soups, roasted nutria, and grilled nutria at many functions," said Chef Parola.

We're not convinced eating nutria meat will ever go mainstream, as heck look at those big orange teeth and long rat like tail. Nonetheless, nutria can be quite tasty. It truly is the other "other" white meat.

Nutritional Value:	Nutria	Chicken	Beef	Turkey
Protein g/100g	22.1	21.4	16.6	21.8
Fat g/100g	1.5	3.1	26.6	2.9
Carbohydrates g/100g	0	0	0	0
Cholesterol g/100g	40.1	70	85	65

From a nutritional standpoint, nutria has much to commend it. According to a state analysis, raw nutria meat has more protein per serving than ground beef and is far lower in fat than farm-raised catfish.

No need to convince Art Cormier. At his home in rural Bridge City, nutria is what's for dinner. "Let me count the ways: meatballs, enchiladas, stir-fry. And of course in Louisiana, a nice sauce piquant," said Mr. Cormier, a retired trapper.

"CROCK-POT" NUTRIA

Source: Chef Philippe Parola

Ingredients

2 hind saddle portions of nutria meat.

1 small onion, sliced thin

1 tomato, cut in big wedges

2 potatoes, sliced thin

2 carrots, sliced thin

8 Brussel sprouts

½ cup white wine

1 cup water

2 tsp chopped garlic

Salt and pepper to taste

1 cup demi-glace (optional)

Directions

Layer onion, tomato, potatoes, carrots and Brussel sprouts in crock pot. Season nutria with salt, pepper and garlic to taste and place nutria over vegetables. Add wine and water, set crock pot on low and let cook until meat is tender. Cook for approximately 4 to 6 hours. Garnish with vegetables and demi-glace. Makes 4 servings.

SOUPE AU RAGONDIN (NUTRIA)

Source: Chef Philippe Parola

Ingredients

Nutria
1 hind saddle nutria meat
2 quarts water
½ cup tomato puree
1 cup red wine
Salt and pepper to taste
1 tsp Louisiana hot sauce
1 tsp red wine vinegar

Roux (mix well)
4 Tbsp flour
2 Tbsp vegetable oil
4 Tbsp corn starch

Mire Poix
1 onion, chopped
1 carrot, chopped
1 celery stalk, chopped
2 cloves garlic

Bouquet Garni
2 whole cloves
½ bunch parsley
4 black peppercorns

Directions

Bring water, seasonings, mire poix, bouquet garni, and tomato puree to a boil. Add nutria hind saddle and simmer for 1 ½ hours or until meat is tender. Remove nutria meat and break meat off bones. Make sure to discard any gristle or silver skin. Strain stock then add roux. Cook slowly for 15 minutes. Slice meat into small pieces, then mix into soup. Slowly cook for another 10 minutes. Add brandy or sherry wine to taste (optional).

SMOKED PULLED NUTRIA

Source: Dave Bureau's award-winning recipe from the Institute of Applied Ecology's Invasive Species Cook-off.

Ingredients

2 large nutria (back quarters)	1 cup kosher salt
1 cup brown sugar	1 gallon water
Woodchips (hickory or alder)	

For barbecue sauce:

½ cup ketchup	2 Tbsp brown sugar
2 Tbsp Worcestershire sauce	1-2 Tbsp vinegar
1 tsp garlic powder	Salt and pepper to taste

Directions

Before smoking, soak nutria in a simple brine. On the stove over low heat, dissolve the salt and sugar in about half a gallon water. Once the salt is dissolved, remove from heat and add another half-gallon of cold water, add nutria, and place in refrigerator. Leave nutria to soak for 24 hours.

Remove nutria from brine and pat dry with a paper towel before placing on smoker racks. A small electric smoker can be used to control both time and temperature.

Smoke nutria for three to four hours at about 190°F. Add new chips about every hour. Nutria will be cooked when the thickest parts are at least 180°F using a meat thermometer. To retain moisture in the meat during the smoking process, close the smoker and add some apple cider in the moisture pan at the bottom of the smoker.

After nutria is cooked, use a fork to shred the meat and separate from the bones. Place shredded meat in a bowl and mix with about a cup of barbecue sauce.

TURTLE SAUCE PIQUANT

Any sort of turtle will do here, but snapping turtle is traditional.

Source: Hank Shaw

Ingredients

½ cup butter	A heaping ½ cup all-purpose flour
2 cups chopped onion	1 cup chopped green pepper
1 cup chopped celery	5 garlic cloves
1 (6 oz.) can tomato paste	1 Tbsp Cajun seasoning
3 to 4 pounds turtle, diced small	
1 cup white wine	1(28 oz. can) tomatoes, diced
4 bay leaves	Salt, black pepper and hot sauce to taste

Instructions

In a large, heavy pot like a Dutch oven, heat the butter over medium-high heat for a minute or two. Stir in the flour, then turn the heat down to medium. Cook this roux, stirring often, until it turns the color of peanut butter, about 10 to 15 minutes.

While the roux is cooking, Heat 6 cups of water in another pot to the boiling point. Hold it at a simmer for now.

When the roux is ready, add the onions, celery and green pepper and stir to combine. Turn the heat to medium-high and cook this, stirring often, until everything is soft, about 6 to 8 minutes. Sprinkle some salt over everything while you do this. Add the garlic, Cajun seasoning and tomato paste and stir to combine. Cook this, stirring occasionally, for 3 to 4 minutes.

Mix in the turtle meat, then add the cup of white wine, the can of crushed tomatoes and the hot water, stirring as you add. Add the bay leaves and bring this to a gentle simmer. Add salt to taste. Let this simmer very gently until the meat is tender, at least 2 hours,

Turtle Sauce Piquant

maybe three.

When the sauce piquant is ready, add any more salt, black pepper, hot sauce and/or Cajun seasoning you want, then serve it with white rice and lots of green onions or parsley. Make sure you have hot sauce at the table; I use Tabasco, but use whatever variety you prefer.

Serve this with white rice and lots of beer, and remember, like all stews, this one's better the day after you make it. It keeps in the fridge a week and can be frozen.

TURTLE OR ALLIGATOR SAUCE PIQUANT

This recipe is from an old-time farmer who never let a turtle get by. If he was traveling along the road checking his crop or Sunday driving, you best believe he would stop his truck without hesitation (don't be behind him) and get the turtle crossing the road to make his favorite turtle sauce piquant.

Ingredients

1 lb. turtle meat or alligator meat	2 large onions, chopped
2 bell peppers, chopped	6 stalks celery, chopped
2 jalapenos, chopped without seeds	1 (6 oz.) cans tomato paste
4 cups of water	2 Tbsp sugar
½ Tbsp basil leaves	2 bay leaves
Cooking oil	½ tsp salt
½ tsp red pepper	1 tsp black pepper
½ tsp garlic	½ tsp onion powder
Vinegar for marinating	1(10 oz.) can Rotel Brand Tomatoes
2 Tbsp roux (optional)	

Directions

A Dutch oven or heavy cast iron pot with cover works best for this dish.

Season the turtle meat with salt and red pepper. Marinate the turtle meat overnight in enough vinegar to cover the meat.

When ready to cook, take the meat out of the marinade and let it drain 10 to 15 minutes. Do not rinse the meat. Season with salt, red pepper, black pepper, onion powder and garlic powder.

Pour about 1/2 the oil in a Dutch oven or cast iron pot and start heat. Put in enough turtle meat to cover the bottom of the pot. Brown the meat on all sides. Continue until all are done, taking out

TURTLE OR ALLIGATOR SAUCE PIQUANT

the meat as they brown.

After all the meat is browned, add the onions, bell pepper, celery and jalapenos and cook until the onions are soft. Add the tomato paste, Rotel tomatoes and 2 cups of water. If you want to use the roux add at this time. Cook on medium heat until the meat turns a lighter brown.

Add 2 to 3 cups of water, sugar, turtle meat, the basil and the bay leaves. Bring to a boil; then reduce the heat to a simmer for 2 to 2 ½ hours (I like to cover the pot) and stir occasionally to prevent scorching and sticking. Serve over rice with a fresh green salad and tomatoes along with a crisp garlic or plain French bread. Does not get much better than this!

If using gator you can use vinegar or this marinate in garlic powder and Cajun seasoning in a covered dish. Add onions, Worcestershire sauce, soy sauce and lemon juice to meat and let marinate overnight in refrigerator. Remove meat from marinade and fry in vegetable oil in a skillet until meat is brown. Follow the rest of the steps.

"Hoo boy! How can anything taste so good look so bad? Huh?"
Justin Wilson

RABBIT AND SAUSAGE JAMBALAYA

Source: Author

Ingredients

1 lb. breakfast sausage

1 lb. smoked sausage, sliced

2 rabbits

2 bunches green onions, chopped, including tops

2 stalks celery, chopped

1 clove garlic, mashed

1 small onion, quartered

Water

1 small box Uncle Ben's Long Grain & Wild Rice (original)

1 cup white rice

½ tsp. salt

½ tsp. black pepper

¼ tsp. cayenne

Preparation

Boil rabbit, celery, garlic, onion, salt and black pepper in enough water to cover until rabbit is tender. De-bone and cut rabbit into chunks. Set aside.

In large skillet, brown and crumble breakfast sausage. Add onions and cook until just tender. Add rabbit to sausage and onion mixture. Add enough water to remaining rabbit broth to make 4½ cups and pour into skillet with rabbit and sausage. Add cayenne and seasoning from wild rice box and bring to a boil.

Add wild rice, white rice and sliced smoked sausage. Cover and simmer for 20 minutes or until liquid is gone.

ALLIGATOR SAUCE PIQUANT

Source: Justin Wilson's "Homegrown Louisiana Cookbook"

Justin Wilson learned to cook from his mother, Olivet, who was of French heritage. "She was a great improviser," Wilson once said. "She'd cook a dish and we'd go 'Mama, what's this here?' And she'd say: 'Chilren, dat's a mus-go. It mus' go down yo' t'roat.'"

Ingredients

5 lbs. Alligator meat, trimmed & cubed	1 cup olive oil
3 cups flour, all-purpose	5 cups onion, chopped
2 cups green onion, chopped	1 cup bell pepper, chopped
½ cup celery, chopped	2 cups tomatoes, fresh/chopped
8 cups water, cold	2 Tbsp garlic, finely chopped
2 Tbsp Worcestershire sauce	1 lemon, juice of
Salt to taste	Tabasco sauce to taste
2 cups dry white wine	6 cups tomato sauce

Directions

Make a dark roux with olive oil and flour. When roux is dark brown, add onion, green onion, bell pepper, and celery; cover and cook until onions are clear, stirring occasionally. Add tomatoes and continue cooking for 10 min; stir often. Add water and stir to make a thick liquid. Add garlic, Worcestershire, lemon juice, salt, hot sauce, wine, and tomato sauce, making sure to mix well. Add alligator, and enough water to cover the ingredients by 2 inches; stir to mix. Bring to a boil, stirring frequently. After it comes to a boil, turn heat to low and cover, checking from time to time, and stir to prevent sauce from sticking. Continue cooking for 3 to 4 hours until meat is tender. Serve over cooked rice or spaghetti with Parmesan cheese.

Freeze leftovers in serving size containers. This recipe is for a party; no one would go to this much trouble if the recipe only fed 4 peoples.

BAKED RABBIT AND VEGETABLES

Source: Author

Ingredients

1/4 cup flour

1/2 tsp freshly ground black pepper

1 tsp onion powder

1 can cream of mushroom soup

1 tsp Italian seasoning

1 cup carrots, sliced

Olive oil, for frying

1 tsp salt

1 tsp garlic powder

3 lb. rabbit, cut up

1 cup mushrooms, sliced

1 cup chicken broth

4 potatoes, peeled and diced

Preparation

Preheat oven to 325°F.

Heat the olive oil over medium heat in an oven-proof Dutch oven. Combine the first five ingredients in a bowl and coat the rabbit in the mixture. Fry for approximately 4 to 5 minutes, or until golden brown. Remove rabbit and drain well on paper towels.

Mix together the homemade mushroom soup, mushrooms, Italian seasoning, and chicken broth in a saucepan; bring to a boil over medium heat.

Place the browned rabbit pieces in the prepared pan and cover the rabbit with the carrots and potatoes. Pour the mushroom sauce over the rabbit, carrots, and potatoes, cover, and bake in the preheated oven for 1 ½ hours, or until the rabbit and vegetables are tender and the sauce is bubbling.

BEAVER POT ROAST

You may be thinking, "Who in the world eats the largest North American rodent?"

Source: Steven Rinella

Ingredients

2 beaver hindquarters

1 onion, quartered

2 sticks celery, chopped

½ tsp pepper

3 bay leaves

4 carrots

3 cloves garlic, chopped

½ tsp salt

½ tsp cayenne

Directions

Put the hindquarters of the beaver in a Crock-pot with carrots, potatoes, onion, garlic, celery and the spices. After five hours in the Crock-pot, your beaver meat should be tender and taste just like a brisket.

Nutrition Facts

Serving Size   100 g

Amount Per Serving

Calories 146

% Daily Value

Total Fat 4.8g   7 %

Total Carbohydrate 0g   0 %

Protein 24g   48 %

Vitamin A   0 %

Sodium 51mg   2 %

Dietary Fiber 0g   0 %

Vitamin C 3 %

Calcium 2 %

Iron   38 %

TEXAS ARMADILLO

Source: CD Kitchen

Ingredients

1 armadillo, cleaned and cut into serving pieces

1 ¼ cup dry white wine

½ cup oil

2 cloves garlic, crushed (optional)

¼ cup butter

Salt and pepper, to taste

½ tsp thyme

½ tsp rosemary

1 medium onion, sliced thin

1 ¼ cup light cream

1 Tbsp brown mustard

1 Tbsp cornstarch

Directions

Mix all ingredients of marinade and add armadillo. Marinate about 8 hours, turning meat occasionally.

Remove armadillo and reserve marinade. Melt butter in deep skillet and brown armadillo pieces. Pour in marinade and bring to a boil. Stir in seasoning, cover and simmer until tender (about 1 to 1 ¼ hours). Remove skillet from the fire and place armadillo pieces on a warmed platter.

Mix mustard and cornstarch, then mix in cream. Return skillet to low heat and stir in this mixture a little at a time. Stir sauce until hot, but not boiling, and thickened. Pour sauce over armadillo. Serve with steamed rice.

ARMADILLO WITH ONIONS & GRAVY

"Florida "Crackers" have been enjoying fried armadillo for more than 100 years. The easy-to-catch animals provided meat for many a pioneer household. They got the nicknames "possum on the half-shell" and later during the Great Depression they were called "Hoover Hogs". Without their shell the armadillo resembles a rabbit but tastes more like fine-grained, high-quality pork. Armadillos are an overlooked food animal, not protected by law, available throughout the year, and good tasting. There's an armadillo near you." Green Deane

Source: Author

Ingredients

1 armadillo, cleaned and cut into serving pieces

1 ½ tsp salt

½ black pepper

½ tsp paprika

½ cup flour

3 Tbsp cooking oil

2 onions, quartered and sliced

2 cups cream gravy

Preparation

Soak meat overnight in salted water (1 Tbsp salt to 1 quart water). Drain, disjoint and cut up. Season with salt, pepper and paprika, roll in flour and fry in oil until browned. Cover meat with onion, add ½ tsp salt and ½ tsp black pepper. Pour in the cream gravy. Cover skillet tightly and simmer for 1 hour.

MUSKRAT STEW

Source: Unknown

Ingredients

1 prepared Muskrat (can be purchased frozen)	2 potatoes, cut up
1 onion, chopped	2 cups canned tomatoes, diced
1 cup canned corn, drained	¼ cup flour
1 tsp salt	½ tsp pepper
5 ½ cups water	3 Tbsp fat or oil
1 tsp thyme, dry	¼ tsp cayenne
Parsley garnish	

Directions

In a pot, bring to boil 5 ½ cups water while frying the Muskrat. Mix flour with salt and pepper. Cut Muskrat into 3 pieces and roll in flour until lightly coated.

In a large skillet or sauté pan, heat fat or oil and fry Muskrat over moderate heat, turning now and then until lightly browned all over. Be careful the flour does not burn, it should be reddish, not chocolate.

Drain fried Muskrat and add to the boiling water, including as much of the flour crumbs as you can, as they will thicken the stew. Stir in the onions, thyme and cayenne. Bring to a boil then simmer for 2-1/4 hours.

Add potatoes and corn. Bring back to a boil and simmer another 15 minutes. Add tomatoes, bring back to a boil and simmer another 45 minutes. Monitor thickness of the stew, keeping in mind it will be noticeably thicker when cooled below a simmer. Add boiling water or boil uncovered as needed to adjust thickness.

Check seasoning and serve hot. Garnish with parsley.

FRIED MUSKRAT

"Not many people have enjoyed the taste of muskrat. Not many people eat them, because you only find them in marshy areas. Most people would be reluctant to try them, because they are a member of the rat family, but muskrats are some of the best meat there is to eat. There is no fat, because they only eat roots in the marsh."

Source: Unknown

Ingredients

6 muskrats

½ cup sage

Flour

3 large onions, quartered and sliced

Olive oil

Instructions

Cut the muskrats into three pieces. Fill a large pot with water then add sage and muskrats. Boil them for 45 minutes.

Take them out of the pot and coat them in flour. Preheat a large frying pan. Add half an inch of olive oil. Place muskrats in the frying pan and add onions. Fry muskrats for about 15 minutes on each side.

LIMONCELLO ROASTED RABBIT WITH OYSTER SAUCE

Source: Author

Ingredients

2 whole rabbits, cut into pieces

Salt, to taste

Pepper, to taste

½ cup olive oil

¼ cup red wine

Preparation

Preheat oven to 350°F. Salt and pepper both sides of rabbit. Heat oil in a heavy skillet and brown rabbit pieces on both sides. Remove rabbit pieces and place in a single layer in a large baking pan.

For the sauce: Pour the olive oil in a small mixing bowl. Whisk in remaining ingredients.

Add wine to the skillet and scrape bottom to loosen all brown bits. Stir in sauce, bring to a simmer and remove from heat. Pour it over the rabbit pieces in the baking pan. Cover with foil, perforate and bake for 40 to 45 minutes. Remove foil and bake an additional 20 minutes or until "fall off the bone" tender.

Limoncello and Oyster Sauce:

Ingredients

½ cup olive oil

¼ cup Limoncello

1 Tbsp lemon juice

½ tsp sesame oil

2 Tbsp oyster sauce

2 chopped garlic cloves

1 teaspoon Provincial herbs

¼ tsp onion powder

½ tsp ground rosemary

Salt and pepper to taste

CHICKEN-FRIED SQUIRREL WITH PAN GRAVY

"One of my favorite mild, white meats." Andrew Zimmern

Source: Andrew Zimmern

Ingredients

3 lbs. squirrel legs and loin pieces

1 cup buttermilk

Lard, vegetable oil or bacon drippings for frying

1 cup minced onion

A few sprigs thyme and rosemary

12 oz. chicken stock

1 cup cream

Salt and black pepper

Instructions

Dredge the squirrel legs and loin pieces in one cup buttermilk. Let rest in the fridge for 12 hours. Remove meat from milk and dredge in well-seasoned flour. Pan fry in a cast iron skillet (I use everything from lard to vegetable oil to bacon drippings). Just make sure the fry pan has ¼ inch of 'oil' so that you are really frying – it makes a difference. Cook until crispy. Remove fried squirrel to a paper towel-lined plate.

Drain skillet. Discard fats. Return pan to medium heat. Add one cup minced onion and a few sprigs of thyme or rosemary. Cook, stirring, picking up the browned bits as you go. Add 12 ounces chicken stock to pan. Bring to simmer, cook for 5 minutes and then add the cream to pan. Bring to simmer. Add squirrel pieces back to the pan and cook in the gravy for 4 to 5 minutes. Season with salt and pepper, and serve.

GOLDONNA SQUIRREL MULLIGAN

By Glynn Harris

Talkin' Outdoors

How I loved those special late fall nights back home. I can still remember the men and boys of the community gathering up down on the banks of Saline Bayou with the squirrels collected since season opened. The cooks would build a fire under a black pot and once the water reached a boil, they'd toss in the skinned and gutted squirrels.

Onions , bell peppers, rice and sorted other additives would be chopped and added to the pot and the cauldron would gurgle and simmer for what seemed like hours until the meat was tender. For a kid like my brother, cousins and me, the tantalizing aroma wafting up from that old black pot was almost more than we could stand. What the men were cooking up was a squirrel mulligan and once the cooks started ladling out steaming bowls of mulligan, we were in culinary heaven.

Since then, I have taken the simple recipe used by those fellows down on Saline and created my own version, adding a little of this and a pinch of that to create what I call my Goldonna Squirrel Mulligan.

I've eaten all sorts of squirrel mulligan over the years prepared by folks who didn't grow up in Goldonna. Peas and corn and potatoes and other foreign stuff is added to their dishes, and most are quite tasty. However, they pale in comparison to mine, in my humble opinion.

A couple of years ago, I cooked up a mulligan for my hunting club buddies down at the camp and George Seacrist took a special liking to my offering.

George has some great squirrel dogs and has no trouble collecting plenty of squirrels, but George is no ordinary fellow. His motto: if

GOLDONNA SQUIRREL MULLIGAN

a little is good, a whole bunch will be better. Keeping in mind the possession limit and gathering squirrels from neighbors, he extrapolated my little 3 squirrel recipe into a 100 squirrel recipe. Here's what he came up with: 100 squirrels, 17 bell peppers, 67 onions, 33 cans of tomato sauce and 67 cans of cream of mushroom soup.

Engaging the assistance of his wife, daughter, mother, daughter-in-law and anybody else who was willing to chop and peel, he spent a whole day on this unusual project and bless your heart if his 100 squirrel mulligan doesn't taste just like my three-squirrel recipe.

Ingredients

3 squirrels, cleaned and cut into quarters

1 large bell pepper, chopped

2 onions, chopped

1 can tomato sauce

2 cans cream of mushroom soup

2 cups rice, cooked

Seasonings to taste.

Directions

Parboil squirrels then rinse.

Transfer squirrels to Dutch oven, cover with water and add vegetables and seasoning. Cook on medium heat until meat is tender. Debone squirrels, cut up meat and return to Dutch oven. Add tomato sauce and soup, cook 1-2 hours on low to medium heat.

Serve over cooked rice.

SQUIRREL STEW

Source: George Graham - AcadianaTable.com

Ingredients

4 Tbsp vegetable oil

4 squirrels, cleaned and cut into pieces

2 Tbsp Acadiana Table Cajun Seasoning Blend (recipe on next page)

2 cups onion, diced

1 cup celery, diced

1 cup bell pepper, diced

2 cups smoked pork sausage, chopped

1 Tbsp garlic, minced

1 cup dry red wine

2 Tbsp Worcestershire sauce

2 cups button mushrooms

3 Tbsp dark roux

1 quart chicken stock

Salt and black pepper to taste

Hot sauce

8 cups long-grain white rice, cooked

1 cup green onion tops, diced

Instructions

In a large black iron pot with a heavy lid over medium-high heat, add the oil.

Sprinkle the squirrel pieces generously with Cajun seasoning and add to the hot oil in the pot. Cooking in batches, brown the squirrel on all sides and remove to a platter.

Add the trinity vegetables along with the sausage to the pot and sauté until the onions begin to brown, about 8 minutes. Add the garlic and deglaze the pot with the wine and Worcestershire. Cook until some of the alcohol burns off, about 5 minutes. Add the mushrooms, roux, and chicken stock. Lower the heat to a simmer, cover the pot and let cook for 1 hour.

Uncover and check to see that there is still plenty of liquid (add water, if needed). Cover and cook for another 1 hour until the squirrel is fork tender and the gravy thickens to coat the back of a spoon.

SQUIRREL STEW

Of all the small game species, squirrel is a delicacy in South Louisiana, and squirrel hunting is a rite of passage for every boy old enough to carry a .410 shotgun. In Louisiana, many rural schools dismiss students on the first day of the season in early October, (along with a short spring season).

In Louisiana forests, there are two predominant kinds of squirrels—the smaller gray squirrels (often referred to as the cat squirrel) and larger bushy-tail fox squirrels (the piney woods squirrel since its habitat is mainly in pine forests). Both are found in abundance in Acadiana, especially in the hardwoods of St. Landry and Evangeline Parishes, and the swamp forests of the Atchafalaya Basin.

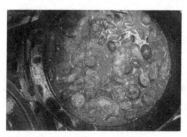

Acadiana Table Cajun Seasoning Blend:

Source: George Graham - AcadianaTable.com

Ingredients

¼ cup salt	¼ cup granulated garlic
¼ cup black pepper	2 Tbsp sweet paprika
2 Tbsp onion powder	2 Tbsp white pepper
1 Tbsp celery salt	1 Tbsp cayenne pepper

Instructions

Add all of the ingredients to a food processor and blend. Pour into an airtight container and store at room temperature for up to 6 months.

VENISON STEW

Source: Courtesy of Emeril Lagasse

Ingredients

3 Tbsp olive oil   2 lbs. venison stew meat, cut into 1-inch cubes

¼ cup all-purpose flour   Essence, recipe on page 329

2 cups onions, chopped   1 cup celery, chopped

1 cup carrots, chopped   1 Tbsp garlic, chopped

1 cup tomatoes, chopped, peeled and seeded   2 bay leaves

1 Tbsp fresh basil, chopped   1 Tbsp fresh thyme, chopped

1 cup red wine   4 cups brown stock

Salt and black pepper   Crusty bread

Directions

In a large pot, over high heat, add the olive oil. In a mixing bowl, toss the venison with flour and Essence. When the oil is hot, sear the meat for 2 to 3 minutes, stirring occasionally. Add the onions and sauté for 2 minutes. Add the celery and carrots. Season with salt and pepper. Saute for 2 minutes. Add the garlic, tomatoes, basil, thyme, and bay leaves to the pan. Season with salt and pepper. Deglaze the pan with the red wine. Add the brown stock. Bring the liquid up to a boil, cover and reduce to a simmer. Simmer the stew for 45 minutes to 1 hour, or until the meat is very tender. If the liquid evaporates too much add a little more stock.

PHEASANT IN WINE SAUCE

Source: Author

Ingredients

2 pheasants, cut up

1 cup all-purpose flour

½ tsp. salt

½ tsp. black pepper

½ tsp. garlic powder

¼ tsp. cayenne

½ cup cooking oil

1 onion, sliced

1 can cream of mushroom soup

1 ½ cups milk

8 oz. sour cream

½ cup white wine

1 small box Uncle Ben's Long Grain and Wild Rice (original)

Preparation

Preheat oven to 300°F. Mix flour, salt, pepper, garlic powder, cayenne and place in a large bowl or bag. Shake or turn pheasant to thoroughly coat with seasoned flour. Heat the oil in a large Dutch oven. Brown meat well on each side. Remove meat and drain the oil. Return pheasant to the Dutch oven. Spread sliced onion over the meat. Combine soup, milk, sour cream and wine and pour over the pheasant. Cover and bake at 300°F for 2 ½ to 3 hours.

About ½ hour before the pheasant is done, cook the rice according to the instructions on the box. Serve pheasant over the wild rice with gravy created from the soup mixture.

VENISON SKILLET STEAK WITH BROWN GRAVY

"My name is Joseph Bernard. I am an avid hunter and outdoorsman. I have had venison this way ever since I can remember; at deer camp or anywhere for that matter. "

Source: Joseph Bernard

Ingredients

1 venison steak

Flour for dredging

Butter or oil for skillet

Salt and pepper

Directions

Roll steak in flour and salt and pepper Add butter, or oil to cast iron skillet. Cook over medium-high heat until crispy (don't flip flop). Add a little more butter or oil, add in some flour and cook until brown. Add water, stir, and simmer until the gravy reaches the desired consistency. Add salt and pepper to taste and some pepper flakes for some heat if you like.

Buttermilk Biscuits:

Ingredients

2 ½ - 2 ¾ cups all-purpose flour

1 Tbsp salt

1 Tbsp sugar

1 ¼ tsp baking powder

7 oz. butter-cubed

1 ¼ cup buttermilk

Directions

Preheat oven to 425°F. Mix flour, salt, sugar, and baking powder together. Add butter and cut into the dry mixture until pea sized. Pour in buttermilk ½ cup at a time until you have achieved a good consistency. Flour your work surface and shape dough into a square about ½ inch thick. Cut into 9 even squares. Transfer to sheet pan or cast iron skillet, pop in the oven, and bake until golden (about 15 minutes).

GRILLED VENISON TENDERLOIN

Source: Author

Ingredients

1 to 1 ½ lb. whole venison loin (back strap)

Olive oil

Salt

Preparation

Coat the venison back strap in oil and salt well. Set aside for 20 minutes at room temperature.

On a hot grill, lay the venison back strap. Keep the grill cover open. Cook 8 to 10 minutes without turning, depending on how hot your grill is and how thick your venison loin is. You want a good sear, with good grill marks. Flip and repeat on the other side.

Do the finger test to check for doneness. If the venison needs some more time, turn it to sides that have not had direct exposure to the grill and cook for 2 to 3 more minutes, checking all the way. Baste with the bbq sauce and cook 2 more minutes on each side.

Remove it from the fire, tent with foil, and let it rest for 10 minutes. Serve with BBQ sauce on the side.

Barbecue Sauce recipe on page 341

NOTES

NOTES

INDEX OF RECIPES

INDEX OF RECIPES

INDEX OF RECIPES

INDEX OF RECIPES

FOOD QUOTES FROM THE BOOKS

"...it didn't seem all that long ago that school had let out for the summer, yet the new school year was halfway through the first six weeks, and Labor Day was only a memory of charcoal-grilled burgers and happy laughter." Eden

"In blatant defiance of cholesterol warnings, she'd started potatoes crisping in a skillet of bacon drippings and quickly stirred up a batch of corn muffins to go with the leftover purple hull peas, thick sliced ham and fresh sliced tomatoes." Eden

"How about some coffee and peanut-butter pie?" she asked. Eden

"Are you sure you don't have time for a quick bite?" she asked. "I fixed milk gravy and homemade biscuits." Eden

"Because her sisters were so weight conscious, she had scooped out tomatoes and filled their ruby red cavities with chicken salad." Eden

"Oatmeal cookies? Mmm, good!" Tess said from her place at the sink where she was slicing tomatoes. "The way to a man's heart is through his stomach, they say. And if that doesn't work, there's always a midnight motorcycle ride—right, Eden?" Eden

"So how about lunch?", Nick said. "I do a great Campbell's soup. And the things I can do with bologna are not to believed." Eden

"I want you to take me to the Revel," she said, "but I wore slacks because I wanted to ride the motorcycle." "Then by all means," he said, "let's take the Harley." Eden

"He took a seat at the counter and ordered a hamburger. When it was served, it was bigger and greasier than ever...just the way he liked it. Jo

"Why do you use white bread, Eden?" Mariah asked. "The additives will kill you. Of course, that cholesterol-filled ham will probably get you first. Watercress, bean sprouts, avocados—they make wonderful, nutritional sandwiches." Mariah

FOOD QUOTES FROM THE BOOKS

"Chicken, coated in a delectable crunchy crust, potatoes whipped mountain high and oozing gravy, and peas swimming in butter—all stared back, virtually untouched, from Mariah's plate." Mariah

"The smell of freshly brewed coffee danced on the kitchen air, along with the fragrance of spices and cooked apples." Mariah

"Mariah and Eden, now alone in the house with only their sisters' promises to return for Christmas to keep them company, sat curled on the sofa eating roast beef sandwiches from paper plates." Mariah

"She had heard Ford holler to the kids that there would be a pizza party after church that night. She could see all the gooey spread of cheese, hear all the laughter, feel all the camaraderie." Mariah

"Placing her arm around Tess's shoulders, she started from the backyard and up the steps to the kitchen. "C'mon. We need a few more sandwiches." Jo, eager to make amends, fell into step beside them. "Watercress and avocado—they make wonderful sandwiches, Eden. You ought to try them." Mariah

"I've got your favorite," she tempted, her lilting voice full of mischief. "Home-baked cinnamon rolls *with* confection icing. And real butter." Tess

"There was a neat trick to shelling peas, but unfortunately, Tess mused wryly, she had never gotten the hang of it." Tess

"With all the meat in this sack," Jo said, "the fire better be in the grill." "Meat?" Mariah exclaimed. "Did you say meat? Don't tell me married life has corrupted you already? I thought you only ate bean sprouts, raw oats and hay." Tess

"The scent of ribs barbecuing on the grill, along with the scent of charbroiled Eden-burgers, signaled it was almost time to eat." Tess

Authors note: I didn't read any of these books. "Steamy" romance novels are not my cup of tea, if you know what I mean. My lovely wife took care of that little "chore" for me. Thank you, Sweetheart!

Made in the USA
Coppell, TX
25 October 2019

10468784R00282